SUNDERLAND
CORPORATION
BUSES
1928-73

David Wayman

Front Cover Upper: This Daimler line-up comprises, in order from the camera, 42, the 1937 "Show" bus with its special livery including gold-leaf "Binns" lettering, and 51/45/49/43/53/46/44/50/47, all in the "streamline" livery. Those without advertising were delivered in December and the others in May 1938. Nos48/52 are absent. It will be seen that on those of the 43-49 batch the cream relief above the destination apertures is slightly shallower and not downswept to a "V" at the centre as with those of the 50-53 batch (and later Daimlers 54/ 55 and Leylands 56/57). *(Copyright Busways Travel Services)*

Front Cover Lower: The introduction in 1966 of the flat fare system with payment by cash or tokens was a highly innovative move. Leyland Panther No53 posed here represents the large number of specially-designed buses purchased to assist the extension of driver only operation to all services. *(Copyright Busways Travel Services)*

Back Cover: No, not a mushroom sprouting in Fawcett Street but an example of the eye-catching style of bus stop sign introduced there late in 1959. The well ladened bus is a Crossley-bodied Guy of the 173-184 batch. *(Copyright Busways Travel Services)*

First published 1997

ISBN 0-9519967-4-6

Published by Northeast Press Ltd., Echo House, Pennywell, Sunderland SR4 9ER.

Printed by: Hot Off The Press, 70 Bondgate, Darlington DL3 7JR.

Origination by: Trendsetters, 59a Yarm Lane, Stockton-on-Tees TS18 3DX.

© David Wayman 1997

Acknowledgments

It has been a time-consuming but enjoyable task to write this work. I sincerely thank all the people and organisations that have expressed interest, willingly made source material available, agreed to the use of copyright photographs and helped with comments and suggestions. My thanks go particularly to:

S Bell (Northeast Press Ltd), S Bradwell, Mrs V Buddle, Busways Travel Services, C Carter, T B Collinge, A B Cross, G Douglas, J Fox, J Fozard, M Fraser, M Hampshire, C Heaps, J Hogarth, R L Kell, the late G Laidler, Greater Manchester Museum of Transport, R Marshall, R McLean, M Morrison, "Oubeck", O Parnaby, H W Peers, the late A Purvis, Ribble Enthusiasts' Club, H Robinson, J Rostron, C W Routh, S A Staddon, G Spoors, B Taylor, A Temple, A A Townsin, Tyne and Wear PTE, W Woodward, A H Wright.

David Wayman
1997

Abbreviations

Dashes and obliques

Where used between two vehicle numbers, eg "88-99", a dash means "88 to 99", and an oblique, eg "88/99", means "88 and 99". Obliques, where used between service numbers and termini, denote that they correspond, eg, "10/11, Pennywell/Ford", means "10 is Pennywell, 11 is Ford". An oblique between the names of two or more thoroughfares denotes a junction, eg, Newcastle Rd/Viewforth Terr = Newcastle Rd at the junction with Viewforth Terr

Bus bodywork codes (descriptive only; not official)

Prefix letters	body type: **H** = highbridge double deck; **L** = lowbridge double deck; **B** = service bus, single deck; **O** = open-top
Figures	seating capacity: eg **"30/26"** = double deck, 30 upper saloon, 26 lower saloon; a single figure, eg **"35"**, is used for single deck buses or the total for a double deck bus where the upper/lower saloon split is not given; a plus sign followed by a figure, eg **"+19"**, denotes standing capacity where above normal
Suffix letters	entrance/exit: **C** = centre; **F** = front; **R** = rear; **D** = dual doorway; **T** = toastrack (ie, open-sided single deck)

Note. The term *saloon* where used in the text denotes a single deck bus, and *'decker* means a double deck bus.

Unladen weights of vehicles

These are usually abbreviated to three groups of figures, eg 7.19.1 (= 7ton, 19cwt, 1qtr)

Some metric equivalents

1d = 0.4166p.   1s 0d (12d) = 5p.   7ton = 7,112kg.   30ft = 9.144m

1 - A Late Start

Until the late 1920s, most of Sunderland was reached conveniently by the Corporation's cheap and efficient tramway system. People usually had no need to wait for a bus, unless they wanted to travel by company bus or that of a small private operator to a point beyond the County Borough boundary. Indeed, Sunderland had no powers to operate motor buses until the Sunderland Corporation Act, 1927, took effect on 29 July that year and granted those powers (among other provisions), although they were confined to the area within the County Borough as extended by the Act. That excluded areas to be embraced by any future extensions, which was to create problems in subsequent decades. The Corporation began to exercise its powers in 1928, using buses and crews hired from the Northern General Transport Company Ltd (NGT) of Gateshead, which had been operating bus services into Sunderland since 1920. Then in 1929, Sunderland Corporation Tramways Department (SCT) acquired motor buses of its own and had no further need to hire from NGT. That, however, was by no means the end of contact between the two concerns and in later years relationships were at times to become somewhat strained as a result of the restrictions imposed by the 1927 Act.

It was a relatively late start to motor bus operating compared with neighbouring municipalities. Newcastle, South Shields, Stockton, West Hartlepool and Middlesbrough, for example, had begun between 1912 and 1921. The decision to start a bus service was made by the Town Council on 11 January 1928 and came about following several years of concern over the tram service from the town centre to the Docks. Passenger traffic was light on that section and as far back as 1924 it had been suggested that trams should perhaps be replaced by buses but the idea was shelved in the absence of the necessary powers. When that obstacle was overcome, the Docks tramway section was abandoned and on 6 February 1928, NGT buses began to run a "temporary circular omnibus service" to the Docks, on hire to, on behalf of and under the terms and control of Sunderland Corporation. Trams had ceased regular operation the previous day although the tracks were not lifted immediately and the cars continued to run at peak times until July 1929. This was the bus route:

Boro' Rd - Hudson Rd - Lawrence St - The Quadrant - Prospect Row - Barrack St - High St E & W - Fawcett St - Boro' Rd

For the journey of exactly two miles a running time of 14 minutes was allowed and the service ran in both directions. The original terms of hire proposed by the Corporation were that it should retain the whole of the amount collected in fares and contribute $1/2$d per bus mile to NGT. This was not acceptable to the NGT board which would agree only to the Corporation's retaining the total traffic receipts and the Company's being paid its working expenses plus 3d per bus mile. From 1 November 1930 the Docks Circle ran in a clockwise direction only, that is, down High Street East and up Borough Road. This proved unpopular and on 20 December 1930, two-way operation was restored.

As far back as 1878, incidentally, Sunderland Corporation had proposed to have a tramway line built to connect Prospect Row (near the Docks) with the town centre and beyond, via High Street East and West, which would have been operated by the Sunderland Tramways Company, using horse-drawn trams. That proposal was never carried out (although some other lines or parts of them were built). Later under the Sunderland Corporation Act 1899, which empowered the Corporation to purchase the Company, a similar line to the Docks via High Street was authorised. Again, it was never built, due to the expense of overcoming roadway alignment problems in High Street East. Ultimately, however, the whole of the East End comprising much of the territory to the south of the river between the centre of town and the South Docks was linked by bus. The area, incidentally, was the original "sundered land" from which the name Sunderland is derived, being separated by the water from the 7th-century monastery on the north side at St Peter's, Wearmouth, later becoming Monkwearmouth and enveloped by the growing Sunderland. The town was to become a Parliamentary Borough in 1832, a Municipal Borough three years later and a County Borough in 1888, with some subsequent changes.

Many tram and bus passengers would comprise workers in the Docks and nearby industries. The East End at that time was a poor neighbourhood comprising many squalid and overcrowded slum dwellings. As with the tram service, it is doubtful whether many residents would often be able to afford the penny fare to the town centre. Originally the Docks Circle service had no set bus stops and was operated on what many years later would be called a "hail

No2, one of the dozen 1929 Leyland-bodied Leyland Lion LT1s, survived into preservation after service in Jersey during 1937-60 and is seen here at a Brighton historic vehicle rally in 1968, restored to original livery. Note the fleet initials on the bulkhead glass above the rally entry number. The registration number on the offside rear window can be seen through the saloon. *(Copyright P. Wrightson)*

and ride" basis. It was then announced on 24 March 1928 that fixed stops would be used. These were to be:

Museum, Norfolk St, Hendon Rd, Orphan Asylum, Prospect Row, Welcome Tavern, Barrack St, Vine St, Old Market, Bodlewell La, Nile St, Havelock Cinema (ie Mackie's Corner)

Some two months after the decision to operate buses to the Docks, SCT and NGT drew up a similar arrangement for a bus service from Castletown on the north bank of the Wear to Park Lane on the southern fringe of the town centre via this circuitous 5.6-mile route:

Castletown - North Hylton Rd - Southwick tram terminus - Alexandra Bridge - Pallion - Kayll Rd - Chester Rd - Park La

The service started on Saturday 24 March. It appears that the agreement applied only to the section of the route inward from the County Borough boundary on North Hylton Road, as Castletown was then in Sunderland Rural District and SCT had no bus-operating powers within it. Some journeys did extend 0.7mile west of Castletown (Stores) to North Hylton. The terminus was at the meeting of the narrow lane later called Grange Road and Ferryboat Lane, some 600 yards east of the riverside hamlet of North Hylton with its 12th-century ferry, due to turning problems west of that junction.

The statistical returns for the brief period from 6 February to the financial year end on 31 March 1928 were modest. This was understandable when only two route miles were being operated, the North Hylton service not being recorded as a Tramways Department operation until 1932. At least, however, for those few weeks in 1928, traffic revenue exceeded working expenses by £63 while a healthy average of 15.1 passengers were carried for each of the 14,898 miles run. From here on, though, after some faltering in the early years the total passenger figures for the buses would increase and reach a peak nearly thirty years later. All principal statistics are tabulated in Appendix 2.

The Corporation still wanted to expand bus services and so on 11 April 1928 approached NGT about running between Sea Lane and a new council housing estate on the south-western outskirts of the town along Durham Road at Humbledon. This was the five-mile route, avoiding the town centre and operated with hired Northern buses from 7 May 1928:

Sea La - Sea Rd - Fulwell (Blue Bell) - Southwick - Alexandra Bridge - Pallion - Kayll Rd - Barnes Park Rd - Durham Rd - Humbledon

The fare for the whole route was 4d, those above 1d being graduated in multiples of 1d and not $^1/_2$d as on the trams. Halfpenny multiples were to be introduced from 1936, however. The service catered for several shipyards, engineering works and suchlike as well as a mixture of residential areas. Seaside traffic was largely seasonal and dependent on the weather.

When the Humbledon - Sea Lane service was commenced, the North Hylton route was changed south of Alexandra Bridge (the title "Queen" being omitted colloquially and in some documents) because the new service covered the Kayll Road - Alexandra Bridge section. Buses from North Hylton then travelled by the more direct route of Trimdon Street, Silksworth Row and Low Row to reach Park Lane. This reduced the route mileage by 1.4 miles to 4.2. At that time the tramway was yet to be extended to Humbledon from Durham Road/Barnes Park Road and transfer tickets between buses and trams were available at two points. One was at the existing Durham Road tram terminus, enabling passengers to have through ticketing by tram and bus between Fawcett Street and Humbledon for $1^1/_2$d. The other was at Kayll Road on the Circle tram route, with a $1^1/_2$d through ticket between Fawcett Street and Pallion Station

Still eager to expand bus operations, just two days later on 9 May 1928, the Council resolved to arrange with NGT to run a service from Park Lane via Wearmouth Bridge then along the coast to the village of Whitburn, about $1^1/_4$ miles north of the Sea Lane tram terminus and outside the County Borough boundary. This was not the first time the Corporation had expressed interest in Whitburn. More than once it had thought of extending its tramway from Sea Lane to the village but nothing had resulted. The idea of a bus service

also came to nothing. By 1928 the Whitburn-based Economic Bus Service, a partnership between G R Anderson and B Wilson (later E W Wilson), was running on a route from South Shields via Whitburn and Sea Lane to Roker (terminating on private land in order to overcome licensing difficulties). In the same year, Anderson and Wilson applied to Sunderland County Borough Council, which at that time was the licensing authority for services within its boundary, to extend their service to Park Lane. This would have meant that the whole of the route that the Corporation proposed to operate through NGT was covered. Economic's application was rejected, but an appeal to the Ministry of Transport was successful. The service did not in fact operate into Park Lane until after the completion of the new Wearmouth Bridge in 1929. Sunderland Corporation never did run a normal service into Whitburn but later the village was to be included in seaside tours. Tentative efforts by the Corporation to acquire the Economic Bus Service in 1932 were to prove fruitless and Economic remained independent until Tyne and Wear PTE days. One further arrangement to be made in 1928 with NGT, however. On 13 August, a shuttle service was commenced between Humbledon and the existing Durham Road/Barnes Park Road tram terminus, buses connecting with trams in both directions. The service lasted only until the 0.7-mile tramway extension to Humbledon was opened on 4 August 1929.

One part of Sunderland that never was reached easily from a tram route was Ashbrooke, along Tunstall Road and a mile or so from the town centre to the south-west. It was always perhaps a sedate and genteel quarter, virtually devoid of industry and less

Like an enormous limousine, the second-hand 1928 Thornycroft LB displays its number, 13, alongside the entrance. There are no doors but there is a half-bulkhead behind the cab. The bugle-shaped horn projects from the cab offside front and the speed limit is given as 20mph. *(Copyright Sunderland Libraries per R Marshall)*

densely populated than many other parts of the town. There was demand for a public transport service and as the area clearly was not viable tramway territory this would have to be bus-operated. In 1925, while the tramway was being extended from the Royalty to Durham Road/Barnes Park Road, the road was closed and vehicles of the Sunderland District Omnibus Co Ltd (SDO) that normally used Durham Road were diverted along Tunstall Road and Alexandra Road, stopping to pick up local passengers. This procedure continued following the re-opening of Durham Road. From December 1926, after being approached by the Corporation, SDO ran additional buses from Union Street in the town centre to Bainbridge Holme Road via Tunstall Road. What this meant, however, was that the Corporation had thrown away the initiative and Ashbrooke became SDO operating territory. From 1931, when the entire share capital of SDO was acquired by NGT, operating control passed to the parent company. In later years this was to be a factor contributing to some of the Corporation's difficulties as has been hinted already.

In anticipation of running its own buses and to assist also with its tramway operations, on 18 September 1928 the Council decided to buy the former premises of D H & G Haggie Ltd, manufacturers of wire ropes, in Fulwell Road. The building was converted to a bus garage, although tram tracks were laid in the yard and used for parking special trams during football matches at nearby Roker Park. On 18 September 1928 also, the local branch of the Independent Labour Party and the Pallion Ward Labour Committee asked the Council to arrange with NGT to provide Pallion with a bus link to the town centre. The Council deferred consideration and Pallion residents had to wait for their bus service to Town.

The sudden death of Mr Archibald R Dayson, Tramways Department General Manager since 1904, occurred on 19 November 1928. Anyone hoping that Mr Dayson's successor would recommend the sweeping away of the tramway system in favour of motor buses was to be disappointed. That process was not to be completed for another 26 years, but in autumn 1928, the Corporation had these three bus services, operated with hired buses and crews as the Tramways Department still had no buses of its own:

Docks Circle
Humbledon - Sea Lane
Humbledon - Barnes Park Rd shuttle service

It was not until 12 December 1928 that the Council decided to advertise for the supply of twelve buses comprising eight new and four second-hand vehicles, all 32-seaters. The chassis manufacturers responding comprised AEC, Maudslay, Karrier, Crossley, Halley, Albion, Guy, Leyland, Dennis, Bristol, Commer and Tilling-Stevens, prices ranging from £760 to £831. Four types chosen for demonstration on 15 February 1929 were the AEC 426, Leyland Lion, Commer F4 and Tilling Stevens B10A2. All were taken over a circular route through Whitburn and the outcome was that twelve new Leyland Lions with Leyland-built bodywork were ordered. Tenders for four second-hand buses were received but not pursued. In the statistics for the year ending 31 March 1929, passenger and revenue averages were disappointing and working expenses exceeded traffic revenue by 19 per cent. A nett deficit of £1,922 was incurred.

Mr Charles Albert Hopkins as took up the post of General Manager and Engineer on 1 May 1929. Previously he had held a similar post with the Wigan Corporation Tramways Motors and Trolley Bus Undertaking although his transport career had begun with Swindon Corporation Tramways in 1905. After moving to the Chatham and District Light Railway Company five years later he had joined Wigan in 1919, becoming General Manager in 1925. There had been 23 applicants for the Sunderland post, the other three interviewees being:

Municipal tramway General Managers: Mr C I Baker (Ashton-under-Lyne),
Mr H Clayton (Preston);
Mr H W Snowball (Rolling Stock Engineer, Sunderland).

The twelve new Leyland Lions, numbered 1-12, were beginning to arrive and within about a week the first seven had been delivered. These were enough to allow the Docks Circle service to be operated by the Corporation and on 8 May the take-over became effective. More arrived within five weeks and SCT buses began to run on the Humbledon - Sea Lane service from 19 June. Although it is not mentioned specifically in any extant report, it seems likely that the Durham Road shuttle service was taken over at the same time. This, of course, had only a matter of weeks to run before the tramway extension was opened.

Leyland Motors had introduced the Lion type LSC originally in 1925, gaining a reputation for reliability and petrol economy. Updated and re-designated type LT1 in 1929, it was a medium-weight model, sharing some features with the contemporary but heavier-duty Tiger TS1 type. The Lion, however, was powered by a new design of four-cylinder overhead-valve engine of the same bore and stroke as the earlier type. Principal details of these and later buses are tabulated in Appendix 1.

As has been mentioned, SCT's first Leyland Lions had bodywork built by the chassis manufacturers, timber-framed as was then usual. Although no doors were fitted, photographic evidence suggests that they may have been specified originally and then removed. The 32 seats were upholstered with attractive red leather. At that time, the town's entire tram fleet had wooden seats! The bus livery below the waistrail was maroon like that of the trams, with cream above. There can be no doubt that the Lion was a wise choice. Leyland's model range from the late 1920s was founded on advanced, sound design principles with good manufacturing practices using high-quality components that were serviceable and durable. Fuel economy was as good and better than that of many competitors' products. Overall reliability and effective service back-up meant that maintenance costs were relatively low.

On 1 July 1929, Mr Hopkins reported to the Tramways Committee that a further eight buses would be needed for service expansion. This would include a route to the new estate of a thousand council houses to be built at Ford, to the west of Pallion. Mr Hopkins also expressed the opinion that Sunderland's tram and bus fares were "wonderful value for money." In fact, at that time, tram passengers could travel up to 1.9 miles for 1d and bus passengers up to two miles, the average being 1.3. No other municipal bus operator could offer a higher average mileage for a penny. Indeed, for some years following the abolition of the trams, Wearsiders were to remain accustomed to relatively cheap bus travel although the situation could remain only for as long as there was efficient operation coupled with high usage. The Corporation was relieved to find itself without the burden of having to pay working expenses to NGT from 4 August 1929. Years later and in a somewhat different form, however, the problem was to come back to stay.

In the late 1920s there was some discussion among operators as to how tramways, sometimes considered obsolescent, should be replaced. Some favoured the trolleybus, because it required indigenous fuel. Others preferred the motor bus on account of its greater flexibility and lower capital investment. On 14 August 1929, Sunderland Council rejected the idea that its trams should be replaced by trolleybuses. Indeed, the question of replacing trams at all, the Docks route having been an exceptional case, was not to be entertained until after World War II and there was to be considerable expansion both before and after that. Motor buses clearly were set to play a secondary role for many years to come. On Saturday 30 August 1929, a 6d Round Tour ticket became available for travel by tram from the Town Hall to Sea Lane, then by bus to Humbledon, and then back to the Town Hall by tram, or *vice versa*. The total distance was nearly ten miles and the ticket represented a saving of 1d on the aggregate of the normal fares for the three journeys.

A tragic incident occurred only five months after the introduction of Corporation buses. At that time, Humbledon-bound buses left Alexandra Bridge by the right-hand prong of a forked junction to reach Pallion New Road. On Thursday 17 October 1929, John Bright, a car shed cleaner acting as spare conductor, fell from his doorless bus as it turned from the bridge. He was then taken on the bus to the Royal Infirmary but it never arrived there because at the Green Terrace/Vine Place junction it collided with a tram and received serious damage. Mr Bright died of his injuries but it was said that the collision did not contribute to his death. Two months later, a boy aged nine years became the first pedestrian to be killed by a Corporation bus when he was run over by Leyland Lion No2 in High Street East. Significantly, most pedestrian fatal accidents in subsequent years were to involve either children or elderly persons. Some seven years after John Bright's fall, an elderly male passenger received fatal injuries after falling from a bus at the same spot. Another Lion, No11, was to be involved in a fatal accident while running along Kayll Road on 30 July 1930, colliding with a motor car and killing a female passenger in it.

One main thoroughfare not yet served by SCT was

Newcastle Road, although company buses ran along it to and from Tyneside destinations. The area was developing and on 11 November 1929 the Corporation commenced a bus service between Newcastle Road/Viewforth Terrace and Noble's Bank Road at Hendon, an area of older housing and dense population to the south-east of the town centre. Previously, Hendon residents had been served, a little remotely, by the Docks trams and buses and the Villette Road tramway section. The new 2.4-mile bus route was:

Newcastle Rd - Wheat Sheaf - Wearmouth Bridge - Fawcett St - Boro' Rd - Hudson Rd - Hendon Rd - Noble's Bank Rd/Mainsforth Terr

After two months the southern terminus was moved 200 yards north to the end of Noble's Bank Road. During this period, too, a used bus was acquired for driver-training and numbered 13. A 1928 Thornycroft LB-type, it was a normal-control model, that is, with the bonnet projecting forward of the saloon so that the instructor could be positioned alongside the trainee. SCT purchased the bus from independent operator W Ankers of Winlaton-on-Tyne at cost of £325, spending £155 on preparing it for service in Sunderland. No official record of the body make seems to have survived but it is believed to have been Thornycroft's own "Tetrarch" type. From February 1930 on football Saturdays all thirteen buses in the fleet were needed to meet service requirements and so No13 was brought into use for passenger-carrying also. While there were to be several Thornycroft lorries in the Department's internal service vehicle fleet over the years, 13 was to remain the only bus of that make ever to be operated by SCT. Mr Hopkins, however, knew something about Thornycrofts as he had operated seventeen of them in his Wigan motor bus fleet.

As to football, Sunderland AFC, then in the original the First Division of the Football League, attracted relatively large crowds to home matches. Opportunities were taken to provide special buses to serve the Roker Park stadium. In September 1929, a service was commenced from near the north landing of the Ferry, a route mileage of 0.6. Like the nearby St Peter's Church, the river crossing could trace its origins back to the seventh century. A 3.1-mile Football Ground - St Luke's Cross via Alexandra Bridge special service was introduced in February 1930. Another regular service started on 10 February 1930, at last linking St Luke's Cross with the town centre via the following 1.7-mile route:

St Luke's Cross - Pallion New Rd - Deptford (Trimdon St) - Town (Union St)

For the 0.65mile west of Alexandra Bridge (South End) to St Luke's Cross it shared the path of the Humbledon - Sea Lane service. East of Alexandra Bridge to High Street West/Low Row it ran the same way as the North Hylton - Park Lane buses. Once again, shipyards and other centres of heavy industry were served, including the large Pyrex glassworks, as well as some densely-populated communities. The service was an immediate success. To 31 March 1930 its average figures were 15.2 passengers and 18.07d per mile, both well above average.

In March, tenders were received for the supply of further new buses from AEC, Bristol, Dennis, Karrier, Leyland, TS Motors (as Tilling-Stevens had become) and Thornycroft. A Dennis blue-liveried double deck demonstrator, new in 1929, was used on the Town - St Luke's Cross service. As a result of its apparent success the Corporation ordered three similar buses and purchased the demonstrator. Eight more Leylands comprising six Lions and two Tigers were ordered also.

The widening role of the bus in Sunderland was now reflected in the title of the Department which was changed to Tramways and Motors, although the name of the Committee remained unaltered. Sixteen drivers and sixteen conductors were employed to staff 13 buses, compared with 92 motormen and 89 conductors for the fleet of 83 trams. By 31 March 1930, bus mileage represented some 17 per cent of tram mileage but the number of bus passengers came to less than 10 per cent of the trams' total. Growth in bus activities is perhaps illustrated by the fact that for the month of May 1930 alone, the total of 446,840 passengers was almost double the May 1929 figure.

This is believed to be PG 6564, the Massey-bodied Dennis demonstrator loaned to and subsequently acquired by SCT in 1930. It is possible to see the upper saloon bench seats for three. The design incorporating set-back upper saloon was about to go out of fashion, although this bus did have the platform and staircase enclosed which was a new idea.

(Copyright Northern Counties, courtesy R Marshall)

Gruss air springs had been fitted to one bus, regrettably not identified in records, and were successful. At that time there was anxiety over the state of the road surface in parts of the town, including Pallion, and so all four Dennises were to be fitted with Gruss equipment, too. It was an early form of air-suspension, made in Glasgow although an American idea, comprising two vertical cylinders mounted on an extension to the chassis frame front dumb irons. Gruss claimed a 65 per cent reduction in the effect of vibration and road shocks and the springs required little attention apart from oiling and inflating.

The buses on order entered service over the high summer period of 1930. In June, the Dennis demonstrator with Surrey registration mark was purchased and taken into stock, keeping its blue livery. The 1930 intake was:

14-19	Leyland Lion LT2	Roe
20/21	Leyland Tiger TS2	Roe
22	Dennis HS	Massey (ex-demonstrator)
23-25	Dennis HV	Massey

Leyland's LT2-type Lion, introduced in 1930, was an improved version of the LT1 although engine and gearbox were unchanged. The highly-reputable Chas H Roe of Cross Gates Carriage Works, Leeds, builder of the 32-seat bodies on Nos14-21, was to supply the majority of SCT's peacetime bus bodywork until 1966. Roe specialised in good-quality teak-framed construction which was be renowned for robustness and long life. A characteristic of Roe bodies built during that period was the provision of rectangular ventilator covers with flared ends, postioned above the side windows. Another typical feature was the "proud" waistrail running along the sides and rear of the body and this was to be a characteristic of most Roe products until the 1960s. Lion 16 was an odd one out. Finished in a livery of mid-red, it is believed to have remained unique in this respect for several years.

Leyland's Tiger was a more powerful and heavier-duty chassis than the Lion. Introduced in 1927, the original TS1 model was intended for bodywork of 27ft 6in length. The TS2 came out in 1928, designed for 26ft-long bodywork but otherwise similar to the TS1. Its exceptionally refined and quiet six-cylinder engine was almost inaudible from the saloon when idling. The pair of TS2 Tigers was acquired in anticipation of the Corporation's obtaining powers to operate outside the County Borough boundary and then taking over the Park Lane - North Hylton service. This development was not to take place until 1932 and even then the service was to be a joint SCT-NGT operation.

Dennis 'deckers 22-25, like the Thornycroft saloon, were the only examples of their make to be operated by SCT. Massey Bros, however, were to supply wartime bodywork, followed by two normal batches in 1946-48. Although some fleet lists have described the 48-seat bodies as highbridge, they were in fact of lowbridge configuration. For a period between 1930 and 1933, they were used on the Villette Road section and as will be mentioned shortly, this had an overhead railway bridge with just 13ft 10in headroom. A normal highbridge bus would have a height of about 14ft 6in, compared with about 13ft 6in for a lowbridge type. Moreover, these

Dennises had sunken gangways at both sides, possibly with centrally-positioned seats arranged herringbone-fashion in one or both of Nos24/25, and transverse rows of three-seat benches (rearmost bench, two-seat) in the remaining one or two. The sunken gangway was, of course, an essential feature of the lowbridge design. Twin gangways were in vogue only for a relatively short period as they took up valuable seating space. It may be however, that they were introduced initially to avoid infringing Leyland patents on lowbridge designs. Nos23-25, of type HV, differed from HS-type No22 visibly at the front end of the chassis where the steering column was was much more upright and the driving position lowered and moved forward. By this means, the amount of space available for the body on the HV was increased to 20ft 9in, 8¾in more than on the HS.

An operating change took place while the new buses were being delivered. On June 26 1930, the Town - St Luke's Cross service was extended 0.45mile via St Luke's Terrace to Westmoor Road/General Havelock Road on the new Ford Estate. Further changes were to take place as the development expanded. In 1930

A Dennis covered-top double-deck bus. Four of this type have just been ordered by the SUNDERLAND CORPORATION.

The bus in this Dennis publicity photograph is believed one of 23-25, new in 1930 and with Massey bodywork. It may be compared with the demonstrator regarding differences in such features as radiator shape and position, and steering column angle.

(Copyright Ribble Enthusiasts' Club)

also, for two reasons, there was concern over the 1.42-mile Fawcett Street - Villette Road tramway section, running via Borough Road, Tatham Street, Suffolk Street and Rosalie Terrace. First, the low railway bridge mentioned earlier precluded the use of double deck tramcars and the single deckers being used were now in a worn state. Second, the track was in poor condition. The Council was faced with the alternatives of (a) withdrawing the tram service permanently and substituting buses, (b) renewing the track and obtaining new single deck cars, and (c) renewing the track, increasing the 13ft 10in headroom of the bridge by at least two feet and operating the service with double deck cars.

It was decided to replace the trams with buses, but this turned out to be only an interim measure. The bus service commenced on 27 August 1930 and there was an immediate and remarkable effect on passenger loadings, despite the fact that some of the residents had petitioned to keep their trams. During the first 26 days of August 1930, the number of tram passengers had averaged 7,746 daily. From 27 to 31 August, the buses carried a daily average of 8,609 and receipts were increased by more than £3 a day. Traffic analyses also reveal that for the remainder of the year to 31 March

1931, the buses averaged 8,750 passengers per day on the Villette Road section. For the full year ended 31 March 1930, the trams had averaged 6,209 but service improvements had increased this to 7,731 for the period from 1 April to 26 August 1930. Even so, the buses came out better.

From September 1930, the Villette Road section was linked with the Town - Ford service. The intensity of the passenger traffic on these sections may be judged by the fact that the basic frequency was five minutes on Monday - Friday and four minutes on Saturday. Yet Mr Hopkins was by no means convinced that the bus was necessarily the permanent solution for Villette Road, a message made clear in his various reports to the Committee. The upshot was that the Council agreed to the purchase of an experimental new single deck tramcar for Villette Road. It was a long, eight-wheel bogie car that had 50 upholstered seats rather than 28 or 34 wooden ones as in the older, short cars. The new one entered service on 11 March 1931, taking the place of a bus on the Fawcett Street - Villette Road section. In his Annual Report for 31 March 1931, Mr Hopkins said that revenue per mile indicated that the popularity of the new car was instantaneous and had been sustained. "This experiment has clearly proved that the majority of the public prefer a modern tram against the modern bus," he concluded.

Road transport at that time was undergoing some radical changes. The Road Traffic Act 1930 was on the statute book and Part IV of it came into force on 1 December 1930. This dealt with the regulation of public service vehicles (PSVs), creating eleven traffic areas, each with Commisssioners who would issue licences and have power to co-ordinate road services. Sunderland was part of the Northern Traffic Area, based in Newcastle and comprising the counties of Durham, Northumberland, Cumberland and Westmorland, with parts of Lancashire and the North Riding of Yorkshire. Part IV also required all PSVs to be examined in order to receive a Certificate of Fitness (CoF) by 1 April 1931. Under Part V, coming into effect on 1 January 1931, municipalities could run bus services without applying to Parliament for permission. They could also operate services outside their own areas by consent of the Traffic Commissioners and they could make working agreements with other operators. Other Parts of the Act were to do with the licensing of drivers and conductors, speed limits and matters concerning other forms of road transport. One of the effects of the Act on Sunderland Corporation was that it could now operate on services to North Hylton and other places outside the County Borough boundary subject to the necessary consent and the granting of licences. Some operators, generally the larger ones, were able to obtain protection for themselves by establishing their "own" territories through area agreements, although to some extent these were virtually already in existence.

For several years during the decade, depressed economic conditions were to have an adverse effect on the Corporation's transport fortunes. Sunderland's principal industry was shipbuilding but much employment was also provided by ship repairing, marine and other heavy engineering, coal mining and port activities. Ships are known to have been built on the River Wear from 1346 and the remains of a primitive oak boat discovered in the river bed at Hylton in 1885 were estimated to be about 4,000 years old. By the twentieth century, Sunderland was styling itself "the largest shipbuilding town in the world" in terms of tonnage launched per year within the local authority boundary. The boom years of World War I had been followed by a slump, but in the late 1920s there came a welcome recovery. This, however, was followed by a drastic fall during 1930-35. The situation was reflected in the bus operating figures for the year ending 31 March 1931. The Docks Circle showed a reduction of 125,431 passengers, representing 8.25 per cent. There was a slight rise in passenger journeys on the Humbledon - Sea Lane service which would have been much greater but for the lack of work in the shipyards along the route. The average revenue per mile on this service showed a fall from 11.08d to 10.55d, representing 4.78 per

cent. Revenue per bus mile at that time needed to exceed 10.2d merely to clear working expenses. The overall picture, though, was by no means dismal. It was the first full financial year of Corporation-owned bus activities and had seen mileage go up by more than 130 per cent. Passenger journeys had increased by nearly 150 per cent. Per mile, the average number of passengers and traffic revenue had risen. Working expenses were a comfortable 74 per cent of traffic revenue.

In June 1931, it was proposed to extend the Noble's Bank Road - Newcastle Road/Viewforth Terrace service to North Hylton via Thompson Road, Southwick, Marley Pots and Castletown, but the application for this was never made to the Traffic Commissioners. On 1 July 1931, some journeys on the Humbledon - Sea Lane route were diverted after leaving Humbledon to reach Ormonde Street via Ettrick Grove and Mount Road, rather than Durham Road and Barnes Park Road, applying only during the morning and mid-afternoon as a facility for schoolchildren. Application was made in December 1931, and refused, for a new service Town - Tunstall Road. As has been mentioned, SDO was already serving the area.

Cheap travel was extended on 24 February 1932. Transfer tickets, which had been available on the trams for three years, were now extended to the Docks Circle buses. It then became possible to make a journey between the Docks and five points on tram routes for a penny. Transfer tickets were available to and from St Barnabas (via Tatham Street), Villette Road (via Christ Church), the Royalty, St Mark's Church and the Wheat Sheaf. The maximum distance involved here was 1.82 miles (St Mark's Church) and the average was 1.65. Previously, these journeys would have entailed two 1d fares. A further facility introduced at about this time was the all-day ticket, priced 1s 0d and valid for journeys of any length by tram and/or bus except on the North Hylton route. The existing 6d Round Tour ticket was to remain available until 1938.

At a hearing before the Northern Area Traffic Commissioners held in Sunderland on 3 March 1932, the Chairman approved an agreement between SCT and NGT to operate a Sunderland - Castletown - North Hylton service, which was the service that had been operated by NGT alone from 1928. However, the Chairman also said that outside its own municipal area the Corporation ought not to have protection but to compete on equal terms. The outcome of this decision was seen on 1 June 1932 the Sunderland (Park Lane) - North Hylton service became a joint SCT - NGT operation. It was Northern's service 48, this being adopted by the Corporation when its own services received identifying numbers in 1953. Return tickets and 12-journey tickets were available between specified points on this service from the commencement of Corporation joint running. The North Hylton - Park Lane return fare was 8$\frac{1}{2}$d and a 12-journey ticket between Castletown (Schools) and Park Lane was 3s 3d.

The Ford terminus was altered to Fordham Road on 31 August 1932, increasing the route length by 0.17mile. Six weeks later, the Tramways Committee received a letter from the Ford Estate Branch of the Houghton-le-Spring Divisional Labour Party (Ford then being in that constituency) suggesting an alteration. The Committee replied that it could not see its way to making a change. On 21 September, the Newcastle Road section was extended by 0.135mile to a new terminus at Charlton Road/Cairns Road. Then on 18 October an experimental service between Southwick Tram Terminus and Elmwood Avenue on the nearby Marley Pots council housing development was started as a tram feeder. The intention was to run it for a fortnight but loadings were so poor that it was withdrawn after only four days. At about this time also, the Ford - Villette Road service was split, buses then running separately on the Town (Union Street) - Ford and the Town (Fawcett Street) - Villette Road sections. The Council agreed to another change on 9 November 1932, substituting the word "Transport" for "Tramways" in the title of the Committee.

The eyes of the Council had been on the Villette Road route since 11 March 1931, when the new single deck bogie tram had started operating alongside buses. In a confidential report to the Committee on 1 July 1932, Mr Hopkins opined that modern double deck tramcars would considerably augment revenue on the service and that the then current operating costs of 11.5d per mile would drop almost to 11d. It was therefore decided to reinstate a full service of double deck trams to the Villette Road section, achievable of course only by renewing the track and increasing the headroom under the Tatham Street bridge. This work was carried out, and following a short suspension of tramway operation with the new single deck car, buses were withdrawn and trams took over on 11 January 1933. The new single decker, incidentally, continued to run on the service with the double deck cars and after a metamorphoric career at Leeds, still survives in the 1990s at the National Tramway Museum, Crich, Derbyshire.

An analysis of the statistics suggest that the argument in favour of trams may not have been so convincing as it appeared. The only full financial year of mixed operation on Villette Road had been 1931-32. During that year, the solitary tram had operated 12.37 per cent of the mileage, carried 13.76 per cent of the passengers and taken 13.47 per cent of the revenue. Although no separate figure for the operating expenses of the new single deck tram has been recorded, the average for all trams was 11.9d per mile for that financial year compared with 10.0d for buses. It could be argued that the advantages of restoring trams to Villette Road were marginal. The Annual Report for 31 March 1932 referred to falling passenger traffic on the Docks Circle route and the Ford section, attributable to unemployment. At that time about 30,000 persons, 60 per cent of those contributing to National Unemployment Insurance in Sunderland, were out of work, with no sign of upturn. The number of bus passenger journeys made during the 1932/33 financial year fell by 8 per cent but the average per mile was down 14 per cent on the previous year. Revenue dropped to 11.2d per mile average. The figures for the trams were down, too, but much less markedly than for the buses.

Bus fares were increased on 1 April 1933 but the effect was less fruitful than anticipated. There was an organised boycott of the buses on the Ford section and on 1 October the fares reverted to their previous levels. Meanwhile, this re-organisation of bus services took place on 24 May 1933, providing a more efficient match of cross-town sections:

Old
Cairns Rd - Town - Noble's Bank Rd
Ford - Town

New
Cairns Rd - Town - High St - Docks - Boro' Rd - Town - Cairns Rd
Ford - Town - Noble's Bank Rd

Unchanged
Docks Circle (Town - Boro' Rd - Docks - High St - Town)

The Transport Committee was again considering the future direction of the undertaking, although there was now no mention of trolleybuses. In a report dated 12 June 1933 the General Manager recommended the continued development of the tramway on which new and modernised cars were entering service. One proposed new tramway section was Wheat Sheaf - Fulwell via Newcastle Road. Had it been built it would have replaced the Cairns Road bus section. Relatively minor extensions to each end of the Ford - Noble's Bank Road route and a new Town (Union Street) - Ettrick Grove service were proposed but not implemented immediately. Another suggested new bus service was one to South Hylton and although this was not to be pursued in the 1960s, the existing one did not in fact become integrated with other historically municipal bus operations until 1995 when a powerful organisation called Stagecoach had begun to dominate the scene.

The early 1930s comprised a period when operators were looking for a possible alternative to the petrol engine. Some advantages seemed to be offered by what was then called the *oil* or *compression-ignition (CI)* engine, soon to be known popularly as the diesel. The findings of some early pioneer diesel operators from 1928 had shown that substantial economies could be made and they would quickly outweigh the diesel's higher initial cost. It was a more reliable type of engine, was cheaper to maintain and could amass much greater mileages between overhauls. SCT, like many others, held back initially but eventually carried out diesel trials. These began on 17 November 1933 when Leyland Lion 14 re-entered service fitted with a four-cylinder Gardner 4LW diesel in place of its original petrol engine. The six-cylinder 8.1-litre diesel engine produced by Leyland, late in 1932 and considerably behind AEC and Crossley, for example, obviously was too large and powerful for the fairly lightweight Lion and the smaller Gardner 4LW was more appropriate.

Gardner already was held in high esteem and although 14's gear change was now a little slower due to the heavier engine, the economy of the 4LW soon began to show. Its fuel consumption over the first five months was 14.29mpg compared with an average of 6.25mpg for the rest of the fleet. Moreover, the Corporation was paying only 5.25d per gallon for fuel oil, including 1d tax, compared with 11.96d for petrol. The cost advantage was reduced as from 8 August 1935 when the tax on fuel oil was increased from 1d to 8d per gallon. Even so, the diesel offered worthwhile savings as may be shown in these figures:

Year(s) ending 31 Mar	Fleet total	Petrol-engined	Diesel-engined	Cost of fuel(s) per bus mile	% of working expenses
1931-33	25	25	-	1.918d	19.0
1939	40	9	31	1.384d	15.4

Turning now to safety, a most unfortunate event occurred in Hudson Road on 15 October 1933 when a boy of five was fatally injured by a Docks-bound bus as the driver was taking action to avoid other children. A verdict of accidental death was returned at the inquest but the jury added a rider implying that the service schedule required excessive speed. The Watch Committee asked the Chief Constable for a special report and in this he reinforced the suggestion. Through the Transport Committee, the General Manager replied, refuting the allegation. He referred to the facts of the case, praised the action of the driver (while regretting its consequence) and said that the Corporation's average service speed was 9.13mph compared with the 10.02mph of seventeen other undertakings he had circulated. Even so, he continued, the Docks Circle schedule had been revised slightly and approved by the Traffic Commissioners. (In fact, the average scheduled speed on that service had been only 8.57mph. The jury's allegation was clearly based on inconclusive evidence, there being no eye-witness accounts of the speed of the bus immediately before the accident.) Children and elderly people continued to be vulnerable to injury and death, the details of pedestrian fatalities involving buses for the first ten years of bus operation (8 May 1929 - 31 March 1939) being:

Sex	Ages	Total	Incidence
Male	5 (two), 6, 7, 9, 13, 71	7	-
Female	3, 7, 64, 80	4	(both sexes) 1 in 659,597 bus miles

Trams comparison, same period (summarised):
12 fatal pedestrian accidents. Incidence 1 in 1.585M tram miles

The local level of unemployment was affecting the buses more than the trams, as the buses served more of the large works premises such as the shipyards. For the year ending 31 March 1934 the figures were depressing. However, a travel facility was made cheaper on 1 April when the all-day ticket was reduced in price from 1s 0d to 9d (6d to 4^{1}/2d for children).

During the same month, a 7.0-litre Gardner 5LW diesel engine was fitted to Dennis 25 and its original petrol engine was subsequently transferred to Dennis 22. During its first 600 miles with the new engine, No25 returned an average of 10.71mpg. This is likely to have been more than double the figure for its petrol unit.

The five-cylinder Gardner 5LW was destined to outnumber all other types of engine in the fleet. Of 236 new diesel-engined buses purchased during 1934-58, 149 were to be 5LW-powered, including four with the 5HLW horizontal version. There were to be fifty with the 8.4-litre 6LW and two with the 5.6-litre 4LW. Of other makes of engine in new buses, 19 were to be Crossley, nine AEC, four Daimler and three Leyland. Gardner represented 85 per cent of engines.

In the trams-versus-buses debate of this period, Mr Hopkins was prominent among the advocates for trams. During 1931-34, addressing various organisations, he said:

■ that the town's tramway system was excellent, compact and an asset to the ratepayers;

■ "We have definitely proved that the travelling public prefer a modern tramcar to a modern omnibus" (a clear reference to events on the Villette Road section);

■ that for densely-populated areas, the tramcar was still the safest and most useful means of moving heavy loads at peak times, although there was room for motor buses and trolleybuses according to local conditions;

■ that while some transport personnel were smitten with 'busitis', modern trams had rapid acceleration, upholstered seating, well-sprung trucks and they rode on jointless track and they had definitely captured the public imagination.

During summer 1934, Leyland Lions 2/4 were withdrawn and sold. SCT had aimed at what was then a reasonably typical life of five years for the type but only these two achieved such a low figure with their original operator. Another two of the 1929 dozen, 7/10, gave fourteen years' service and the average age at withdrawal for the whole batch was 8¹/2 years. No2 emigrated to Jersey where it was re-registered J 9008. In 1960 it was acquired for preservation by Michael Plunkett and took part in early rallies of restored heavy vehicles. It was to return to Sunderland in 1979 for the transport centenary celebrations.

The summer of 1934 was a poor one with a cold Whit weekend and a wet August bank holiday. From midsummer's day the Docks - Cairns Road service was extended 0.9mile to Sea Lane on Sundays and holidays. At the end of July, two Guy Wolf type CF20 normal-control single deck chassis were delivered, fitted with Guy 'toastrack' bodies for use on local tours from Sea Lane tram terminus. Originally the Traffic Commissioners refused a licence to operate them. The Corporation appealed successfully to the Minister of Transport. Like Lion 16, the Wolves were finished in bright red with lining-out. They were always known both officially and colloquially as *tram-o-cars*, not toastracks. (Tramocars Ltd was a Worthing-based company then operating small vehicles on seaside tours, its title being adopted for appropriate usage by some other operators.)

Originally SCT's Wolves were un-numbered and identified only by their registration numbers, GR 1156/1157. Weather permitting, they operated until the end of September on the Coast Tour from Sea Lane along the sea front to Whitburn at a 2d fare and on the Town Tour at a fare of 6d. Despite the adverse weather and the short season, the tours were considered a success and were to be extended. The Town Tour ran around this circuit:

Sea Lane - Whitburn - Shields Rd - Thompson Rd - Alexandra Bridge - Pallion - Ford - Hylton Rd - Kayll Rd - Barnes Park Rd - Alexandra Rd - Grangetown - Hendon - Docks - High St E & W - Wearmouth Bridge - Wheat Sheaf - Roker - Sea Lane

On 16 August 1934 the Council made the momentous decision of approving the purchase of two Daimler COG5 chassis powered by the Gardner 5LW engine and fitted with Roe double deck centre-entrance bodywork. It marked the beginning of a relationship with Daimler that was to last for some three decades although its effects continued for many more years. Another 180 Daimler chassis were to join the fleet to 1966, comprising 55 per cent of new vehicles. Perhaps significantly, Mr Hopkins and the Chairman of the Committee, Alderman R Dixon Jeffrey, had been

The second member of the first pair of Guy Wolf tram-o-cars, new in 1934, here shows its open sides and canvas screens. A second pair was delivered in 1935, differing only in minor details. The seating arrangement over the rear wheels is noteworthy. A trip along the sea front in a tram-o-car would have been, er, bracing! (Copyright Sunderland Echo)

Here Daimler 26 is in its sixteenth year and wearing the early post-war "plain", non-streamlined version of red and cream, its final livery. A conventional windscreen wiper has been fitted for many years, the conductor's stirrup has been moved to the dumb iron and the autovac has been replaced by a lift pump (under the bonnet). The angle-iron diagonal stay at the front of the canopy (fitted to several COG5s by the Corporation) is not intended to support the upper saloon floor but to restrict relative movement of the "floating" cab. As standard with the pre-war Daimlers, the half-drop windows have been replaced by top-sliders, a single spot lamp is fitted and a revised type of bonnet side panel without louvres has been fitted. This bus and its twin, 27, carried an advertisement for Young's, the then Ford dealers, in place of the usual "Binns" exhortation at the rear. Typical Roe body features include the proud teak waistrails of both saloons (the upper one being omitted on new production from about 1948) and, until 1942, the ventilator covers with flared ends (above the lower saloon windows).

(Copyright R Marshall)

among those present at a demonstration 30-mile run from Newcastle to Morpeth and back on Tuesday 2 December 1930 involving one single deck and two double deck Daimler petrol-engined buses with the then newly-introduced fluid flywheel and preselective gearbox. It seems clear that the Sunderland representatives were impressed by the advanced Daimler transmission and this may well have influenced subsequent decisions.

Once again, on 9 November 1934, the Council considered seeking powers to operate trolleybuses but no further action was taken. Then on 28 December the Corporation applied to start a new service, Town - Chester Road (Grindon Mill Inn), 1.2 miles west of Kayll Road and in a developing area. It was already served by NGT and SDO buses going beyond the boundary and SCT's application was refused. Municipal buses were not to reach Grindon until post-war years. By mid-December 1934, however, the two new Daimler COG5s had been delivered as Nos26/27. They heralded a new age in Sunderland's transport.

2 - Two New Ages

Sunderland Corporation's Leyland Lions and Tigers of 1929/30 had been ahead of many of their competitors technically. In the words of Charles Hopkins, they would not be improved upon for some years to come. The Daimler COG5 was in a somewhat different class but it could hardly have been bettered for the way in which it combined economy and reliability with distinctive and refined specification. Sunderland's first two examples had the following features and characteristics which, as the COG5 was to be the pre-war standard, moved the fleet into a more advanced era:

Daimler chassis
robustness, good reliability, low maintenance costs

Gardner 5LW engine
outstanding economy and dependability

Preselective 5-speed gearbox
quick, easy gear changes

Fluid flywheel
smooth starting from rest under all conditions

Roe teak-framed bodywork
sound construction, durability, long and trouble-free service

Centre entrance and Y-shaped dual staircase
rapid loading and unloading

The Daimler Company had pioneered alternatives to the layshaft gearbox and friction clutch. Development of the preselective epicyclic gearbox had been carried out by W G Wilson and indeed Sunderland Corporation, among others, generally referred to it as the "Wilson gearbox", whatever its make. The fluid flywheel was a form of hydro-dynamic transmission coupling developed by Daimler under Vulcan-Sinclair patents. Following three years of successfully combining preselective gearbox and fluid flywheel in its motor cars, Daimler marketed the combination as standard for bus chassis in 1930 and this was a significant milestone in transport history. AEC, Crossley and later Guy and Leyland were to offer the option of preselective gearbox with fluid transmission.

On Daimler buses until 1953, gears were preselected by means of a lever set in a quadrant arrangement on the right of the steering column. Ratio positions were marked 5-4-3-2-1-N-R (four speeds from 1943) and the lever was moved into the required position at any time in advance of the change of ratio. A baulking mechanism prevented inadvertent selection of reverse. There was no clutch pedal and what looked like one was actually the gear-change pedal which engaged the pre-selected gear ratio. It had to be depressed the full length of its travel or else it would shoot back beyond its normal position, possibly causing injury. If the vehicle was stationary and in gear, the engine would idle through the fluid flywheel. Then when the accelerator pedal was depressed and engine speed rose to about 600rpm, the

flywheel would take up the drive and the bus would move away smoothly. When the engine was idling in neutral the passengers would hear a "whooping" sound varying in pitch and tone from the fluid flywheel. Then as starting gear was engaged there would be an audible "clunk" and the flywheel sound would cease. A similar audible effect was to characterise buses with succeeding types of epicyclic gearbox and fluid transmission, even into the 1990s. The characteristic radiator shell with fluted top was a feature of Daimler buses into the 1950s.

Chas H Roe's design of centre-entrance double deck bodywork was noteworthy, favoured by some other operators, including the Corporations of Blackpool, Burnley, Grimsby, Wallasey, West Hartlepool and two Yorkshire companies, from 1930 until the early post-war period. However, they did not all adopt it as standard and some specified it in the products of such other coachbuilders as Brush, Burlingham and English Electric. The staircase design was developed and patented jointly between Chas H Roe Ltd and Mr J C Whiteley, the Grimsby undertaking General Manager. There was a pair of one-piece outward-opening doors, operated manually, hinged to the inner end of each entrance bulkhead and left open in service.

Normally at this time the Roe double deck body featured a "recessed V-front" profile, incorporating forward-facing windows in V-form. At the rear, the centre-entrance 'deckers had a centrally-positioned emergency door. Winding half-drop side windows were fitted and were to be standard on SCT 'deckers until 1942, although most were replaced by top sliding vents post-war. At the rear, 26/27 did not carry the customary advertisement "Shop at Binns" but publicity for a local car dealer featuring the slogan "Young's for Ford".

SCT was to have no further problems with low bridges and so these and future buses were of highbridge layout. Decisions were made to order three and then two more Roe-bodied Daimlers, which were to be delivered in July-September 1935 (Nos28-30) and December (Nos31/32). They differed only in minor details from 26/27. One change was that the engine stop was now on the left of the cab and not on the steering wheel hub. No30, fitted with a reconditioned engine from new, apparently was damaged during

Guys' new guise. The 1935 pair of tram-o-cars were fitted with 20-seat saloon bodies built by local coachbuilder F Blagg in 1938 and given fleet numbers 3/4, initially being used on the Town - Alexandra Road service with driver-only operation. Here, No4 poses at the Wheat Sheaf in revised form but during its final year of service. By the standards of later decades it would be regarded as a minibus. *(Copyright R Marshall)*

This early wartime picture of 1935 Daimler 28 shows that the precautionary white edging needs touching-up. The name of the undertaking has been overpainted and two of the half-drop windows are stuck diagonally, a frequent occurrence and one of the reasons for their subsequent removal. *(Copyright Busways Travel Services)*

delivery and returned to Roe for repair. Daimler fuel consumption averaged a creditable 10.8mpg. Performance was surprisingly lively and although the Gardner engine was mounted rigidly at that time, the fluid flywheel absorbed much of the vibration and it was well within acceptable limits.

Results for the year to 31 March 1935 were encouraging, a fall in unemployment helping to produce increased loadings and revenue other than on the joint North Hylton service. Not for the first time, Mr Hopkins said that fares were too low with up to 1.83 miles (Museum - Cairns Road) for 1d. Cheap travel was in fact extended on 1 May 1935 when a 1d universal fare was introduced on working days up to 9am, available for any distance in one direction by bus and/or tram with one transfer of vehicle. In some cases, well over four miles could be travelled. In a special report six months later, Mr Hopkins said that no conclusions could be reached about additional traffic created. Falling unemployment had led to more journeys anyway and many passengers would travel earlier in order to beat the 9am deadline for the cheaper fare. He urged the Committee not to introduce any more concessions.

Network expansion took place on 8 May 1935 when the Ford - Noble's Bank Road service was extended 1.2 miles southward via Commercial Road and Ocean Road to Grangetown, bringing that route length to 4.45 miles. Buses shared the Grangetown terminus with trams which reached it via Ryhope Road. Across the river, the Humbledon - Sea Lane bus terminus was altered to Seaburn Camp, 0.4mile to the north, increasing that route mileage to 5.4. At the end of that month, two new tram-o-cars entered service, registered GR 1774/1775 and similar to the 1934 pair. In June they were joined on their tour work by Thornycroft 13 which had received a new English Electric 29-seat bus body in a striking livery of cream and red, featuring winding full-drop windows and a folding roof. A new

circular tour was commenced at Whitsun 1935, running from and to Sea Lane via Fulwell, Shields Road and Whitburn for a fare of 4d. On Sundays and holidays during the summer from 8 June there was an extension of the Docks - Cairns Road service 1.3 miles to Seaburn Camp rather than to Sea Lane only as in 1934. Dennises 22-25 were withdrawn in 1935/36 (details in Appendix 1).

A further change to the Ford service took place on 4 December 1935 when it was extended south and east from Fordham Road to Hylton Road/Kayll Road. Transfer tickets were available between buses and the Circle trams, so providing through-booking facilities to Hylton Road/Trimdon Street and the Royalty on the north and south sides of the Circle respectively. In both cases the transfer fare was 1^1/2d, a saving of a halfpenny to the Royalty. This facility was to be extended to Town via either side of the Circle as from 22 July 1936.

A total of five more Roe-bodied Daimlers were ordered for 1936, three arriving in summer (33-35) and two in December (36/37). Again, they were the same as the earlier ones except that they had the rear destination indicator set in the upper saloon panelling. Daimler was making much of the CO-type chassis in its advertising at this time, emphasising such advantages as the "elimination of driver-fatigue". Other municipal operators placing orders up to wartime included neighbours Newcastle, South Shields, West Hartlepool, Middlesbrough and Stockton, and big cities Belfast, Birmingham, Manchester, Edinburgh and Glasgow. Earlier in the year a new company named Transport Vehicles (Daimler) Ltd had been created to concentrate on building chassis for buses as distinct from cars.

In February 1936, Newcastle's Transport Committee Chairman proposed before the Royal Commission on Local Government on Tyneside that there should be a unified public

11

authority responsible for Tyneside passenger transport, to include South Shields and Whitley Bay. No action was taken but the idea was to be revived post-war and would then have embraced a vastly larger area including Sunderland. Nothing of the kind was to come into existence, however, until the Transport Act, 1968, created the Passenger Transport Authorities and their Executives, although Sunderland was not to be incorporated until 1973.

There were further increases in the annual passenger and revenue figures to 31 March 1936. Working expenses per mile had fallen slightly, too, and the nett balance had returned to a credit figure after two years of debit. Although bus operations were growing healthily, trams were still the town's primary transport mode. On the tram-o-cars, the new Whitburn circular tour had been the most popular during the previous summer. The summer of 1936, however, was inclement and this had an adverse effect on all services to the seaside. Tram-o-cars particularly felt the impact although a new tour along the coast to South Shields and a circular tour incorporating Grindon were introduced, both at a fare of a shilling. Fortunately, matters improved on Bank Holiday Monday 3 August

The two 1937 Crossley Mancunians had English Electric bodies of striking if not handsome appearance, employing features first seen on Blackpool trams four years previously and some Sunderland trams from 1934. Clearly an attempt to "streamline" a basically box-like shape, the design incorporated symmetry into various features, although subsequent modifications were carried out. All 1937-42 buses with the twin apertures had them repeated at the rear, with a single indicator above the entrance. The English Electric emergency door was on the offside, immediately behind the front bulkhead. No25, the second of the pair, reveals the slightly more forward position of the entrance and the two steps from ground level to the lower saloon floor compared with three on the Roe bodies.

(Copyright GEC Traction, courtesy R Marshall)

when Durham County Agricultural Show was held at Seaburn. Record receipts were taken on all services and for the buses this meant increases 34 per cent on the corresponding day in 1935 and 75 per cent on the average of each other Monday during the financial year. The trams took nearly four times more money than the buses. Illuminations in Roker Park (that is, the public pleasance and not the football stadium nearby) during 12 September - 4 October provided a further benefit. On the four Saturdays included, bus receipts were 44 per cent more than on the corresponding days in 1935. Over the whole illuminations period, they were up by 40 per cent. By now, the tide had turned for Wearside industry. The Board of Trade, under the British Shipping (Assistance) Act, 1935, could give financial aid to stimulate the economy and modernise that industry under the "scrap and build" scheme. Sunderland benefited from this and the transport figures were to reflect it. So dawned another kind of new age, although it was to be relatively short-lived.

1937 was a joyous year for Sunderland. Mr Hopkins referred to the "renewed prosperity" and for buses, his Annual Report for 31 March that year showed the highest increase in passengers since 1931, the highest average passenger journeys per mile since 1932 and the highest ever traffic revenue. Local unemployment was falling significantly and shops, services and leisure businesses were enjoying much better trade. The Wearside situation epitomised the national one where output per worker was 20 per cent greater than in

1929. Prices dropped a little but wages remained stable. The balance of payments was favourable. In Sunderland, pride was boosted further by the football team which, already League champions for 1935/36, won the FA Cup on 8 May 1937. Four days later there was the Coronation of King George VI to celebrate, the Massey body framing of Dennises 22/24 going up in smoke (along with five old tramcar bodies) on a commemorative bonfire. On the transport scene there were new Corporation buses and trams of the latest designs, comfortable and attractive. Attitudes locally were positive and optimistic.

Despite obvious satisfaction with the Daimlers, it had been decided to order two double deckers with *Crossley* special drop-frame chassis and *English Electric* double deck centre entrance bodywork, although four more Roe-bodied Daimlers were to be ordered before the year-end. About 1930, Crossley Motors Ltd of Gorton, Manchester, had appeared set to remain among the PSV market leaders. By 1936, the firm was struggling to maintain its prestige. Away from the Manchester area it had lost ground and while still in a potentially strong position, that potential was never to be realised. The two Crossley 'deckers arrived in April 1937 and their appearance was in keeping with the mood in the town. They were given the vacant numbers 24/25, out of sequence with the Daimlers. Preston-based English Electric had also built not only the tram-o-car body of Thornycroft 13 but (with its predecessor) had manufactured or supplied the car bodies and/or equipment for some 90 vehicles in the tram fleet since 1900. The bodies of Crossleys 24/25, like the Roe bodies, had a centre entrance and dual staircase, there now being a joint patent on the staircase design held by Roe and English Electric. The seating distribution was slightly different. With Roe it was 26-over-22 but as the English Electric entrance and staircase were positioned a little more forward the seating was 25-over-23. Probably the most striking feature of the English Electric bodies, however, was that they were fully-fronted with twin windscreens and a nearside 'cab' door giving access to the engine. Moreover, in plan view their panelling formed a 'V'-shaped 'nose' at front and rear after the fashion of the latest English Electric trams. This streamlining effect was then being applied to objects varying from railway locomotives to toothbrushes. On a bus or tram it was a purely a styling feature with publicity value but virtually no aerodynamic merit. Some other seaside towns adopted it, most notably Blackpool (on trams and buses). The full front impeded access to the engine and for this reason Sunderland's 24/25 were to be converted to normal half-cab layout by wartime.

1937 Daimlers 38-41 had SCT's first curving-profile Roe bodies as illustrated here by 40 at the coachbuilder's premises. The entrance arrangement with doors that were normally left in the pushed-open position, the Y-shaped staircase and the seating layout can be seen. In the upper saloon the third to sixth nearside seats are single ones. Note the louvred bonnet side panel, later replaced on all SCT's pre-war Daimlers. The style of fleet name shown was abandoned from 1938. This centre-entrance, twin-staircase design facilitated quick passenger movement at stops but the penalty was reduced seating capacity. *(Copyright holder uncertain)*

These two Crossleys were finished in a new livery of red relieved by cream for the upper saloon window surrounds and for some streamline markings. They featured twin destination apertures at both ends, the nearside front and offside rear ones later being altered to show only the initials 'SCT' in white on the glass which was then painted blue. Internally, mouldings and fillets were of the usual mahogany with leathercloth trim and moquette seats, all of which became the fleet standard until the war put a stop to it. The chassis was of Crossley's Mancunian design and had that concern's six-cylinder 8.365-litre indirect-injection engine. Problems led Sunderland (and others) to convert their Crossley engines to direct injection during the war. 24/25 had the optional four-speed preselective gearbox with a left-hand quadrant on the steering column. An obsolete feature was the centre accelerator pedal with which Crossley persisted until the end of pre-war production. Compared with the Daimlers, Sunderland's pair of Crossleys gave less value as they were more troublesome, consumed more fuel and had relatively short lives. Their performance was livelier, however, due to their 100bhp engines and 6.5 to 1 rear axle ratio compared with 85bhp and 5.2 to 1 respectively of the Daimlers. One of the latest four Daimlers ordered, No38, arrived a week before the Crossleys and 39-41 followed by the end of May. Their Roe bodies incorporated the new and graceful curving frontal profile that generally was to be a Roe characteristic in peacetime years until 1968. The new Daimler quartet had the mostly cream livery of the earlier Daimlers and not the red-based garb of the Crossleys. Upon repainting, these and other cream-topped 'deckers emerged with red roofs.

Another event of Coronation Day 1937 was the opening of a new 0.8-mile tramway extension from Fulwell (Blue Bell) via Dykelands Road to Seaburn (the Sea Lane area now becoming known by this name). This new line made it unnecessary for the Docks - Cairns Road bus service to be extended to Seaburn Camp at holiday periods. The trade press was reporting events in Sunderland regularly at this time. New trams, the tramway extension and the new Crossley and Daimler buses of 1937 all received coverage. *The Transport World* described Sunderland's undertaking as "one of the most enterprising in the country". The proportion of diesels in the fleet,

incidentally, was now some 57 per cent comprising 19 buses. Nationally the average was about 50 per cent.

At this time a new council housing development was taking shape at Hylton Lane on a hill to the south of the expanding Ford Estate. The Council was eager to develop new, healthier housing areas in a town where deaths from tuberculosis were double the national average and the infant mortality rate (92 per 1,000 in 1935) was some 60 per cent above average. On 4 August 1937 a new bus service, circular via Ford, was commenced to the edge of the Hylton Lane scheme. To and from Town the route length was 2.1 and 2.4 miles respectively. There was a $1^1/2$d transfer facility between Front Road and the Royalty via the Circle tram route from Kayll Road. At the same time, the Cairns Road - Docks service was cut back to Cairns Road - Town and the new Hylton Lane service linked with the Docks Circle section clockwise (Town - Docks via High Street, return via Borough Road), shown below as 'a'. From 16 November 1938 the route was extended, omitting the Ford detour, buses then follow the one-way clockwise course through the new estate shown as 'b' below. Route mileage became 2.2 from Town in both directions.

a Docks Circle - Town - Hylton Rd - Millfield - Fordham Rd - Fordfield Rd - Front Rd/Hylton Rd, returning direct via Hylton Rd (full length)
b Hylton Rd - Hadleigh Rd - Hartford Rd - Holborn Rd - Hylton Rd, then as westbound

Coronation time in Fawcett Street, May 1937. Approaching the camera are Leyland Lion 15 and Daimler 36, five months old and with a single spot lamp but still lacking "Binns" advertising. Following behind is a Sunderland District forward-entrance Brush-bodied AEC Regent while outside the Town Hall is one of the rebuilt pair of trams acquired from Mansfield District in 1933. *(Copyright Sunderland Echo)*

The Grangetown - Ford service ceased running to Hylton Road/Kayll Road when the Hylton Lane service was first commenced and the route within Ford was extended in the form of this clockwise one-way circuit, making the route 5.1 miles long:

Westmoor Rd - General Havelock Rd - Fordfield Rd - Front Rd/Westmoor Rd (terminus) - Westmoor Rd (full length) then as westbound

A more speculative service between Town (Museum) and Alexandra Road/Ashbrooke Range, 1.7 miles, was launched on 4 August 1937 also, via Toward Road, the Cedars and Glen Path. The venture was a flop. Figures per mile averaged only 1.3 passengers and 1.6d. It was withdrawn on 21 September but to be revived later. At that time Ashbrooke Range, a westward link between The Cedars and Alexandra Road, was closed to motor traffic and not until it was opened in 1954 could the slight detour via Glen Path be omitted.

There were more service revisions on 15 December 1937. The Hylton Lane route was cut back from Docks to Town and the Cairns Road service again linked with the Docks. By this time a further new bus had been running for a fortnight, but what a bus! Numbered 42, it was the Daimler COG5 that had been exhibited on the Roe stand at the Commercial Motor Show, Earls Court, London. This was the show at which Daimler introduced two new chassis features. One was a lubrication system by which every depression of the brake pedal would distribute oil to one part of the chassis, in turn. The other was a "float-mounting" arrangement whereby the engine was mounted flexibly rather than rigidly although as mentioned, the fluid flywheel already effectively dampened much of the engine vibration.

The appearance and detail specification of No42 made it the star of the fleet. Its seats were upholstered in green moquette, those downstairs having high backs. Decorative mirrors graced the lower saloon front bulkhead as with some of the trams. Stanchions were covered with a fawn plastics material. The 1930s-style artistry was completed with highly-polished walnut trim. A livery unique to this bus was applied, comprising red with three cream bands and cream on the roof and lower saloon rear corner panels at window-level. No42 was acquired as transport for the committees of the Council when on their tours of inspection and suchlike. In between times, it earned its keep on *works special journeys* when the seating was protected with dark brown covers! The war, of course, was to put an end to such preferential treatment for a bus. Until 1950 it could be identified from afar by virtue of its "Binns" lettering which was gold leaf on red. The arrival of 42 rounded off an outstanding calendar year.

1938 began with another look at the future. The fact that some operators were replacing their trams with motor buses or trolleybuses had not escaped the Council which was anxious to avoid being too much out of line with trends elsewhere. A report from Mr Hopkins advised keeping the tramway as the major element of the transport system. Both track and rolling stock were in excellent condition, he said. The cars had unbeatable acceleration, could carry more passengers, were more economical and gave better financial results than the alternatives. Mr Hopkins did suggest, however, that reserves should be built up in order to cater for any possible future change of policy.

Indeed, bus mileage and passenger figures were still creeping upward as shown in the Annual Report for 31 March 1938. Mileage operated was now practically half the trams' figure. Working expenses per mile were the lowest so far, helped somewhat by the economy of diesel engines. The Daimlers' average of 10.8mpg has been mentioned, the Crossleys returning 9.5mpg (extrapolated). Fuel oil had been only 5d a gallon in 1935 but by 1938 had risen to 11.88d. Petrol-engined buses had never averaged better than 6.25mpg and during 1936-38 petrol cost about 15 per cent more than fuel oil. A factor affecting 1938 passenger traffic slightly was the opening by the London & North Eastern Railway in 1937 of a new station at Fulwell, but named Seaburn. Prior to this, most rail passengers for Seaburn would have changed to tram at Monkwearmouth or Fawcett Street and Mr Hopkins mentioned that these were now lost. He did not say that as the new station was on the Humbledon - Seaburn route and almost a mile from the beach, the buses would benefit. That service actually gained more than 216,000 passengers and its receipts per mile rose from 10.83d to 11.03d per mile during the year. The Roker - Seaburn tramway section lost some 145,000 passengers and 0.4d per mile. There was also a small loss of traffic on the Docks section due to partial depopulation of the East End, but this was balanced by gains on the sections to which the residents had removed. Some new housing stock replaced the old within a year and so part of the lost Docks Circle traffic was recouped.

Seven new buses ordered in 1937 were delivered during May

This animated scene captured from outside the museum possibly in 1939 includes Leyland Lion 17 driven by Tommy Wilson with Conductors Charlie Tonkinson (left) and Charlie Parnaby on the footpath. Behind is one of the 1937 Daimlers, 38-41, with Driver Joe Ward standing at the cab door. The bus on the left is Daimler 37 and the tram one of the octet of cars acquired from London Transport in 1938, new to Ilford Corporation in 1932.

(Copyright holder not known.)

1938 as Nos43-49. Again they were Roe-bodied Daimler COG5 chassis of standard layout but modified appearance, with livery and destination apertures broadly similar to those of the Crossleys. One of the new Daimlers, 47, was to set a record by covering the longest span of service ever achieved by any bus in the fleet, not including rebodied ones, becoming the last pre-war Daimler still in service when withdrawn 183/4 years after its delivery.

A 2d universal transfer return fare was introduced on 8 June 1938, replacing the existing 1d universal transfer single (but not the transfer singles between specified stages). The new tickets were issued up to 9am weekdays and could be used for a journey of any distance on two vehicles, with later return. This extended cheaper travel to the whole day providing an outward journey was made during the morning peak. A further development at this time, less welcome, was the issuing of a Government circular to transport undertakings advising them on air raid precautions (ARP). It covered such matters as sheltering passengers during journeys, avoiding obstructing emergency vehicles, screening headlights, protection of fuel supplies, training staff in first aid and decontamination, and dispersal of vehicles. Within nine months nearly 250 Sunderland transport employees had become qualified in ARP work. That 1938 summer was a poor one for the seaside and this was shown in the passenger and revenue figures. The autumn illuminations were also affected by inclement weather and, for another reason of course, were not to be switched on the following year.

On 8 August 1938, the Town (Union Street) - Ettrick Grove bus service was started at last. On the 400-yard Chester Road/Western Hill - Cleveland Road stretch the buses paralleled the Circle trams, resulting in a slight leakage of passengers to the buses. The full 1.8-mile route was:

Town (Union St) - out via Northumberland St, return via High St W - Low Row - Chester Rd - Cleveland Rd/Ettrick Gr

It was decided at this time to have the second pair of tram-o-cars, GR 1774/1775, rebodied as 20-seat saloons and numbered 3/4. A small local coachbuilder, F Blagg & Co of Hartley's Buildings, Hylton Road, successfully quoted £516 for the two bodies. It was specified that they should be suitable for driver-only operation as they were intended for use in due course on a revived Alexandra Road service. There may also have been an intention to use them on the tours when appropriate because they were fitted with full-drop strap-controlled opening windows in the fashion of railway carriages. Further new buses were delivered in December 1938, comprising Roe-bodied Daimler COG5s numbered 50-53, identical other than for one minor detail to the previous seven.

It was implied earlier that the relationship between Sunderland Corporation and the Northern General Transport Company along with its subsidiary, the Sunderland District Omnibus Company, was at times uneasy. For much of 1938 and until January 1939 it was almost hostile. Understandably, each operator was anxious to safeguard its own interests and while the inner parts of the town and the tram routes were not areas of contention, the other parts along the main arterial roads were. There had been negotiations between SCT, NGT and SDO during 1938 concerning services and fares along Durham, Chester, Tunstall, Ryhope, Newcastle and North Hylton Roads. Deadlock was reached, however, following NGT opposition which had led to the Corporation's withdrawal of its application for a licence to run a new service from Town to North Hylton Road/Burntland Avenue in order to cater for the new Marley Pots housing estate. The grounds for the objection were that it would compete unfairly with NGT's existing Sunderland - Washington - Newcastle service through that area, and also the joint SCT-NGT service to North Hylton. In retaliation, the Corporation gave notice of its intention to terminate the joint running agreement for the North Hylton service, drawn up in 1932. Each operator then applied to run that service on its own. These applications were withdrawn upon the making of a new agreement between the Corporation and the companies. Under this, joint operation of the North Hylton service would continue and in return for concessions from the Corporation, (a) NGT would not oppose any application by SCT to run a Town - Marley Pots service; (b) NGT and SDO would withdraw their appeals against the granting of the licence for SCT's Ettrick Grove service; and (c) neither company would oppose a new application by

Union Street, possibly also in 1939, with Leyland Lion 18 leaving and Daimlers 36 and 39 waiting, both having been repainted with red roofs. 36 shows the position of the lower saloon emergency exit on all SCT's Roe centre-entrance bodies, and of the rear destination aperture on 33-42. With 26-32 it was at the top of the lower saloon emergency exit.
(Copyright holder not known)

SCT to operate again to Alexandra Road.

The bus war was over, but expensive preparations for a longer and much more destructive kind of war were still going ahead. During the year ended 31 March 1939, SCT spent £1,366 on ARP, representing more than five per cent of the nett joint revenue balance. Work included the building of staff shelters at depots and concreting the bus depot yard to make it suitable as a decontamination centre. It was hoped that at least some costs would be reimbursed by the Government in due course. The Annual Report for 1938/39 was the first in which the term *Transport Department* was used. Average working expenses per mile were the lowest they were ever to be at 8.978d. While this was meritworthy it was not the best. Of 69 municipalities for which figures are available, Sunderland came 13th from the lowest which was Blackpool, showing 7.54d. The highest was Eastbourne with 13.78d.

A new service was commenced and another revived on 3 May 1939. The new one was Town (High Street West/Havelock cinema) - Marley Pots, following this 1.9-mile route:

Town - Wheat Sheaf - Southwick Rd - Sunderland Rd - Carley Rd - Collingwood St - Goschen St - Beaumont St - Faber Rd - Beechwood Cres

The other service was of course the previously short-lived Town - Alexandra Road one. It was now extended by some 200 yards to Alexandra Road/Ledbury Road in order to cater for new private housing and the recently-opened Eye Infirmary. The two 20-seat Blagg-rebodied Guy Wolves, 3/4, were used with driver only. Crew-operation would not have been economical as the area served was not densely-populated, there was little industry and the route was too near others on which trams and SDO buses ran. At that time, buses without conductors, single deck only, were restricted to not more than 26 seats. The method of fare collection was rudimentary. Tickets were issued from the type of rack used by conductors and the driver wore the ticket punch and cash bag. Mr Hopkins had gained experience of the driver-only principle in Wigan where some of his Thornycrofts had been operated without conductors. West Hartlepool had also used that system previously. In the light of developments in years to come the use of driver-only operation now was perhaps a portent.

Sunderland's final pre-war Daimler COG5s, Nos54/55, ordered five months previously, entered service in August 1939. No55 always heralded its approach with the raucous sound of a klaxon horn. The declaration of war of 3 September was obviously going to bring about many changes but not all at once. Blackout measures had been implemented two days previously and British Summer Time was extended to the night of 18/19 November. From 17 September there were service reductions as a result of fuel rationing. Final departures from Town at night were brought forward to 10.15, amended to 10.30 from 29 November. There were reduced frequencies after 7pm. The Cairns Road - Docks Circle service was split at Town, buses then running independently on each section. From 23 September services from Town to the following destinations were suspended: Hylton Lane, Ettrick Grove, Marley Pots, Alexandra Road. Fortunately an additional fuel ration was obtained, allowing the Corporation 87^{1}/2 per cent of normal requirements and so Town - Hylton Lane was recommenced on 4 October, followed four days later by reduced services from Town to Marley Pots (Sundays excepted) and to Ettrick Grove (daily). On 3 November and 23 December respectively Ettrick Grove (daily) and Marley Pots (Sundays excepted) were fully restored.

Failure to observe the blackout was an offence and regulations were enforced strictly. They had a severe impact on transport operators. Blue varnish was applied to window interiors (some operators used amber). The blue had a drastic effect during daylight and so the varnish was removed from about half the surface area. When suitable interior lighting masks became available the varnish was removed entirely. Other requirements were:

■ Extremities (eg, mudwings) marked with white edges.

■ Illumination from side and rear lights obscured and reduced to 2-in opening.

■ Stop lights reduced to 1-in diameter.

■ Lamp reflectors blackened.

■ No illumination of number plates or destination indicators.

■ Direction indicators (where used) reduced to ^{1}/8-in illuminated strip.

■ Bulb to be removed from offside headlamp [not then generally fitted to SCT buses].

■ Nearside headlamp masked with opaque cardboard with 2-in aperture and partial blackening of reflector.

From 22 January 1940 a new type of headlamp mask was brought into use. It took the form of a hood with apertures, giving better illumination of the road without making the beam visible from the air. On 29 January the built-up area speed limit of 30mph was

The final two pre-war buses, Blagg-bodied Crossleys 22/23, were acquired for the North Hylton service although this became double deck-operated during the war. 23 here poses at Seaburn when new, showing off considerable brightwork.
(Copyright Busways Travel Services)

reduced to 20mph during darkness. Further regulation changes in October 1940 allowed the use of the masked headlight on moving vehicles during air raid alerts, although the sidelight aperture had to be cut down to a diameter of one inch. Later the rules were relaxed a little and destination blinds could be partially illuminated. In the street, obstructions like lamps posts, telegraph poles, trees and junction boxes were at least given white markings.

At the outbreak of war, two single deck Crossleys were on order. They were delivered a month later and have been referred to variously as Alpha and Mancunian models. With 32-seat bodywork built locally by Blagg, they were numbered 22/23 in sequence with double deck Crossleys 24/25 and although powered by the same 8.365-litre Crossley engine, 22/23 had the four-speed constant mesh gearbox and not the preselective unit. They were obtained for the North Hylton service and nominally were replacements for Leyland Tigers 20/21 although those two were to remain in service until 1944. At the seaside, the promenades were still open to the public but the beaches were declared prohibited areas on account of the threat of invasion and so were cordoned off with barbed wire. The tram service along the Roker - Seaburn sea front was suspended on 5 December 1939 when the military authorities closed Whitburn Road at Cliff Park, a strategic vantage point. Trams then terminated at Roker. A replacement bus service from Town (Bedford Street) using a different 2.05-mile route was substituted the following day, to be altered on 17 December. Some journeys were extended by a further 0.15 mile to the new concert and dancing establishment, Seaburn Hall, as required. These are the route details:

Town - Wheat Sheaf - Roker Av - Gladstone St - Roker Baths Rd - Roker Park Rd - Seaburn (Park Ave/Chichester Rd), extended by 0.1mile 17 Dec 39 to Seaburn Terr/Whitburn Rd

The first of the two Crossley single deckers, 22, was adapted for driver-only operation in 1952 and here loads in that guise at the Town (Borough Road) terminus for Alexandra Road. A straight waistband has replaced original cream flashes, most of the polished metal has been removed or overpainted, the front wings have been clipped and the seating capacity increased from 32 to 34. Crossley 103, left, has been repainted green but that livery was never applied to any bus with a registration number below GR 7501. After disposal, Crossley 22 became a caravan in the Cambridge area and may have survived with a preservationist into the 1990s.

(Copyright R Marshall)

The list below shows the position at the end of 1939, after just some ten years of own-bus operations. 46 vehicles made up the Corporation bus fleet, excluding tram-o-cars, running the services mentioned (tram services also included). Locations are shown on the 1960 map.

14 single deck (11 petrol-engined): 8 1929/30 Leyland Lion, 2 1930 Leyland Tiger, 2 1935 Guy, 2 1939 Crossley
32 double deck (all diesel-engined): 30 1934-39 Daimler, 2 1937 Crossley.

Bus services	Tram services
Alexandra Rd - Town (Boro' Rd/Museum) (suspended)	*Circle - Roker - Seaburn (suspended Roker - Seaburn)
Cairns Rd - Newcastle Rd - Town (Boro' Rd/Museum)	Durham Rd - Town - Fulwell - Seaburn
Docks Circle	Durham Rd - Town - Southwick
Ettrick Grove - Chester Rd - Town (Union St)	Grangetown - Ryhope Rd - Town - Fulwell
Ford - Pallion - Deptford - Town - Hendon - Grangetown	Villette Rd - Tatham St - Town - Southwick
Humbledon - Pallion - Southwick - Fulwell - Seaburn Camp	*Circle section: High St W/Station (N End) - Hylton Rd - Kayll Rd
Hylton Lane - Hylton Rd - Town (Union St)	- Chester Rd - Western Hill - New Durham Rd - Fawcett St
Marley Pots - Wheat Sheaf - Town (High St W)	
North Hylton - Castletown - Southwick - Deptford - Park Lane	
Seaburn - Park Ave - Town (Bedford St)	

3 - Blackout, Grey In

Shortage of male labour led to the engagement in 1940 of female bus and tram conductors. A new recruit here poses in a gloomy Daimler 45, blue varnish being applied partially to its windows. *(Copyright Sunderland Echo)*

Fuel rationing and shortages of materials, particularly rubber and metal, created difficulties for all transport systems. Additionally for some there was the disruption caused by enemy action. The first air raid on Wearside took place on 21 June 1940 and Sunderland was to be among the seven most heavily bombed towns and cities in the country. On the east coast only Hull received more damage. A German map of Sunderland obtained after the war identified 26 targets comprising the docks, shipyards and other industrial premises, power and fuel installations, railways and of course the two Wear road bridges and rail bridge. The townspeople were to suffer heavily in the raids, 267 civilians being killed and more than 1,000 injured. A thousand houses were destroyed, another 3,000 were rendered uninhabitable and 32,000 otherwise damaged. Amid all this the buses and trams rendered invaluable service despite some disruption. There was damage to Transport Department property and vehicles but no buses or trams were destroyed.

SCT was an undertaking on which unduly heavy burdens fell because of the greatly increased need for essential war workers' transport. Wearside's average annual shipping wartime tonnage launched was 70 per cent higher than that for each of the four "busy" years to 1939, representing 27 per cent of UK merchant shipping output for the war period and exceeding the total for the Tyne, the Tees and Hartlepool put together. The increased work in the Wear shipyards and associated industries imposed severe pressures on the transport system. Over the war years the trams' passenger figure was to increase by 37 per cent while both the bus figure and the number

of bus employees were to double at least. The bus fleet became 35 per cent larger and bus mileage operated rose by 23 per cent despite service cuts.

Before the end of 1939 it had been realised that the bus fleet would need to be increased. By February 1940 orders were placed for four more Roe-bodied Daimler COG5 chassis. That was the beginning of an intriguing sequence of events which will be unfolded in due course. Meanwhile, the blackout was causing particular problems on the Humbledon - Seaburn Camp service and from 10 January 1940 longer running times were allowed after 5pm. Alexandra Bridge was particularly dangerous with its roadway enclosed in a tunnel of lattice girders and a disused railway deck on top, gaining practically no benefit from any moonlight. At the same time, the Docks Circle service was given more running time during the day. As to the blackout, there were vehicle collisions but more seriously, some pedestrian fatalities. During the year to 31 March 1940, five of the nine fatal accidents involving Corporation buses and trams took place during darkness and elderly persons were the most vulnerable. The situation was repeated nationwide and was a cause for great concern. A further serious matter was the amount of interior damage being caused to SCT buses by vandalism.

In an unsolicited report dated 9 February 1940 Mr Hopkins reminded the Committee that if hostilities escalated, military fuel usage along with the loss of American tankerage would greatly intensify the fuel shortage. Buses were more vulnerable than trams in this respect and this would lead to more stringent bus service cuts, he stated. Already, the Department was facing increased costs of some £8,000 for the approaching financial year. The actual results for 31 March 1940, however, were encouraging from the performance point of view. Mileage, passenger and revenue figures all showed increases and working expenses had gone up by less than revenue.

There was no delivery date available for the four Daimlers in hand and the Department was now stretched beyond its limit due to the increasing need for essential workers' provision. Accordingly, four spare double deckers were hired from Manchester Corporation for £25 per month hire charge plus 1d per mile. Delivered to Sunderland about 8 July 1940, these buses were not considered to be in good condition and two of them remained on Wearside for only two months. There were, incidentally, to be further links between the two undertakings: soon after the war, Sunderland bought six trams from Manchester and, at the time of the hiring of the four Crossley buses, Manchester Corporation employed a relatively young and promising technical assistant called Norman Morton who will be mentioned again.

SCT did hire in further buses later but it also had some of its own vehicles commandeered by the War Department in 1941 and subsequently loaned out others. Leyland Lion 10 is known to have been one of those commandeered, being returned by November 1941. It has not proved possible to trace further details. The three remaining tram-o-cars were adapted for use as ARP mobile canteens and hired to the Ministry of Home Security. Sunderland's Leyland Lion 18, Tiger 21 and Guy Wolves 3/4 were loaned to South Shields Corporation at various times. Soon after the war Crossley saloon 23 was to be loaned to South Shields for eight months. All known details are given in Appendix 1 and income from hiring out is tabulated in Appendix 2.

As male employees left the Transport Department to join the armed forces a labour shortage arose and on 27 June 1940 the Transport Committee decided to engage female conductors on buses and trams. The age group was set at 21-30 years and initially at least, married women whose husbands had jobs were excluded. From 10 July, wounded servicemen in hospital blue uniform were allowed free travel on Corporation transport. Ten days later new regulations were introduced, prohibiting operators from disposing of any mechanically-propelled vehicle without a licence (tramcars and trolleybuses excepted). Further regulations to do with the displaying of names on vehicles were introduced also, in order not to assist possible enemy parachute invaders. The test was whether a name could be read from the air or from a slow-moving vehicle. Sunderland, like many others, displayed only "Corporation Transport" and the name of the General Manager until after the war. Destination indicators could show the names of thoroughfares providing they did not reveal the identity of any particular district, military establishment or munition works.

August 1940 came and the much-needed Daimlers were still not ready but Roe had nearly completed the bodies and approached Sunderland Corporation for a payment on account. The Council agreed on £1,500, somewhat less than half the total cost of the four bodies. News about the chassis was to become worse. Coventry, home of Daimler and other vehicle builders, suffered heavy bombing particularly on the night of 14 November 1940, and the Daimler works were badly damaged. Production did recommence gradually but following further attacks on 8 and 10 April 1941 there was virtually

total devastation of Daimler. Bus chassis-building was not to start again for nearly two years.

Early in 1940, widespread abuse of Sunderland Corporation's 2d universal transfer return ticket was causing concern. Despite precautions taken by redesigning the ticket, some passengers were still finding ways of using it to make a different return journey from their outward one. Moreover, no other operator offered such absurdly generous value as this 2d facility, reported Mr Hopkins. More than two million of the tickets were being issued each year and it was costing the Department an estimated £8,447 in annual revenue. He recommended going back to the 1d morning universal transfer single ticket. No action was taken until 1 January 1941 when the 2d universal transfer return ticket was abolished and replaced, not by a 1d ticket but by a 1$\frac{1}{2}$d transfer single, valid for any distance with one transfer of vehicle (bus-tram or same type of vehicle) per journey and available as follows:

■ Mon - Sat up to 9am;   ■ Mon - Fri 4.30 - 6pm;   ■ Sat 11.30am - 1pm

Later in the year, Mr Hopkins was to boast in the trade press of the enormous value represented by Sunderland Corporation's fares, not least the universal transfer facility. Meanwhile, the results for the year ending 31 March 1941 were generally favourable. Bus mileage was still catching up on tram mileage and other bus figures showed increases too.

In view of the Daimler situation, on 11 June 1941 the Committee authorised Mr Hopkins to try to obtain four Leylands or AECs instead, although military priorities had brought all bus production virtually to a standstill. On the labour front, the flow of employees away to military service had slowed a little from 1 February 1941 when bus driving had become a reserved occupation. By the end of July that year, nevertheless, operators were feeling keenly the effects of staff shortages. SCT had seen 180 bus and tram men joining HM forces, being replaced by 100 women. Clearly the shortfall in Sunderland as elsewhere placed tremendous demands in difficult conditions on all grades of staff. The burden on bus drivers during the blackout was eased slightly from 15 September 1941, when two masked headlamps were permitted instead of one, but rear lights now had to be dimmed by a sheet of tissue paper or equivalent.

Soon afterward, Leyland Lions 7/10/17 had 28 perimeter seats installed and could take a further 28 standing. Perimeter-seated single deckers were permitted to carry more than the usual eight standing passengers on journeys up to ten miles long on specific

The first buses delivered to Sunderland Corporation under wartime arrangements were 56/57, "unfrozen" Leyland Titan TD7s with standard Roe bodywork originally intended for four Daimler chassis. The other two similar bodies ended up at West Hartlepool on AEC Regent chassis. Originally in wartime grey primer finish, No57 is seen here in 1950 wearing post-war livery alongside (left to right) Guy 64 and Daimlers 26/42. Sunderland Corporation seemed to have an ambivalent attitude to Leyland (and later Crossley) front wheel nut guard rings but their absence probably did nothing to enhance appearance.

(Copyright R Marshall)

19

services. On 25 September 1941, the Committee authorised further service curtailments and the final departures from Town then became 10pm Monday - Friday, remaining at 10.30 during weekends. From October 1941, twelve passengers were allowed to stand on conventionally-seated buses, providing this did not exceed half the seating capacity. Sunderland was spared that irksome wartime requirement, the conversion of ten per cent of its fleet to producer gas operation, as only operators with 150 buses or more were caught by it. At various points during the war other curtailments and adjustments to services were made for economy reasons, whether of fuel or materials, although it seems clear that some records of these changes may not have survived. Those known to have taken place between 22 October 1941 and 2 December 1942 are summarised here.

22 Oct 41	Some peak time jnys withdrawn on: Hylton Lane, Ettrick Grove, Marley Pots, to provide better facilities for workers from Docks to: Ford, Grangetown, Marley Pots, Hylton Lane.
30 Oct 41	Town terminus of Cairns Rd service moved from Boro' Rd/Museum to Bedford St (saving 400yds per single jny).
6 Nov 41	Peak time jnys withdrawn on 22 Oct now restored as workers' jnys provided were not sufficiently patronised.
10 Nov 41	A few jnys cancelled on various services.
15 Dec 41	Restoration of services to level as before 10 Nov.
30 Jan 42	Some jnys to be cancelled on some services, including Marley Pots.
1 Jun 42	Some bus stops suspended to save fuel.
2 Dec 42	Docks Circle: suspended 9.15 - 11.30am and after 6.40pm. Town - Cairns Rd: jnys restored 7 - 9pm. Town - Seaburn: Mon - Fri frequency 15min, Sat 10min. Town - Marley Pots: off-peak frequency 30min, no Sunday service before 1pm. Town - Ettrick Gr: as Marley Pots but Ettrick Gr Sunday service suspended at a later date

Mr Hopkins reported on 30 October 1941 that a licence had been obtained to buy two Leyland chassis for fitting with two of the completed Roe bodies intended for Daimlers. The two other bodies, he added, had been "allocated elsewhere", meaning that they had been sent to another undertaking by the Ministry of War Transport which controlled the distribution of new vehicles through the purchase licensing system. Leyland was one of the builders authorised by the Ministry of Supply to re-start chassis assembly, using up stocks of "frozen" parts.

By this time a new and standardised design of bus body had been produced by the Ministry of Supply in conjunction with the National Federation of Vehicle Trades. Of simplified construction, it made optimum use of scarce materials and labour and was to be described colloquially as "utility" (a term then applied to manufactured goods). The design was to be adopted by a number of coachbuilders, each interpreting the details differently so that it was possible to distinguish between the various makes. Not all the "unfrozen" chassis had this type of bodywork. SCT's Leylands

were a case in point as their Roe bodies were purely of pre-war design. Some alterations were necessary to make these two bodies fit the Leyland chassis. The modifications added £50 to the cost of each body and the Leyland chassis each cost £52 more than the Daimler quotation. Further buses were hired from the London Passenger Transport Board, one in December 1941 and two in April 1942, all with open rear staircases. When the second pair arrived the remaining two Manchester buses were sent home. The three Londoners stayed in Sunderland until August 1942. At some time during 1942 also, a single decker was hired from Leigh Corporation in Lancashire.

On 26 March 1942 the Transport Committee decided to withdraw special bus journeys for dance-goers at Seaburn Hall, subject to the approval of the Regional Transport Commissioner (a wartime designation). The reason given was that the risks being run by British merchant seamen in bringing supplies of fuel to the country were too great for it to be used for the convenience of pleasure-seekers. Although precise records are lacking, a post-war application for dance journeys to be restored does imply that the withdrawals were made. The annual figures for 31 March 1942 showed several rises. While these included working expenses, they had risen by less than traffic revenue. There was, however, a small nett deficit from bus operations. The rise in the number of passengers carried was some four times greater than the rise in the mileage operated.

The Corporation's first new bus since autumn 1939 arrived in the early spring of 1942. It was No56 of the pair of Roe-bodied Leylands, followed by 57 in mid-June. A third Leyland, 58, arrived two weeks later, surprisingly because Mr Hopkins had not even had time to report officially to the Committee that he had been able to obtain it! This bus had a Leyland rear-entrance metal-framed body, of Leyland's supremely attractive outline introduced in March 1936 with a gently curving frontal profile and from late 1937 a well-rounded rear roof dome. 58 was diverted from an order of Western SMT, Kilmarnock, finished to that operator's specification including black stanchions, and its seating capacity of 56 was to be standard in the SCT fleet until 1952. The three Leylands introduced the overall grey primer body finish common to all new buses delivered to SCT during the war. There were variations between coachbuilders in the

One further new "unfrozen" Leyland TD7 joined the SCT fleet and was numbered 58. Its handsome 56-seat metal-framed Leyland body was one of eight distributed among four English operators but ordered by Western SMT and featuring that operator's protruding destination box and other details, including a side indicator over the platform, latterly disused. In this 1953 shot at the Black Road parking ground, 58 illustrates the 1950 livery of red with three cream bands and reposes alongside the Roe-bodied TD7 acquired second-hand from Stockton in 1950 and given the number 25, held previously by a 1937 Crossley and a 1930 Dennis. The body of 25 was one of three originally intended for West Hartlepool on Daimler chassis, one body going to that undertaking (on a Leyland TD7 chassis) and the other coming to Sunderland on Guy 59. Here 25 sports an experimental red and cream format, intended as a prototype for the new green livery, and is wearing a radiator insulating jacket although the date is October. Alongside are ex-Blackburn Guy 5, Guy 66 and a Daimler CWA6.

(Copyright D S Burnicle)

20

The Corporation's first wartime Guy, 59, had a Roe body of pre-war design with normal teak framing. Although it was of Sunderland's standard 48-seat centre-entrance layout, the detail specification was that of West Hartlepool for whom it had been intended on a Daimler chassis and was generally similar to the body on 25, the ex-Stockton Leyland Titan TD7. Among the differences from SCT specification were top-sliding window vents instead of winding half-drops and straight mouldings without streamline flashings, although it was possible for Sunderland's destination apertures to be incorporated. Also originally grey, after the war it was repainted in the "plain" livery then later in the 1950 revised version and in 1954 along with five utility Guys received a new body. *(Copyright R Marshall)*

Wartime damage to buses resulted in Crossley 25's running with boarded-up windows upstairs at the nearside rear and on the nearside of the emergency exit, probably following the May 1943 episode. The removal of the full front was, however, by design! White edging and masks on the headlights (no longer twins) and sidelights are noteworthy. *(Copyright Busways Travel Services)*

precise shade of grey used, and 58 had red beadings. Although by this time some operators were receiving new buses with so-called utility bodywork, SCT still had one more new bus of pre-war body design to come.

All three Leyland chassis were of the Titan TD7 type. The Titan had been introduced in 1927 as the TD1, gradually being modified until the TD7 (and equivalent Tiger TS11 single deck) emerged in autumn 1939. Hardly can a forward-engined double deck bus have been surpassed in terms of smooth running. Some Wearsiders may have enjoyed TD7 travel already, as SDO had placed five in service during mid-1940. The engine was the extremely refined Leyland 8.6-litre unit, fully flexibly-mounted in the TD7. There was little audible mechanical clatter, the principal sound being the pleasant induction roar, accompanied by an attractive and soothing siren effect, like that of a humming top, produced by the clutch-ventilating holes around the perimeter of the flywheel. Along with the agreeable crooning of the four-speed constant mesh gearbox, especially in helical third, the full orchestration was a glorious selection of aural pleasures! Gear-changing was slow, however, SCT drivers not being trained in the use of the clutch-stop, and so the Leylands were less popular than the "easy-change" Daimlers (although the author has found the converse to apply elsewhere).

Mid-1942 was also a time of considerable alarm concerning rubber supplies. From 1939 Government propaganda had urged economy with many materials, particularly imported ones, but following the loss to Japan of Malaya and other parts of the Far East, the enemy had control of 90 per cent of the world's natural rubber resources. The Government now stressed the greater need to conserve it and within a few months the Ministry of Supply would not allow vehicle tyres to be renewed unless the tread was worn

completely smooth.

Following Committee authorisation to make "discreet enquiries", in late 1942 Mr Hopkins was able to order six AEC Regent chassis. They were not to be delivered for nearly five years. Early in 1943, the remaining pre-war style wartime bus arrived and comprised a unique combination of chassis and body. Numbered 59, it was a Guy Arab of the type later called Mark I, with virtually standard centre-entrance 48-seat Roe bodywork. The body was in fact built to the specification of West Hartlepool Corporation but with Sunderland destination indicator layout. Mention has been made of the sequence of events surrounding these Roe bodies and it is given in abbreviated form below:

Year	Month	Operator	Event	Fleet No(s)
1940	Feb	Sunderland	ordered 4 Daimler chassis, 4 Roe bodies	
	Mar/Apr	W Hartlepool	ordered 3 Daimler chassis, 3 Roe bodies	
1941	Apr		DAIMLER PRODUCTION HALTED	
1942	Jan	W Hartlepool	received two of the Sunderland bodies on AEC chassis	34/35
	Mar/Jun	Sunderland	received the other two Sunderland bodies on Leyland chassis	56/57
	Jul	W Hartlepool	received one of the W Hartlepool bodies on Leyland chassis	36*
	Jul	Stockton	received one of the W Hartlepool bodies on Leyland chassis	85
1943	Jan	Sunderland	received the remaining W Hartlepool body on Guy chassis	59
1949	Dec	Sunderland	acquired the Stockton Leyland	25

*Privately preserved as at 1997

21

In this fascinating wartime study of Mackie's Corner (on the left, Havelock cinema beyond) blackout markings are much in evidence. The buses are Daimlers, 48 leading with show bus 42 cornering and one of 26-37 behind. Dated 1943, the photograph was clearly taken before the May air raid in which 42 was seriously damaged and then repainted. *(Copyright Busways Travel Services)*

Sunderland Corporation's Guy Arab 59 had one of the first 500 such chassis built under the Ministry of Supply's instructions and to a specification agreed between itself, the Ministry of War Transport and the Technical Committee of Operators. Guy Motors Ltd of Wolverhampton had introduced the Arab model in 1933. It did not sell widely but in any case, at the request of the War Office, from 1936 Guy gave up much of its civilian business to concentrate on military vehicle production (of which it had had 25 years' experience). Only a handful of bus chassis were then produced until 1942 Guy was directed to build the first 500 fully wartime (not unfrozen) bus chassis. The first chassis was reviewed in the trade press during November 1942 when. Lightweight materials such as aluminium were not available for bus construction and this meant increased chassis weight of some 18 per cent over the pre-war Arab. Guy would have preferred to fit the Gardner 6LW engine but supplies were restricted and so the 5LW was standard, although a minority of wartime Arabs did have the six-cylinder unit. It seems that all Sunderland's wartime Guys had the 6.25 rather than the alternative 5.6 to 1 rear axle ratio. No59 sported the usual short bonnet of the 5LW Arab I and its pre-war style Roe body suited the chassis well.

It had been announced in December 1942 that Daimler double deck chassis were now available. The 22 utility-bodied Guys and Daimlers that were to join the SCT fleet during 1943/44 are tabulated below for clarity but fuller information is given in Appendix 1 as usual.

60/61	Daimler CWG5	Massey
62-66	Guy Arab II 5LW	Massey
67/68	Guy Arab II 5LW	Pickering
69/70	Guy Arab II 5LW	Massey
71-73	Daimler CWA6	Duple
74-79	Guy Arab II 5LW	Massey
80/81	Guy Arab II 6LW	Massey

Daimler chassis were now being produced at a temporary base in Wolverhampton. The new wartime model was based on the design of the well-proven pre-war COG5 and the wartime chassis, designated CWG5, at 4.6.0 weighed only 6cwt (7.5 per cent) more than the COG5. The Gardner 5LW engine drove through a four-speed preselective gearbox and the rear axle was made by the well-known Kirkstall Forge & Engineering Company of Leeds. Rounded hub covers distinguished the Kirkstall from the Daimler rear axle as fitted to some of the of the later CW-type chassis. Sunderland's CWG5s, 60/61, entered service in March/April 1943. They had Massey Bros bodywork which, as with SCT's future 1943/44 bodies, were of the "standard wartime specification". This included the following among 35 itemised details:

- timber framing using oak, ash, mahogany or teak except for the longitudinal rails which could be of pitch pine [a few builders had dispensation to build steel-framed bodies from existing stocks, but none were delivered to SCT];
- all exterior panels, including the roof, to be of 20-gauge SWG steel; interior side-lining panels not permitted;
- panels could be shaped but not beaten [accounting for the shell-backed appearance of the rear roof domes];
- upper saloon emergency exit (at rear) not glazed but panelled; this requirement reversed 1943 [after the delivery of 60/61];
- windows fixed direct to the framing; only one half-drop window per side (usually spring-clip controlled) in each saloon;
- seats to be upholstered in leather [as with 60/61] or other suitable substance but in 1943 a shortage of materials led to the introduction of wooden-slatted seats.

Although 60/61 were the town's first true wartime buses they were by no means as austere as may be imagined. The 5LW engine was mounted flexibly and there was hardly any noticeable difference in noise and vibration between the CWG5 and the COG5. The CWG5's standard rear axle ratio was 5.75 to 1 but the author's

March and April 1943 saw the delivery of SCT's first two buses with utility bodies, Daimler CWG5s 60/61. The uncompromisingly angular body conformed to the Ministry of Supply's basic specification but as may be seen here, Massey Bros managed to mitigate some of the harsher visual effects by the use of thicker pillars, careful raking of the front and rear profiles and the curving of the lower edge of the windscreen. In this Bedford Street view 60 is newly repainted in the 1950 style of red livery. Exceptionally for utilities, they (and Massey-bodied CWG5s elsewhere) had top-sliding window vents from new and in this picture 60 has had its upper saloon quantity doubled.

(Copyright R Marshall)

impression is that the SCT pair had the optional 6.75 version. Despite the total weight being ³/₄ton more than the average COG5, with their reasonably smart acceleration up to a top speed of barely 30mph and good hill-climbing ability, they were clearly much lower-geared than the COG5s. On one unforgettable occasion in 1956, after rounding the adversely-cambered Watson Street bend at Pallion slowly but in top gear, 61 picked up admirably as it passed climbed the short rise of about 1 in 14 still in top, accelerating gently all the way up! In service, 60/61 harmonised with most other fleet members. Seating was comfortable, giving good support to the back and legs, and the wartime crudities became evident perhaps only in extremes of temperature when the lack of insulating materials had its effect. SCT had rear destination indicators, not normally a utility feature, fitted to all its new wartime bodies at a cost of about £4 per body.

Figures for the year ending 31 March 1943 again were favourable, all major results showing increases once more. On the buses' side the nett balance of £24,464 was nearly four times greater than the previous best in 1938. On a more sombre note, the night of 15/16 May 1943 saw a prolonged and intensive air raid on Sunderland. A land mine destroyed buildings in Fulwell Road, damaging the bus depot and all vehicles inside. However, compared with the scenes of mangled buses following raids on London, Birmingham and Coventry, for example, Sunderland's fleet escaped fairly lightly. Daimler 42, the 1937 Show bus, came off worst with damage to 29 windows, many panels, pillars and rails, both front wings, radiator, roof and other features. A full repaint was carried out upon repairs. Daimler 49 suffered least

with only one broken window. All other buses suffered varying amounts of damage between those extremes. Daimler 45 was bad enough to need a full repaint, and roof repaints were carried out on Crossley 25 and Daimler 26. Presumably Guy Wolves 3/4 were at South Shields at this time as they were not included in the claim made under the War Damage Act, 1941. The total value of the fifty buses concerned prior to being damaged was put at £52,043.

In order to maintain services pending repairs, hurried arrangements were made to borrow buses from Newcastle, Stockton and Middlesbrough Corporations and Darlington Triumph Services Ltd which had a depot in Sunderland. There appears to be no surviving record of the details. At the Committee meeting on 27 May it was minuted that Mr Hopkins commended Foreman T Craig, Driver V Bradshaw and Driver R Evans for trying to rescue vehicles and prevent further damage. The Town Clerk sent appropriate letters to the men.

More rigours of wartime bus travel were felt in Sunderland from July 1943 when the first two utility-bodied 5LW Guys entered service (62/63). Their Massey bodies and those of subsequent utilities did have wooden-slatted seats. People would be unaccustomed to the discomfort, though, as a significant minority of Corporation trams still had wooden seating in one saloon, or both. Massey Bros used fairly broad slats, unlike the narrower ones to be seen later in Pickering and Duple bodies. While these wooden-slatted seats provided reasonable support, when the bus was in

Delivered October 1943, Massey bodied Guys 64/65 were the first to have upper saloon forward-facing window vents, Daimlers 61/61 and Guys 62/63 having only fixed panes at that location although the vents were part of the original MoS specification. In this 1950 picture, 64 has been prepared for recertification and in fact failed by the vehicle examiner who insisted that the upper saloon should have four window vents. It will be seen that the lower saloon half-drops were retained and that there is an additional step at the forward edge of the nearside front wing, believed to be for the benefit of three particularly small conductresses. No other bus received one, the destination indicator handles being lengthened instead. In this view the adjacent Daimlers are 32 (out of use) and 26. *(Copyright R Marshall)*

23

Pickering bodies were fitted to Guys 67/68, also new in October 1943. On this glorious 1950 midsummer evening, a gleaming 68 picks up at the museum. Noteworthy details are the treatment of the window vents and, compared with Massey examples, the destination apertures. By this time, 68 had received a 6LW engine in place of its original 5LW. Eight years later it was to be rebuilt as an open-topper.

(Copyright A B Cross)

First and last. The final new wartime Guys were 80/81 which were 6LW-powered and also had some different body features, including the exterior mouldings about midway up each saloon and the ventilator covers at cantrail level. 81 here stands in front of centre-entrance 59, the first wartime Guy, which like 81 now wears the 1950-style livery and has also acquired an unpainted radiator, so helping the appearance. The service to Red House, destination of 81, was commenced on 21 January 1952, five months before the taking of this picture.

(Copyright R Marshall)

motion the human frame felt every vibration and each imperfection of the road surface. Fortunately the Gardner engine had flexible mountings in the Guy Arab and while this model was perhaps not up to the standard of the Daimler CWG5, the amount of vibration transmitted to the bodywork was tolerable.

Unlike Roe-bodied 59, Guys 62/63 were of the Arab II variety with the now-standard longer bonnet, irrespective of engine type, as first used on the relatively few 6LW-engined Arab Is built. In an attempt to minimise the effect of the protrusion, the front wings were swept forward at their leading edge although they did not reach the foremost extremity of the radiator shell. By special dispensation, long-bonneted Arabs were slightly over the legal maximum length. Massey utility bodies featured a full sliding window in the bulkhead behind the driver. If this were left only slightly open, especially on a Guy, at least one regular young passenger would enjoy positioning himself where he could best savour the characteristic warm oily aroma wafting through to the saloon!

Further Guys and Daimlers arrived during the last three months of 1943 although not all in numerical order. Massey-bodied Guys 64-66 introduced the luxury of inward-opening vents in the upper saloon front windows. 66 broke down at Blackburn on 20 December when on delivery from Massey's at Wigan and was not collected until 4 January. 69/70 and the later 74-79 were Massey Guys again while Guys 67/68 were bodied by R Y Pickering of

Wishaw in Lanarkshire, a concern little heard of in bus circles during peacetime although it supplied four utility bodies to nearby SDO and in post-war years was to do work for NGT and Tynemouth & District. The Duple-bodied Daimler CWA6s, 71-73, were powered by the AEC 7.7-litre engine which was non-standard in SCT's fleet. Although believed to be derated it was a somewhat lively unit and those buses, which appear to have had the 5.75 to 1 rear axle ratio, were high performers. Unlike the Leyland 8.6, however, the AEC 7.7 was a noisy runner, emitting a pronounced "thump" with each revolution. Being mounted rigidly, it made its presence felt to passengers on those wooden-slatted seats. The front bulkhead was trimmed with grey patterned moquette (clearly from pre-war stocks) but this did little to reduce the effect. The design of seat was probably the best, Duple having carried out tests involving three employees of varying height sitting stripped in a bank of wet sand. From the moulds obtained, an average measurement was calculated and a suitable template formed. Where the Massey body design used boldness effectively, Duple used subtlety and restraint and its utility body was admired for good looks, given the circumstances. Duple's utilities tended to be robust, too, the framework incorporating a very substantial lower saloon waistrail and all timber being treated with preservative. One day in 1965, long after the disappearance of SCT's utility Daimlers, the author was waiting at a breezy bus stop on the outskirts of Aberdeen when to his delight along came a local Duple-

Regrettably this wartime Massey-bodied Guy cannot be identified but it is not 62/63/80 or 81. The picture conveys the impression of dowdiness created by the grey primer finish which in Massey's case was darker than most others. The name of the undertaking is omitted and that the General Manager's name appears below "Corporation Transport".
(Copyright Busways Travel Services)

Some wartime buses underwent changes during the 1940s and 1950s before being rebuilt or rebodied early during the green livery era from 1953. Left to right here at the Black Road parking ground are 74/66/63/65, with 62 behind 74. As shown, 74/66 (along with 75-79) received a modified form of front destination aperture about 1951 and it may be compared with the original as on 63/65/62. No66 had previously received a 6LW engine and had also been repainted in the 1950-style livery, keeping its original apertures (like those of 63, alongside), but was altered to receive the revised indicator display during accident repairs. 66's style of "Binns" lettering with the larger initial and final letters was unique among utilities, making it easily identifiable until rebuilt and repainted green in 1954. All buses in this picture have received the under-canopy service number box, fitted summer 1953. It will be seen that 62/63 lack upper saloon front window vents. *(Copyright R L Kell)*

bodied CWA6, twenty years old but still doing stalwart work.

By the time Sunderland's CWA6s had entered service there were promises of an easing of transport difficulties. Mr Ernest Bevin, Minister of Labour and National Service, had said on 28 September that oil supplies were better, rubber supplies were going to be better and that more new buses were to be provided. *The Transport World* subsequently implied that bus operating had become the Cinderella of the war effort. Plainly this was true and because of problems still to be encountered, it was to be a long time before Cinders would go to the ball! Tyre supplies were still causing anxiety and the Ministry of Supply said that expected deliveries of synthetic rubber from the USA would ease the situation only a little.

The annual statistics for 31 March 1944 again were generally positive. Mileage increased by 0.4 per cent while passenger journeys went up by nine per cent. Bus mileage was still creeping up on tram mileage although the trams were still carrying double the total number of bus passengers. The average number of bus passengers per mile was a record 15.53 and still to rise even higher. It became possible to lengthen the Cairns Road service by some 400 yards to the Alston Crescent/Ambleside Terrace junction on 31 July 1944. The route length was then again 1.9 miles as it had been before its Town terminus was cut back from the Museum to Bedford Street in 1941. There was a subsequent petition *against* the extended service but the Transport Committee left it in place. Some years later there were to be objections to other bus services from private housing estate residents. As to the section along Newcastle Road, first being extended to Cairns Road and now Ambleside Terrace, it had seen only 9.95 passengers per mile in 1935. Within ten

years this had risen to 14.36 and from 2 October 1944 the basic service frequency was six minutes.

The Corporation's final two new wartime buses, 80/81, Massey-bodied Guy Arabs, arrived in August 1944. Surprisingly they had 6LW engines, the first but by no means the last buses in the fleet to have this 8.4-litre unit. The surprise lay in the fact that 6LW Guys had normally gone to operators with hilly territory. This did not describe Sunderland as the steep hills like Stoney Lane and Castletown Bank were relatively short and the 700-yard Humbledon Bank was not particularly steep at about 1 in 14. The whole terrain was within the capabilities of the 5LW Arabs (and in post-war years NGT was to run eight-ton five-cylinder Guys on long climbs of up to 1 in 8). However, the more spirited performances of Corporation 80/81 helped with timekeeping during busy periods, made them

Doxford's shipyard (right) is seen, looking west in this view, also on 4 May 1945. Guy 65 is now leaving (centre left) with a fair load. It will be seen that the "Binns" advertisement appeared at the rear only on the utilities, although it was applied to the front soon after the war and before the grey was overpainted with standard colours. Waiting on the right fork from Alexandra Bridge (right) is Daimler 31, showing the rear destination indicator mounted at the top of the lower saloon emergency exit, a feature of 26-32. *(Copyright Busways Travel Services)*

popular with drivers and heightened the enjoyment of riding on them. At this time it was possible again to use aluminium for panelling and even with their heavier engines they weighed a little less unladen than the 5LW Massey-bodied Guys and Daimlers. 80/81 differed in some body details from earlier Masseys and the less staccato 6LW engine sound and deeper exhaust also note assisted identification.

On 17 September 1944, after the Allies had broken through the Siegfried Line, Belgium had been liberated and German troops were retreating across Europe, Britain's blackout was replaced by the "dim-out". Some street lighting was allowed and public transport was permitted to be adequately lit again. Subsequently headlamp masks were dispensed with but lamps were required to be be extinguished on the instructions of a police officer. By October 1944 all the Leyland Lions and Tigers had been taken out of service, their withdrawal having covered ten years. Apart from Lion 3, scrapped 1938, all went for service elsewhere and only Tiger 20 ran as other than as a PSV. Some kept going into the 1950s at locations as far south as Jersey in the case of Lion 2, now preserved, and as far north as Inverness-shire in the case of Lion 15. Originally built for an estimated life of only about five years, circumstances caused them to show that they were capable of running for much longer. Their longevity was a tribute to the soundness of their original design and construction.

At the end of 1944 the part-day suspension of the Docks Circle was lifted and a basic 20-minute service introduced. Early in 1945, Daimler introduced its own 8.6-litre diesel engine. Chassis fitted with it were designated CWD6 and Sunderland Corporation was to have some. Guy and Daimler had already been joined by Bristol as wartime chassis suppliers but one of the first additional chassis makes available was Crossley. In March 1945 the Ministry of War Transport said it was ready to receive applications for that make of chassis with Crossley's own bodywork. Sunderland was successful in applying although in this case the bodies were not to be built by Crossley but by Cravens Railway Carriage & Wagon Company of Darnall, Sheffield. More than a year was to pass before they were delivered, however.

For the year ending 31 March 1945, Sunderland Corporation's statistics again showed upward trends. The average passengers-per-mile figures for buses and trams became all-time records and the increase in the total number of passenger journeys was almost three times the increase in operated mileage. However, the rise in working expenses was more than double the rise in traffic revenue. Regrettably, industrial relations at this time became strained. There was a dispute about new schedules to be introduced on Tuesday 3 April 1945 and some 600 bus and tram employees began unofficial strike action on Easter Monday, 2 April. The matter was referred to arbitration and troops were called out on the Thursday to take shipyard and engineering employees to work. The strike ended on Saturday 7 April, the transport workers keeping to their old schedules pending the arbitration decision. On Sunday 29 July, however, a further unofficial strike began, the dispute being about one bus service only. Work resumed on Saturday 4 August which was bank holiday weekend. During this action the employees' unions asked the Council to hold an enquiry into the administration of the Transport Department. This was done and the findings, published in February 1946, will be summarised shortly. An honour for Mr Hopkins during 1945 was his election April as Vice President of the Municipal Passenger Transport Association for 1945/46. Then in January 1946, following the death of the President, Mr Hopkins became Acting President until taking over the Presidency for 1946/47.

The war in Europe was over on 8 May 1945 but there could be no immediate reversion to pre-war standards of service. Within a few days the Regional Transport Commissioner wrote to Mr Hopkins, saying that Sunday morning services other than workers' journeys were not yet to be restored and that the 10pm curfew would remain in force. No change in the situation came about until July and anything resembling pre-war levels of service was not possible until December. There was to be a long wait for the better situation which it was hoped peace would bring. Then when the days of austerity were finally over there were other problems, serious ones, for public transport.

Pictures of SCT unfrozen buses in wartime grey are rare, but this one shows Leyland 56 unloading behind grey utility Daimler 60 at Ford terminus on 4 May 1945. The handwritten caption on the back of the print reads: "60 bus arrived 4.44pm, left 4.45pm. 56 bus arrived 4.44pm, left 4.48pm." The little boy on the right seems to recognise someone!

(Copyright Busways Travel Services)

4 - Peace But No Rest

By the time of the surrender of Japan on 15 August 1945, Britain was beginning to realise that transport had played a wartime role more vital that may have been realised at the time. The manufacturing industry had produced about half a million heavy vehicles, 80,000 light vans and cars, 75,000 carriers and armoured cars and 25,000 tanks; but only 5,000 double deck buses, of which Sunderland Corporation had received 26, representing only about 0.5 per cent. During the war, average bus operating costs throughout the country had risen by the following approximate percentages: lubricating oil, 80; fuel oil and petrol, 50; materials and spare parts, 40; platform staff wages, 30. New buses, moreover, were costing nearly 45 per cent more. Yet in Sunderland as almost everywhere else, fares were still at their 1939 level other than for the withdrawal of some cheap facilities here and there. SCT passengers had seen their 2d universal transfer return ticket replaced by a 1^1/2d transfer single although this still gave extraordinary value. During 1939-45, SCT's bus

Massey Bros were quick to shake off appearances of wartime austerity immediately after the utility period. Curving lines and radiused lower corners to the windows replaced the squareness of the previous few years' designs as exemplified here by 1946 Daimler CWD6 No15, the first of four. Its livery may be termed the "post-war streamline" version. These Daimler-engined buses kept their original destination apertures and streamline mouldings until withdrawal. *(Copyright holder not known)*

operating figures had undergone these percentage rises: working expenses, 115; traffic revenue, 118; passenger journeys, almost 110. Mr Hopkins predicted that 1939 fares could not be kept for much longer and events were to prove him right.

It was also clear to operators that fleets were going to need massive intakes of new vehicles to replace time-worn ones and to allow for post-war development. In Sunderland, however, at the war's end the situation was reasonably good. Of the 58 double deckers in the fleet, 26 vehicles (45 per cent) were up to three years old; 25 (43 per cent) were six to nine years old; only seven (12 per cent) were ten or more years old. For the next few years the Corporation was going to need every new bus for service expansion. Only four double deckers were to be withdrawn before 1952. Almost everywhere, the demand for public transport continued to rise in those early post-war years. Television, private car ownership and other social changes would make their impact later. In the meantime, Wearsiders were generally facing a period of social and economic stability. Most people available for work had secure jobs and some would see, years later, the end of the traditional heavy industries on the Wear and the building of an enormous motor car factory with a *Japanese* title. In the July 1945 general election most of them contributed to a Labour landslide victory and while this had implications for the future of public transport in the region, these were never fully put into effect.

As Appendix 2 shows clearly, during the first nine post-war years Sunderland's buses would gradually overtake the trams in importance until the trams disappeared. The town was to see an enormous housing programme implemented, creating new residential areas mostly around the periphery. Along with the restoration of pre-war service levels, this meant that the growth in bus and tram mileage would be greater than the growth in passenger journeys. Never again would the average number of passengers per tram and bus mile reach the 1945 figures.

Trams ran along the sea front again from 4 June 1945. The bus service that had replaced the suspended tram section in 1939,

Town - Seaburn via Park Avenue, kept running all day at weekends but only at peak times Monday - Friday. Other Sunday bus services were improved later. The Alexandra Road service was restored on 15 October 1945 with a southward extension of 0.85mile to Grangetown. Again, it was operated by Guy Wolves 3/4, augmented or replaced at peak times and on Saturdays by Crossley saloons 22/23 which had been supplanted from the North Hylton service by double deckers during the war. All late-night services were extended from 10 December 1945 when the final departures from Town became 10.45 Monday - Friday and 11 o'clock at weekends.

As from the end of 1945 bus operators (and hauliers) were free from all restrictions and controls on obtaining vehicles. A huge upsurge in orders followed and for several years, supply could not keep up with demand, leading to long waits for desperately-needed new buses. There was to be a wider choice of makes and types, but for more than ten years Sunderland Corporation would stick to names already seen in the fleet other than for Leyland and with the addition of the six AECs ordered in 1942. On 1 January 1946 the limit of standing passengers on buses was reduced from twelve to five off-peak. The peak limit went down from twelve to eight on 27 May 1946. SCT was still eager to restore pre-war operating standards and some frequencies were increased where practicable from 21 January 1946. On a tragic note, utility Massey Guy 75 proved unlucky twice at this period. A cyclist was fatally injured in a collision with it in Bridge Street on 31 January. Three weeks later, 75 knocked down and killed an eight-year-old boy in Stoney Lane (see Appendix 3).

The Transport Committee's report into the administration of the Department, mentioned previously, was published in February 1946. Among the points raised were:

1 Employees should not have to meet the cost of unavoidable damage to vehicles. While this had already been agreed by the Committee, there was no consensus as to the definition of the term "avoidable".

2 Occasionally, bad language had been used between some officials and employees. The Committee deplored this and said that in future it would

constitute a serious disciplinary matter.

3   Mr Hopkins had been asked to hear employees' complaints weekly. In the absence of agreement, the complaints would be referred to a committee comprising employees' representatives, their union and the Corporation.

Further evidence of the return of peace was seen in early March 1946 the Ministry of Transport dropped the term "War" from its title. Then later that month Sunderland rejoiced in the arrival of four new buses that almost seemed to push the war further into the background. They were the four Daimler CWD6 chassis with eye-catching Massey bodywork, re-using old numbers which in this case were 15-18. Other builders were still producing "relaxed" utility designs as sanctioned by the Ministry of Supply early in 1945, but Massey Bros had now cast aside their unashamedly squarish wartime style and were producing a curvilinear product that perhaps just stopped short of being flamboyant, although the framing was based on the utility pattern. Refreshingly different from wartime drabness, a new livery format with streamline effect enhanced the overall impression. It was virtually a red and cream version of Rochdale's blue and ivory layout. Seats were upholstered in red leathercloth which was to be Sunderland's post-war standard generally until green was introduced in 1953. Simulating materials and other colours were to be used in later years.

As was said previously, the CWD6 chassis was powered by Daimler's new 8.6-litre diesel engine, designated type CD6 and compact enough to fit into the same space as the Gardner 5LW and the AEC 7.7-litre. Development of the Daimler unit had begun in 1936, the war impeding some of its progress, but by 1946 some other firms were moving ahead. AEC already had a 9.6-litre engine and Leyland was about to produce a 9.8. Nevertheless Daimler, celebrating its golden jubilee in 1946 and planning return to Coventry where it would occupy a shadow factory at Allesley, extolled its engine's virtues of durability, economy and smooth running. Sunderland's four CWD6s had the builder's own rear axle, now to be standard on Daimlers in the fleet. The Daimler engine in the CWD6 was certainly much more quiet and refined than the AEC unit in the CWA6.

Some service changes were made on 11 March 1946, permitting more efficient use of vehicles and crews and providing through-running to the Docks instead of operating the Docks Circle independently. Here are the details:

Old	*New*
Ettrick Gr - Town	Ettrick Gr - Town - Boro' Rd - Docks
Marley Pots - Town	Marley Pots - Town - High St - Docks

The statistics for the year ending 31 March 1946 showed little change from the previous year. Mr Hopkins again warned that the increasing costs of operating would inevitably lead to fare rises before long. A further move toward pre-war standards was made on 1 April when final weeknight departures from Town became 11 o'clock. Two days later, the Town - Hylton Lane service was extended by about 200 yards to Nookside (Holborn Road/Holborn Square), catering for an area of new prefabricated housing. The basic service frequency was doubled to five minutes and Holborn Road was used both ways, omitting Hadleigh Road southbound.

Another driver-only operated service was started on 3 May 1946, running on Friday to Sunday evenings only with one of the Guy Wolves, 3/4. Traffic revenue averaged only 6.45d per mile which was below the level of the driver-only Alexandra Road service, itself well below average. Driver-only services needed to clear about 13d per mile just to break even. The new service was withdrawn on 9 February 1947. This was its 2.45-mile course, paralleling the Seaburn Camp - Humbledon route south of St Luke's Cross:

Ford - St Luke's Rd - Pallion Rd - Kayll Rd - Barnes Park Rd - Durham Rd - Humbledon

In contrast, two summer days in 1946 broke records, condensed as follows:

Sat 22 Jun (all records)

passengers :
buses   118,142 (trams 206,513);   buses av 16.65/mile (trams 29.17)
receipts :
buses   £667 (trams £928);   buses av 22.57d/mile (trams 25.11d)

Sun 7 Jul (Sun records)

passengers:
buses   74,737 (trams 152,985);   buses av 16.17/mile (trams: 24.68)
receipts:
buses   £458 (trams £742);   buses av 23.77d/mile* (trams 29.66d*)
(* records, any day)

Another summer incident, and a most serious one, took place on the afternoon of Friday 19 July when the bus depot was severely damaged by a fire which was thought to have started in the trimming shop. Fourteen buses were driven to safety. Driver Charlie Parnaby, although off duty, lived nearby and was among those who assisted. One bus, believed to have been unique centre-entrance Guy 59 which was over a pit for maintenance and without some wheels, received extensive damage externally but was returned to service after repairs.

The three Crossleys of type DD42/3 ordered during the spring of 1945 finally arrived in September 1946, numbered 19-21. Appearance-wise, their Cravens bodies were dull compared with the Masseys delivered six months earlier. Cravens had used a "relaxed utility" design, although they had never built any true utility bodies. The seats were frameless and while upholstered, they were barely more comfortable than the wartime wooden-slatted type due to their being somewhat hard and having fairly upright back squabs. These three buses were part of a Ministry of Supply contract with Cravens for 70 bodies on Crossley DD42/3 chassis (meaning Double Deck, 4-wheeled, 2 wheels driven, type 3), Bolton Corporation receiving the entire remainder. The bodywork was steel-framed and while these Cravens products compared unfavourably with the 1946 Masseys for style, they made up for it in durability. Apparently it was never necessary even to remove the panels from the Cravens bodies other than in cases of collision-damage and they never needed any remedial treatment.

The Crossley DD42/3 chassis had excellent riding characteristics with a constant mesh gearbox that was easy to handle. Regrettably, what let Crossleys down was the direct-injection six-cylinder 8.6-litre engine, designated type HOE7/1 and replacing the pre-war VR6 unit. Its development had begun in the late 1930s but as with Daimler's engine, the war had delayed its introduction. In 1944

Cravens of Sheffield produced a much more utility-like but steel-framed design on 70 Crossley DD42/3 chassis in 1946. Sunderland received three examples of which 21 was the numerical last, seen here on a dull 1950 midsummer's day loading in Union Street alongside market stallholders occupying the site of the bombed Empress Hotel, later to be used as a bus station. The Crossley radiator shell carried the chassis-maker's Coptic cross motif but not the name. All three buses kept their original destination layout until withdrawal although 19/21 had the name glass blanked off about 1960. They received pre-war Gardner 5LW engines during 1953-55. The appearance of the width of these buses was exaggerated by the absence of taper in plan view at the front of the upper saloon. *(Copyright R Marshall)*

the Crossley 8.6-litre HOE7 prototype was fitted to a pre-war Manchester double decker for testing. It showed itself a reliable and smooth runner with good performance and low fuel and oil consumption. Yet this did not correspond with the post-war experiences of operators running production examples in service. The matter remained a mystery for nearly fifty years but thanks to the efforts of Crossley historian Michael Eyre, light has been thrown on it. Evidently the design of cylinder head for the prototype Crossley HOE7 had incorporated by arrangement some advanced features originating with the well-known Swiss manufacturer, Saurer. The Crossley managing director would not agree to paying royalties on production examples and so Crossley's own design of cylinder head was concocted hurriedly, avoiding any resemblance to Saurer's principles. The result was an engine with a restricted flow of inducted air. It lacked power, was inefficient and uneconomical, used lubricating oil excessively and suffered from localised overheating with consequent leakage of oil and water, and worse. As to reliability, by the time SCT became aware of problems with Crossley engines there were six more in the pipeline.

Several service extensions took place during the autumn of 1946. They were:

11 Oct.: Town - Seaburn via Park Ave
   Again extended to Seaburn Hall as required

19 Oct. St Luke's Cross - Football Ground
   Most journeys operated from Fordham Rd (0.5mile west of St Luke's X)

21 Oct. Seaburn Camp - Humbledon
   Extended from Humbledon to Springwell Rd/Somerset Rd

The extension from Humbledon served the new council housing development at Springwell and increased the route length by 0.45mile to 6.3 miles. Springwell was linked with the town centre by the Durham Road tramway section which for some residents meant a lengthy walk or a change from bus to tram at the Prospect Hotel. Some bus journeys, especially peak time extras, continued to terminate at Humbledon. Two days after the Springwell extension was introduced, pre-war Crossley 25 was withdrawn after sustaining a fracture of the chassis frame. Subsequently it was cannibalised for spare parts.

At the end of the war Sunderland Corporation, like most other operators, had reason to be grateful to the women who had worked as conductresses under the onerous conditions of wartime. On 8 November 1946 the Transport Committee held a farewell dinner for the two hundred longest-serving of the 800 who had conducted on the buses and trams during the war. The maximum number employed at any one time had been 300 and with the return of men from military service this had fallen to sixteen. Recruiting difficulties, however, were to mean that more women would have to be engaged in the future. At the dinner, a response to the toast of "the visitors" was made by Mrs Rosina Cleete, the most senior conductress. The toast of the Transport Committee was proposed by

Six more Crossley DD42/3 chassis were delivered in April 1947 as 9-14, and how different were their metal-framed Crossley bodies from the Cravens products! The standard Crossley design of the period incorporated stepped and swooping coach-like features. Note the low-positioned bonnet and radiator, and deep windscreen giving an excellent forward view to the driver, although the high bulkhead waistrail impeded passengers' view. When new, 9-14 had a larger style of fleet numeral than standard. Interestingly, their front destination apertures followed utility layout and were never modified. 10, here crewed by Driver Frank Fowler and Conductress Rosina (Renee) Cleete, waits in High Street West during 1952 before a trip to Red House North, wearing the 1950-style livery with new coat-of-arms minus diamond background. By this time similar bus 13 had been fitted with a pre-war Gardner 5LW engine, the others of the 9-14 batch receiving the same treatment during 1953/54. *(Copyright R Marshall)*

Miss Molly Parker who had been awarded the British Empire Medal for her wartime service. (Other details about her are given in Appendix 3).

On 28 November 1946 the Government's Transport Bill was introduced in the House of Commons. Under the Bill, the British Transport Commission was to be established. It would have general powers to carry passengers and goods by road, rail and inland waterways and also to provide port facilities within Great Britain. The Bill preceded the Transport Act, 1947, under which later the railways and parts of the bus-operating and road haulage industries were to be nationalised. Reference has been made already to the plans that were to be made for almost total nationalisation of buses in north-east England from part of the North Riding to the Scottish border. This certainly exercised the minds of Sunderland Town Council although nothing was discussed in open forum yet. Subsequently approaches were made by national representatives of bus companies opposing the Bill but the Council took no action.

Problems of a different kind stretched the Transport Department's resources early in 1947 when a prolonged spell of exceptionally severe weather gripped the country. Sunderland had heavy snowfalls in January and February accompanied by extraordinary frost. Tramlines were blocked and bus services disrupted. On some occasions buses deputised for trams. A further heavy blizzard occurred on 13 March, bringing more chaos. The weather cost the Department an estimated £6,000 in lost revenue, repairs to damage and suchlike. There was also a severe coal shortage which added to the misery. In contrast to the two record-breaking summer days the previous year when sun-seekers had flocked to Roker and Seaburn, people now made for the beaches in search of washed-up sea coal.

As to longer-term policy, a momentous decision was made by the Council on 11 January 1947. Following completion of the planned lengthening of the existing Durham Road section, no further tramway extensions would be made. Trams would then be replaced gradually by motor buses. Later that month, tenders were accepted from Daimler and Massey Bros for twelve bus chassis and bodies respectively, both concerns submitting the lowest quotations. Seventeen months were to elapse before these vehicles were

Docks-bound Daimler 52 pulls up at Mackie's Corner and illustrates the post-war version of the streamline livery as applied to the Roe bodies of 43-57. Omitting cream from the upper saloon windows and until 1950 applying black to both waistrails, this was an amended version of the original carried by those up to No55. Both trams visible are second-hand examples, 3 (behind the bus) being ex-London, originally Ilford Corporation, and 38 (creeping in on the right) an ex-Manchester "Pilcher" car which dates this picture after May 1947. The short trousers, long socks (often in "concertina" shape!) and helmet worn by young boys are evocative of the period.

(Copyright Sunderland Echo)

delivered. Although plenty of Daimlers were to be acquired over the next two decades, this was to be the final order to go to Massey Bros from SCT.

24 February 1947 saw a further bus service extension. The Nookside route was lengthened by 0.75mile to Grindon (Mill Inn). It is not known precisely when, but during this period Grindon was linked with Docks via High Street and the Marley Pots service was cut back from Docks to Town. As has been mentioned, the Grindon Mill Inn was on the route of NGT and SDO buses on out-of-town services. Plainly, the companies regarded the Corporation's extension as an encroachment on their own exclusive territory, notwithstanding that Grindon residents may have benefited from a link with Hylton Road. It seems clear that NGT had its eye on a planned Council housing development to the north-west of Grindon. The situation was to become uneasy and ultimately the Chairman of the Traffic Commissioners would have to exercise a Solomon-like judgment. It was one that was going to leave the company smirking and the municipality smarting, or so it appeared.

The Annual Report for 31 March 1947 showed bus mileage up by the largest amount since 1931 and now 90 per cent of tram

Here the green light is showing at Mackie's Corner for two utility Daimlers in their first post-war garb. Leading is 72, middle member of the handsomely-proportioned Duple-bodied CWA6 trio and following is 61, second of the Massey-bodied CWG5 duet. The CWG5 model was relatively smooth-running and had tolerable noise levels, thanks to a flexibly-mounted 5LW engine. However, the CWA6 was a thumping good bus, its somewhat rough AEC 7.7-litre unit being mounted rigidly although much livelier than the 5LW. Note the differences in roof structure, destination aperture sizes and "Binns" styles and format. It is possible to see the wooden-slatted seats in 72, and the dark area toward the rear of 61's upper saloon is caused by the emergency window which is still panelled and not yet glazed. Standing at the north end of the railway station behind is tram 23, one of three rebuilt in 1925 from single deckers new in 1900. The saloon car (right) is a mid-1930s Morris Eight. Tizer (as on side of 61) has survived but whatever happened to Tattersall's soups?

(Copyright Sunderland Echo)

mileage. Passenger journeys increased by the greatest figure for ten years although tram loadings were still considerably heavier. Mr Hopkins remarked that many of the buses were of "ancient vintage" and although well-maintained and giving good service, they would need to be replaced soon. Buses new at that time were additions and not replacements. Many other operators were running fleets of greater average age than Sunderland's and the pre-war Daimlers were patently capable of soldiering on for some years to come, as events would prove. Mr Hopkins once again referred to the low level fares and said that this was responsible for operating losses of 2.353d and 2.533d per mile respectively on the Ambleside Terrace and Seaburn via Park Avenue sections. Another troublesome factor was the shortening of working hours in commerce and industry which was tending to compress the peak periods and creating problems with the organising of workers' services.

As to new buses, six Crossley DD42/3 chassis were delivered in April 1947, the same as Nos19-21 of 1946 but with bodies of vastly different appearance. Numbered 9-14, they had Crossley's own highly distinctive steel-framed bodywork of the "Manchester" style, incorporating some features originating with that city's streamline specification dating back to 1936. These characteristics, adopted as standard on early post-war Crossley bodies, included a drooping lower window line at the front corners upstairs and stepped waistrails below the rearmost two windows on each side of each saloon. This latter detail had a structural function in the lower saloon as it accommodated the long diagonal stays reinforcing the wheelarch area, the corresponding upper saloon windows being treated the same simply to match. The lower radiator and bonnet line of post-war Crossleys enabled a deep windscreen to be fitted. While the Crossley body design exploited this the Cravens did not, and neither make incorporated a low bulkhead waistrail. Crossley bodywork of this period also developed a reputation for robustness, utilising the builder's patent design of exceptionally strong metal body pillar comprising two L-sections separated by a zig-zag insert spot-welded to them and incorporating hardwood packing where necessary for panel attachment.

About six weeks after the arrival of these Crossleys some more new buses entered service, highly distinctive in a different way. Roe-bodied with standard teak framing and numbered 82-87, they comprised the half-dozen AECs ordered in 1942 when the price quoted was £1,109 per chassis. That figure had now risen by 52 per cent! The chassis was of the Regent Mark III variety, type O961/2, possibly the most refined double deck model on the market at that time. It was the provincial version of AEC's O961 species best known as London Transport RT-type chassis, developed from 1937 and of which nearly 5,000 examples were to enter London service by 1954. Powered by the AEC 9.6-litre engine, transmission was through an AEC air-operated preselective gearbox with selector lever set in an H-shaped "gate" arrangement on the left of the steering column. Outwardly the higher bonnet and radiator distinguished the provincial O961/2 Regent III from the London O961. SCT's half-dozen were among the earliest O961/2 specimens

to be completed and the chassis type probably had the most handsome frontal features of any contemporary double deck model. The bodywork introduced to SCT the Roe patent "safety" staircase, a design for rear-entrance bodies (except utilities) dating from 1936 incorporating also a uniquely-shaped window. To be a standard Roe feature for some years to come and modified a little in the mid-1950s, it had two landings which were arranged so that the boarding passenger mounted the first two stairs straight ahead, then turned left through 90 degrees to climb five more straight stairs and then turned left again to mount the final stair and stand in the upper saloon gangway. This design almost eliminated the possibility of a fall from

"Two pound a bob the tomatoes," they shouted from the fruit stalls, the shawl-clad old "willick woman" sat quietly selling her shell fish from a barrow (right) and the fare for the 4.25 miles from Union Street to Thorney Close was 3d (1.25p). AEC Regent Mark III 86 prepares to make the journey, its appearance enhanced by the gleaming chrome of its radiator shell and front wheel nut rings. There were six of these refined buses, 82-87, the only AEC double deckers ever to join the fleet. A non-standard style of fleet numeral, smaller and silver rather than gold leaf, was carried until their repaint in the 1950-style livery. Although teak-framed as normal, they were SCT's first to have rear-entrance Roe bodies with the distinctive staircase window. As with all SCT's Roe bodies of 1938-50, the twin front apertures were repeated at the rear. In 1952, No86 was to be the first bus painted green. *(Copyright R Marshall)*

the staircase and off the open rear platform. Due to the layout the offside rear bulkhead encroached more than a foot into the lower saloon, reducing the inward-facing offside wheelarch bench from the usual triple to a double seat. The loss was made good upstairs where the rearmost nearside seat was a triple rather than a double one.

A ride on a Regent III was always to be relished. With ample power and quick gear-changes, when driven hard these buses could almost leave some other types standing. Internal and external finish was to Roe's usual high standard. They were smooth and fairly quiet when running, emitting some euphonious gearbox sounds and an audible "gulp" with every change of ratio. Drivers liked them because of their high performance, easy steering, effective air brakes and the light operation of the air-assisted gear-change pedal. A picture of Sunderland's No83 on Wearmouth Bridge, newly in service without advertisements, was used in contemporary AEC publicity.

The two remaining Guy tram-o-cars, GR 1156/57, out of use with the Department since 1939, were fitted with 20-seat saloon bodies suitable for driver-only operation and numbered 1/2 in July 1947. Local builder F Blagg had received the order in March 1946 but the bodies were produced by Associated Coachbuilders (ACB) at their Southwick river bank premises. Established in late 1946, its directors included Sir Myers Wayman (a former Mayor, not related to the writer), Alderman W S Martin (a former Transport Committee member), Mr E Steel (founder of a Pallion crane-building concern), Major D Nicholson and Mr H Lane. It seems clear that ACB, which built bodies for goods vehicles as well as PSVs, acquired the business of F Blagg. Certainly, the ACB bodywork fitted to 1/2 was

Almost identical bodies to those on Nos3/4 were fitted to the first pair of Guy Wolves in 1947, although they were built locally by Associated Coachbuilders which was the successor to F Blagg. These two were now numbered 1/2, the second being caught here on a private hire. *(Copyright holder not known)*

practically identical to that fitted by Blagg to 3/4 in 1938. It was intended that 1/2 should be used by Committee members instead of taxis, as well as on normal service which meant the Alexandra Road route. ("Queen" was added to "Alexandra Road" at about this time, though never shown on destination blinds.)

Two 1943 Pickering-bodied Guy Arab I 5LW double deckers were acquired from Blackburn Corporation and entered SCT service on 1 January 1948 as Nos5/6. They were fairly standard in Sunderland and blended well with the other utilities. At this time, too, the Town - Marley Pots service was showing a 14 per cent passenger rise on the previous fiscal year while the average bus network figure was nine per cent, and on 26 January 1948 frequencies were increased at the busiest times. Only Ambleside Terrace showed a decrease and this was less than one per cent. Petrol was still rationed and new cars were in short supply which helped to keep up the demand for public transport. In 1948 the volume of road traffic nationally was still below the figure for 1937. The Annual Report for 31 March 1948 also showed that the increase in working expenses was three times the increase in revenue, leading to a general rise in fares later in the year. There were difficulties with recruiting and keeping enough platform staff and service levels were maintained only by considerable overtime working. The ogres of sharply rising costs and staff shortages were to harass much of the transport operating industry for years to come.

Sunderland's population was drifting gradually to the west. A vast housing programme was in operation, generally moving people away from the older areas that lay toward the sea. Most of the space available for new houses was beyond the western fringes and some boundary changes were made accordingly. The Springwell housing area has been mentioned and by 1948 the new Thorney Close development was under way immediately to the west. It was to be served at its southern periphery by a further projection of the Durham Road tram service (the final tramway extension) and then by the lengthening of the Docks - Ettrick Grove bus route which would penetrate the estate. The first new length of tramway, Humbledon - Plains Farm (Durham Road/Grindon Lane), within reach of the lower part of Thorney Close, was on reserved track and had come into operation on 21 February 1948. As an interim measure, the Ettrick Grove bus service was extended 0.7mile to Humbledon (Durham

Road/Shrewsbury Crescent) on 10 May 1948, despite protests from Ettrick Grove/Cleveland Road area residents who feared being left behind by full buses coming down from Humbledon. NGT also unsuccessfully opposed the licence application for this extension.

The summer of 1948 held an exciting treat for young bus observers. Early in July the first of the dozen Massey-bodied Daimlers arrived, numbered 88-99. Like the 1947 all-Crossleys they were certainly eye-catching. Daimlers 88-99 had the Rochdale-like livery format of 1946 Massey Daimlers 15-18 and although the basic design of the 1948 bodies was similar, there were styling detail differences. In contrast to the Crossley and Cravens bodies, however, after about seven years the new Masseys like the utilities needed rebuilding, due largely to the rotting of unseasoned timber framework. There were no such problems with the chassis as they were of the CVG6 type and true to Daimler tradition, robust and reliable. 'V' denoted 'victory', that is, post-war design and 'G6' meant that a Gardner 6LW engine was fitted. The CV-type chassis frame was of a reinforced box section $11\frac{1}{2}$in deep which, said Daimler, reduced deflection and helped to prolong body life. Components were designed for heavy duty and every detail had been conceived with maximum serviceability in mind. Other manufacturers, of course, claimed similar virtues for their products and probably with justification for bus chassis and bodywork designs had now come of age, so to speak, manufacturers having had ample experience from which to learn. Many vehicles of this era were to prove capable of some two decades' reliable service although SCT did not hold on to post-war buses for so long.

Expected fare increases took place on 27 September 1948, affecting buses and trams but not the universal transfer ticket and children's fares. The minimum adult fare throughout the system was now $1\frac{1}{2}$d although the maximum distance that could be travelled for this amount was 2.02 miles on the trams and 2.45 on the buses. Here are the details:

Increased by $\frac{1}{2}$d

buses	1d ordinary, $1\frac{1}{2}$d & 2d normal transfer
	$1\frac{1}{2}$d & 2d ordinary on Town - Seaburn via Park Ave service
trams	1d to $2\frac{1}{2}$d ordinary

Increased by 3d

buses & trams	9d all-day ticket

The Ministry of War Transport's system of allocating buses did not always seem logical and although in 1944 Sunderland was allocated two 6LW-powered Guys which seemed an extravagance among sixteen five-cylinder examples, Blackburn Corporation with terrain that was almost mountainous by comparison had been allocated two short-bonneted Arabs with 5LW engines in 1943. Understandably the Lancashire concern disposed of them early and they migrated to Wearside, entering service on 1 January 1948 as 5/6. They had Pickering bodies, generally similar to those on Sunderland's 67/68, but with leathercloth-covered seats and some minor differences. As Blackburn's front indicator layout was convenient for SCT it was retained as shown here by 6, previously Blackburn 57, on Sunday 7 June 1954 in John Street while doing Seaburn - Town short workings. The ex-Blackburn pair had no rear indicator and from 1955 until withdrawal two years later both were used for driver training, never receiving the green livery. *(Copyright R Marshall)*

32

The Springwell terminus of the service from Seaburn Camp was moved 0.2mile to Somerset Road/Grindon Lane on 11 October 1948, bringing the route length to 6.5 miles for which the fare was only 5^1/2d. Five days after this change the death occurred in hospital of the General Manager, Mr Charles A Hopkins, aged 62 years. He had been ill since June and his deputy, Mr Henry W Snowball, AMI Mech E, took charge during this period. As a tribute, all Corporation buses and trams stopped for one minute at 11am on Tuesday 19 October, the day of the funeral. In effect Mr Snowball remained in control as his appointment to the post of General Manager was confirmed by the Council on 8 December. A native of Sunderland, he had served his apprenticeship with local marine engineers Geo Clark Ltd of Southwick, subsequently becoming a draughtsman with another concern. While with the Royal Northumberland Fusiliers during World War I he had been awarded the Distinguished Conduct Medal. After further experience in shipbuilding Mr Snowball had become Rolling Stock Engineer with the Tramways Department in 1926 and Deputy General Manager in 1945.

On its way from the Docks to Thorney Close, 103 represents the six Liverpool-style Crossley DD42/7C models of 1949, Nos100-105. Its appearance differs from that of the 1947 Crossleys in several ways. The metal-framed Crossley body lines are straight and highly functional, it is of four-bay rather than five-bay construction, the name "Crossley" appears on the radiator shell and although the front destination and name glass apertures are the same, the "Binns" format does not feature the larger first and last letters. Beneath the floor there is a synchromesh rather than a constant mesh gearbox and under the bonnet the HOE7/4 type engine differs from the HOE7/1 in some details. Semaphore direction indicators, troublesome and later blanked off, and a sliding cab door were unique to this batch in the fleet. Crossleys 100-105 were to be fitted with pre-war Gardner 5LW engines during 1953-55, the final Crossley of all to receive one being 103. *(Copyright A B Cross)*

More new buses were going to be needed by early 1949 to provide for Thorney Close. The reason for the apparent delay is uncertain but it was not until 8 December 1948 that the Transport Committee dealt with the matter. Only Crossley could promise delivery by the required date. This firm was given an order for six complete buses but only because it had assured Mr Snowball that existing difficulties with "engine details" on the earlier post-war Crossleys (9-14, 19-21) had been cured by "modifications and improvements". Crossley had moved a few miles from the old Gorton works in Manchester to a former shadow factory at Errwood Park, Stockport, during early 1947. Then in 1948, Crossley Motors (along with the Maudslay Motor Company) had been taken over by AEC, the organisation then becoming Associated Commercial Vehicles Ltd, generally known as ACV, on 1 October 1948. The only other supplier offering reasonably quick delivery was Guy, quoting June/July 1949. It could supply the Arab Mark III chassis with Guy-built bodywork on Park Royal metal frames and Meadows 10.35-litre engine of type 6DC630 which was then a new option, more readily available than the usual Gardner. Neighbouring NGT and its subsidiary Tynemouth were to place in service small numbers of Meadows-engined Guys but replacement engines were fitted to all in the mid-1950s. Obviously there was a parallel here with SCT's experience of post-war Crossley engines which were also to be replaced.

The need for new buses was acute but the need for platform staff was chronic and severe. As mentioned previously a small number of conductresses had been kept on after the war but by late 1948 the Corporation was appealing to former wartime clippies to consider returning. There was some response and by the end of the year the number of tram and bus conductresses had risen to about thirty. The problem, however, was becoming endemic throughout much of the industry, particularly among the municipalities and in London. Training costs were rising due to the increasing turnover of labour, most recruits in Sunderland as elsewhere staying only for a relatively short time. With plentiful employment in other industries offering comparable wages without unsocial hours, public transport could hardly hope to compete. In years to come a bold and innovative SCT General Manager was to adopt a radical approach to try to cure the malaise for good, as will be described.

At the end of 1948, the formation of the proposed Area Board for the north-east was going ahead and in January 1949, Sunderland Corporation was asked by the Road Transport Executive to submit any plans or suggestions in connection with it. On 4 February 1949 a working party of the Road Transport Executive surveyed Sunderland's transport network and conferred with Council members and transport officials. Despite intensive planning, consultation and some preparation, the idea was never to reach fruition. There was stiff opposition from the BET Group which included NGT and its subsidiaries. Neither were municipalities won over despite the extent of Labour control among them. The matter was to drag on for two more years and then a new Conservative Government dropped it .

The new Crossleys were registered on 1 February 1949. Numbered 100-105, they differed from the previous Crossleys in several respects as detailed in Appendix 1. Moreover, other than for destination indicators the bodywork of 100-105 was basically to the specification of Liverpool Corporation. Apparently this was not then on general offer but accepted by Sunderland for quicker delivery as Crossley was completing 25 buses for Liverpool at that time. It was not unheard of for an operator to accept another's body specification in order to speed up delivery. At 7.19.0, Crossleys 100-105 were the heaviest-ever 7ft 6in-wide buses in the SCT fleet. Their synchromesh gearboxes emitted more of a pronounced whine than that of the earlier constant-mesh Crossley 'boxes. The "modifications and improvements" mentioned in correspondence from Crossley to Mr Snowball included little more than a higher-speed fan and the re-positioning of the dynamo. Major details and output figures were unchanged and despite Crossley's assurances, the problems were not solved.

The arrival of 100-105 allowed the Docks - Humbledon service to be extended westward on 7 February 1949 via Springwell to Thorney Close (Theme Road), 5.7 miles from the Docks (via Borough Road). From Humbledon the buses ran via:

Receipts per mile on the lengthened service went up from 17.2d to 19.4d during the few weeks to 31 March 1949, reflecting the rapid movement of families into the new estate. Indeed, later in the year Sunderland's 1,000th post-war council house was to be opened ceremonially at Thorney Close. On the day that the bus service was lengthened, the final extension of the Durham Road tramway came into operation. This meant that both Springwell and Thorney Close were linked with Town by buses penetrating them centrally and by trams running along the southern edge of both. The trams offered an advantage in cost and distance, fares to Town being 2^1/2d for 2.91 miles from Durham Road by tram compared with 3d for a meandering course of 4.25 miles from Theme Road by bus.

In Mr Snowball's first Annual Report, for 31 March 1949, increases were again shown for mileage, passenger journeys, revenue and working expenses on the buses. Bus mileage was now just 1.6 per cent less than the tram figure. Mr Snowball expressed concern about bus depot accommodation, twenty vehicles having to be parked overnight on vacant land alongside the building. For several years to come, however, relief was to lie only in palliatives.

The summer of 1949 was dry and sunny which brought about additional passenger traffic for both buses and trams. On Saturday 3 September the seaside illuminations were recommenced and on that day a record total of £2,510 was taken in bus and tram fares and 373,372 passengers carried. The records do not break down the figures between modes but the passenger total exceeded the previous best of 22 June 1946 by some 48,000. However, a substantial amount of the extra revenue collected on 3 September 1949 was swallowed up by overtime rates for the platform staff. At this time Sunderland's fares still compared favourably with those of many other municipalities, including some north-eastern neighbours.

On 21 November 1949 the Town - Alexandra Road service was diverted to run through the new Hill View council housing estate to the west of Grangetown, via Sea View Road, Sea View Road West, Hereford Road, Westheath Avenue and Woodstock Avenue. This increased the route length from 2.45 to 3.07 miles. The driver-only Guy Wolves, 1-4, were now inadequate for the loadings and normally the 1939 Crossley saloons, 22/23, were used with conductors. The average number of passengers per mile went up from 6.9 at 31 March 1949 to 10.8 within two years. Traffic revenue, however, remained below working expenses.

The Transport Department was reminded by the licensing authority in December 1949 that all buses delivered during the war years would have to be re-certified within 18 months. The total, including unfrozen buses and the two from Blackburn, came to 28. Of these, seventeen were re-certified within four months and the continuing programme was three buses per month. The repair work on the Massey utility bodies of Guys 62/63/65/70 was carried out by the Tramways Section at Hylton Road Car Works. After treatment these differed from the others in such details as mouldings around the frontal area.

Sunderland Corporation had now been operating its own buses for twenty years. During the previous ten, operated mileage had risen by 118 per cent and the number of passenger journeys by 221 per cent. The 102-strong bus fleet was very mixed and although the age profile had changed since 1945, it was still better than many. The were also *three* standard double deck liveries! A summary of services and particulars of fleet and liveries as at the end of 1949 are given below.

Service list, 31 Dec 49

Thorney Close - Docks via Boro' Rd	Grindon - Docks via High St	Town - Ambleside Ter
Town - Seaburn via Park Ave	Town - Marley Pots	Town - Alexandra Rd
Ford Estate - Grangetown	Springwell - Seaburn Camp	S'land - N Hylton (joint with NGT)

Fleet age profile, 31 Dec 49	Up to 3 years	37 vehicles	(36.3%)
	4 to 7 years	28 "	(27.5%)
	8 to 12 years	21 "	(20.5%)
	13 or more years	16 "	(15.7%)
Chassis make totals	6 AEC, 18 Crossley (3 types), 51 Daimler (5 types), 24 Guy (3 types*), 3 Leyland		
Engine make totals	9 AEC (2 types), 18 Crossley (3 types), 4 Daimler, 64 Gardner (2 types), 3 Leyland, 4 Meadows**		
Body make totals	2 ACB, 4 Blagg, 3 Cravens, 12 Crossley, 3 Duple, 1 English Electric, 1 Leyland, 33 Massey,		
	4 Pickering, 39 Roe (some makes with different types)		
	*Guy Arab I and II 5LW counted as one type	**Petrol; others diesel	

Double deck liveries	**(post-war to 1950)**		
Livery type '	**1 - plain**	**2 - pre-war streamline**	**3 - post-war streamline**
roof	red	red	red
u/d window surrounds	red	red	red
u/d panels	cream	red with cream partial down-sweep front and rear	red with cream waistrail band fully down-swept at front
cantrail-level band	red	cream	cream
l/d window surrounds	red	red	red
l/d panels	red with cream waistrail band	red with cream waistrail band in form of coach flash	red with dream waistrail band fully down-swept at front

Type & fleet Nos of buses bearing each livery

1		2		3	
Daimler/Roe	26-41	Crossley/Eng Elec	24	Daimler/Massey 15-18, 88-99	
all-Leyland	58	Daimler/Roe	43-55		
Guy/Roe	59	Leyland/Roe	56/57		
Guy & Daim utilities	60-81, 5/6				
Crossley/Cravens	19-21				
all-Crossley	9-14, 100-105				
AEC/Roe	82-87				

Horizontal beadings - all liveries: black where separating red and cream
Note. Centre-entrance Roe-bodied buses had the lower saloon "proud" waistrail painted black during early post-war period
Special livery: Daimler/Roe 42, red with three cream bands until 1950

5 - When He Said Jump

New Year's Day 1950 was a memorable one for votaries of pre-war Leyland designs. Sunderland Corporation placed in service another TD7! This was the 1942 unfrozen example with West Hartlepool-specified Roe centre-entrance body that had been allocated to Stockton, mentioned earlier. Sunderland numbered it 25 and painted it in the "plain" livery. Twenty-four days later 1935 Daimler 30, a bus of "ancient vintage" in Mr Hopkins's terms, was withdrawn although most other pre-war Daimlers were to go on for a few more years. On 26 January 1950 the Transport Committee took the first step in implementing its tramway replacement policy by deciding to convert the Fawcett Street - Villette Road via Tatham Street section to bus operation later in the year. Committee members Alderman D Cairns JP and Councillor W H Sheehan had been on the Tramways Committee in 1930 when the decision to abandon the Villette Road tram service had been made for the first time, albeit temporarily.

Oh what delight! The Corporation's number of 1942 Leyland Titan TD7s was increased by 33 per cent at a stroke with the purchase of Stockton's 85, becoming 25 in the SCT fleet as from 1 January 1950. Its Roe 48-seat centre-entrance body was of Sunderland's basic pre-war standard but to the detail specification of West Hartlepool where, but for the war, it would have served on a Daimler chassis. The bodywork was completely non-standard at Stockton and it was rumoured to be something of a "jinx" bus there. SCT was to standardise on the size of destination aperture carried by 25, although this bus had no side or rear indicator. It lasted for seven years on Wearside and became the final surviving centre-entrance bus in service when withdrawn, still in the red livery applied in 1952.
(Copyright R L Kell)

The Transport Department was having severe peak-time problems during this period. These arose from the Council's policy of completing house-building on the new estates before dealing with schools, leaving many hundreds of children to travel by bus or tram from their new homes to school. The children's journeys overlapped with those of many workers and the transport services were being strained to breaking point, exacerbated by shortage of vehicles and crews. Early in February 1950 four new Roe-bodied Daimler CVG6s, ordered in autumn 1949, were delivered as 106-109. Daimler-Roe was well-tried combination of chassis and body makes, one indeed that was to outnumber all others in the fleet. The livery of 106-109 was a revised format of red with three relieving cream bands. This layout was to become standard for a couple of years and was applied to all except "streamline"-liveried buses, pre-war Daimlers 26/27/30/32 and ex-Stockton Leyland 25, which will be mentioned specially in due course. In July 1947, Chas H Roe Ltd had been acquired by Park Royal Vehicles Ltd, and then in 1949 this company itself had been purchased by Associated Commercial Vehicles Ltd, making Roe part of an empire comprising chassis-builders AEC, Crossley and Maudslay along with coachbuilders Park Royal and the Crossley coachworks. Roe was to continue to produce its own designs until the late 1960s although evidence of the Park Royal relationship was to be seen in the SCT fleet within a few years.

The new Pennywell housing estate to the west of the Ford and Hylton Lane Estates was being built by the end of 1949. At that time it was outside the County Borough boundary and so sanction was therefore sought and obtained under Section 101 of the Road Traffic Act 1930, along with a road service licence, for the Corporation to begin serving Pennywell with buses. Well away from NGT and SDO territory, the new operation started on 27 January 1950 and was in effect an extension of the Grangetown - Ford service. The existing

The driver turns the indicator of 108 to "Town" at Seaburn, Guy 80 behind picking up on a short working of the Springwell service to Hylton Road Schools. 108 was the third of four Daimler CVG6s, new in the summer of 1950 and with Roe bodywork similar to that of the AEC Regents of 1947, but with detail differences. These Daimlers introduced the livery of red with three cream bands and although the chromed radiator shell improved appearance, the absence of black on the beadings separating the main colours, while an economy measure, may have been retrograde aesthetically.
(Copyright C Carter)

1937 Daimler 42 finally lost its special livery complete with gold leaf "Binns" lettering in favour of the post-war "plain" livery during January 1950, a month before the introduction of the revised red and cream layout. This rare picture shows it in the livery it wore only briefly for incredibly, by the end of 1950, it was repainted in the new style of red relieved by three cream bands. *(Copyright R Marshall)*

Replacing the pair of Blagg-rebodied Guy Wolves, 3/4, two Roe-bodied Guy Arab Mark III 6LW models entered service in May 1950. Within three years they were re-engined 5LW and then altered by Roe for driver-only operation. Here the second one, 8, after both alterations and a repaint still in red, loads for Alexandra Road via Hill View at the Town terminus. The diamond-shaped sign reading "PAYE. Fares ready please" can be seen on the nearside bulkhead window. Subsequently the second of two new Binns stores was to be built on the site bordered by the hoardings where the previous one, destroyed by a bomb, had stood. *(Copyright holder not known)*

route through Ford, now used for alternate journeys, comprised a four-sided one-way clockwise circuit as given here with the new route through Ford to Pennywell:

existing: south along General Havelock Rd - west along Fordfield Rd - north along Front Rd - east along Westmoor Rd

new: west along Westmoor Rd - south along Front Rd - west along the westernmost section of Fordfield Rd

The Pennywell route turned right at the end of Fordfield Road and terminated at St Luke's Road/Prestwick Road, 3.75 miles from the town centre (3d fare) and 5.95 miles from Grangetown (5d fare). Although the new service to the first phase of the development at the north-eastern corner of Pennywell had been implemented painlessly, that was not to be the case with the rest of the estate. It was expanding rapidly and eventually would house a population of some 10,000, equivalent to half that of Durham city. NGT, however, would lay claim to Pennywell's south-western side to within about 400 yards of Chester Road at Grindon. This was to be the cause of some wrangling.

Mr Snowball's Annual Report for the year ending 31 March 1950, the undertaking's fiftieth, showed small increases in the total number of bus passengers carried and average revenue per bus mile, with a slight drop in both average number of passengers and average working expenses per bus mile. Bus mileage was now 107 per cent of tram mileage. The accommodation problem was about to be relieved a little by the renting of vacant land belonging to the National Coal Board at Black Road between the Wheat Sheaf and Wearmouth Colliery, to be used for overnight parking with fuelling

facilities. It came into use on 14 August 1950 and would last until 2 December 1954. Outside garaging was detrimental to bus bodywork and the permanent answer lay in new covered accommodation, said Mr Snowball. A further anxiety lay in the shortage of 60 to 70 bus and tram conductors. It was feared that without an improvement in the situation, augmented summer services would be jeopardised.

Two new single deck Guy 6LW Arab III chassis with Roe 35-seat bodies, intended for the Alexandra Road service, were registered on 19 April 1950 and numbered 7/8. Efforts to buy suitable second-hand single deck buses had come to nothing. 6LW engines in buses weighing only $6^{1}/2$ tons seemed extravagant, for most of the utility Guys weighed at least a ton more and had only the 5LW. Nos7/8 had a Guy-built four-speed preselective gearbox with fluid coupling, as Guy preferred to call it. The Guys' gear selection was by means of a lever like a conventional gear stick with a spherical knob instead of a flattened one as used on Guys with layshaft gearboxes. These two Guys were the final new buses to be delivered with the town's coat-of-arms on the traditional cream diamond-shaped background. A revised version of this heraldry was about to be introduced and with just a few early exceptions, the diamond background was discontinued. The arrival of 7/8 paved the way for the withdrawal in December 1950 of the two Blagg-rebodied Guy Wolves, 3/4.

Petrol was de-rationed on 26 May 1950 and within a year, consumption of it nationally was to increase by 11 per cent. This was to make a significant impact on bus travel in due course. The growth in private car ownership and the promotion of the motor car as a desirable and available symbol of affluence and success were about to begin, although SCT was to be behind some other operators in

A palliative to the chronic problem of bus depot accommodation was brought into use on 14 August 1950, lasting for four years, when National Coal Board land at Black Road was rented for parking, usually of buses for peak time and special duties. This view includes the fuelling facility (toward right, beyond buses) and the buses are believed to be (from left of front row): 52/68/53/39/54/67/47/50/45 (all Daimler COG5 except 68/67, which are Guy Arab II); then (rears to camera, right, both Daimler CWA6s): 72 (with altered platform window), 71 or 73; then (extreme right): line of Daimler COG5s headed by 43. Left of the fuel pump and hut is tower wagon GR 5930. The second row includes Leyland 25 (third from left), Guy 63 (front visible right of centre) and Daimler 55 (last on right). Most buses have insulating jackets but the boxes on the lamp standards (example in front of bus 39) house cables which when plugged into a socket in the cab of each bus will power a heating element in the radiator during severely cold weather. *(Copyright D S Burnicle)*

feeling the effects. One factor that did affect the town's bus and tram receipts during 1950 was poor summer weather with rain on each bank holiday from Easter to August! During that same summer, Manchester-style Crossley 13 was off the road for five months, awaiting an engine part. It was decided in August to replace 13's Crossley engine with a Gardner 5LW. Mr Saunders, the Gardner representative in the north-east, acted as consultant. With its replacement engine, 13 sounded very much like the Bristol 5LW-engined buses in some other fleets and vibration was within tolerable limits. While the Transport Department did keep a small stock of spare Gardner engines, it is almost certain that the 5LW put into 13 came from pre-war Daimler 30, withdrawn the previous January. As to Crossleys, subsequently all other post-war examples were to be 5LW-powered.

This period, however, was plainly a vexing one for Sunderland Corporation. New housing developments were either being built or planned generally to the west of existing populated districts and at that time were outside the County Borough boundary. This applied to Pennywell, mentioned previously. The new housing estates were mostly for the benefit of residents from the older areas of the town served from the turn of the century by Corporation trams and later by the buses. Probably with some justification, the Corporation believed that it had a right to continue serving those residents in their new homes. It promoted the Sunderland Extension Bill in Parliament, a section of the Bill being concerned with the Corporation's obtaining monopoly powers to run buses in the added areas just as it did within the existing boundary. Objections were lodged by the British Electric Traction Company on behalf of NGT and SDO, and by the Passenger Transport Association. The Chairman of the Transport Committee, Alderman George Lumsden JP, gave evidence to the Committee on Private Bills in the House of Commons. Although the Bill was then modified to exclude those parts of Sunderland Rural District comprising the villages of Castletown, North Hylton, South Hylton and East Herrington, the monopoly clause was included and the Bill proceeded. Alderman Lumsden also appeared before the House of Lords Select Committee on 5/6 July 1950, and their Lordships recommended that the Bill should proceed subject to the withdrawal of the monopoly clause. This now meant that the Corporation would have to continue to obtain approval under Section 101 of the Road Traffic Act before applying to serve new and planned housing developments in the added areas just as would have been the case if the boundaries of the County Borough had not been extended.

During August 1950, both SCT and NGT applied to operate buses to those parts of Pennywell not served by the Corporation's existing route via Ford. The Licensing Authority accepted that NGT had been operating along Chester Road bordering the south side of Pennywell since 1921 (although prior to 1950 it had comprised only green fields) and concurred that for this reason the Company, as well as the Corporation, was entitled to serve the new development. Mr S W Nelson, the Chairman of the Authority, pointed out that as NGT's proposed fare to the town centre was 4d single and 7d return compared with the Corporation's peak time universal fare of three halfpence, the company would need to reduce its fares. The Authority's final decision was that both parties should arrive at a suitable compromise in order to provide the public with the best service.

Meetings between the two operators then followed. Ultimately it was agreed that NGT would operate into the southern part of Pennywell from Park Lane via Chester Road and Nookside, and the Corporation would alter its existing Docks - Hylton Road - Nookside - Grindon service to continue right along Hylton Road and through the centre of Pennywell to a terminus at Prestbury Road on the western extremity of the estate, 3.2 miles from Town. Nookside would lose its bus connection with Hylton Road, and Hylton Lane Estate would lose its bus service altogether. The Licensing Authority accepted the proposals and the new services were to commence on 8 January 1951. Those people affected adversely by the Hylton Lane and Nookside withdrawal did not find the new proposals acceptable and they expressed their feelings at councillors' ward surgeries and elsewhere. Action would be taken before long.

August 1950 also saw the golden jubilee celebrations of Sunderland's municipal transport undertaking. A commemorative booklet was produced and a jubilee dinner held in the Seaburn Hotel. Alderman Lumsden, still fresh from his Parliamentary encounter, spoke of the need to substitute trams with buses and to build a new, first class bus depot. The first of those aims was to be fulfilled within just over four years, but the second was a different matter. In autumn 1950, the six new buses ordered in February as tram replacements were delivered, comprising Roe-bodied Daimlers again (110-115). Mr Snowball wanted to standardise on Gardner engines and this meant a choice of only two chassis makes, Daimler and Guy. The arrival of the six new Daimlers brought about the closure of the Villette Road via Tatham Street tramway section on 5 November 1950. The replacing bus service was an extension of the Ambleside Terrace - Town route which now carried on via Tatham Street to Villette Road, 3.32 miles from Ambleside Terrace. Trams now ran Southwick - Grangetown (previously Villette Road) and Fulwell -

The beginning of the end for the trams began on 6 November 1950 when buses took over the Town - Villette Road section as an extension of the existing Ambleside Terrace - Town bus service. At the Villette Road terminus on the first day of bus operation Driver George Richmond climbs into the cab of 1948 Massey Daimler 92, fresh from its first repaint, while Conductress Bel Duke looks along from the platform edge. Bus 92 was to be the first of its batch of twelve to be rebuilt in 1956 and in this picture its offside front tyre, although normal for that period, would be well beyond the legal limits of wear in later decades. It is just possible to see the way in which the post-war streamline livery was applied to the nearside lower saloon panelling. *(Copyright Sunderland Echo)*

Fawcett Street (previously Grangetown).

That question of a new bus depot came up again at the beginning of 1951. The Council considered building it on land near St Luke's Road at Pallion where a new trading estate was already taking shape. However, nothing came of the idea. On the positive side, a new bus station was built on the bombed site of the Empress Hotel in Union Street and came into use on 18 December 1951. Only four services were able to use it and in one direction only. They were those to Pennywell, Prestbury Road, Thorney Close and the replacement for Hylton Lane which will be mentioned shortly. For the year ending 31 March 1951, bus passenger and mileage totals were up by nearly ten per cent. Bus figures were now outstripping tram figures due to the beginning of tramway abolition and the gradual shift of population to the new housing areas. There was little change in passenger *volume,* although the buses still lagged behind. As was now the pattern, buses were significantly more economical to operate than trams, despite a 9d tax increase on vehicle fuel.

A single deck-operated all-night service was commenced on 2 April 1951. It was intended primarily for miners at Wearmouth Colliery and its timings were arranged to suit their shifts. The service ran hourly between 11.30pm-5.30am as shown in 'a' below. The service clearly fulfilled a need, although during its first year the receipts per mile were only 12.36d which was some 10d below overall average. Nevertheless was to be extended on 12 May 1952 as shown in 'b' and subsequently a considerable working economy was to be effected, as will be described later.

a Southwick Rd/Wayman St - Wearmouth Bridge - High St W - Hylton Rd - Holborn Rd - Springwell Rd/Durham Rd, returning direct - Durham Rd - Town - Southwick Rd/Wayman St

b Southwick Rd/Wayman St - Wearmouth Bridge - High St W - Hylton Rd (westerly) - Prestbury Rd terminus (turn around) - Hylton Rd (easterly) - Portsmouth Rd - Grindon La - Telford Rd - Thorney Close Rd - Durham Rd/Springwell Rd, returning as previously.

In the meantime there were calls from residents of Nookside and Hylton Lane for their lost bus service to be restored and on 9 April 1951, the situation was eased by a revival of the Town (Union Street) - Hylton Lane link. Buses showed the destination "Helmsdale Road" because, as if to confuse matters, "Hylton Lane" was now being displayed by buses running on a short working of the Prestbury Road service terminating in central Pennywell (Hylton Road/St Luke's Road)! Reference to *Hylton Lane* in subsequent pages here may now be taken to mean *central Pennywell,* unless qualified by the word "Estate". The Helmsdale Road service ran around this clockwise circuit through the estate:

Hadleigh Road - Helmsdale Road (terminus) - Holborn Road - Hylton Road

The summer of 1951 was another one of inclement weather, especially over the bank holiday periods, with the usual adverse effects on bus and tram services to Roker and Seaburn. The Springwell - Seaburn Camp bus service was to show increases for the financial year although this was clearly due to other, non-leisure traffic. A sea front bus tour from Seaburn Camp to Harbour View was operated when the illuminations were on between 8 September and 20 October. Working expenses were covered but passenger traffic was disappointing and the service was not repeated.

Twelve new Roe-bodied Daimlers began to arrive in September 1951, numbered 116-127. They were the first buses in the fleet to be 8ft rather than 7ft 6in wide and 27ft rather than 26ft long. The greater width had been legalised in 1946 for approved routes only, a restriction that was lifted on 1 June 1950 when the 27ft length for new double deckers was made legal also. Single deckers were allowed to be 30ft long under these changes and some operators

Partly for tram replacement on the Villette Road section, a further six Roe-bodied Daimler CVG6s were obtained in November 1950 and numbered 110-115, represented here by 113 in John Street on 16 April 1952. The first new buses to appear with the new coat-of-arms minus cream diamond, they differed in some details from the previous four. Note, for example, upper window corners, headlamps, type of sliding window vent, painted radiator shell and the transposition of destination and name glass apertures. *(Copyright R Marshall)*

had hoped that this would apply to double deck buses too. The Government adopted a more cautious approach, however, and those bus-owners had to wait another six years. On Roe double deck bodies the lower saloon windows were now slightly deeper and the upper saloon ones were enlarged to be of the same depth which improved an already attractive appearance. The revised body style, which had been optional for three years, was known as Roe's "Pullman" design and many commentators have regarded it as a classic of its kind. 116-127 had a single, larger destination aperture at front and rear without any fleet name glass and were SCT's first new buses to be fitted with the then newly-introduced 'K'-type modification to the Gardner LW range, giving increased power. Subsequent new Gardners in the fleet had this modification and most existing engines were altered to include it when overhauled.

The advent of the new Daimlers made it possible the Wheat Sheaf - Southwick tramway section to be converted to bus operation. Owing to the poor condition of the bridge over the railway near the foot of Southwick Road, from 19 March 1951 it had been closed for widening and rebuilding, making it necessary for the Town - Marley Pots bus service to be diverted temporarily. The shortage of buses had ruled out the replacement of trams immediately and so matters were arranged to allow for three trams to cross the bridge each morning to operate a shuttle service up to Southwick, returning over the bridge at night. Passengers had to walk through the bridge works in order to change between the trams. With four Daimlers already delivered (116-119), on 3 September the shuttle service became bus-operated. When the road was re-opened six months later a completely new bus service was introduced, of which more shortly.

Fares were increased on 3 December 1951. The new structure was based on 1d per mile with a minimum of $1^1/2$d for any journey up to a distance of $1^1/2$ miles. Graduations were then in halfpence. Several new short stages were introduced in an attempt to avoid deterring short-distance passengers. The average fare charged per mile now worked out at 1.01d on the trams and 1.07d on the buses. These figures compared with 0.65d and 0.82d respectively in 1946. At this 1951 fares increase, too, the shilling all-day ticket was abolished. The last day of 1951 saw the withdrawal of pre-war Crossley 24. There were still ten older Daimlers in service, their Roe bodies being in somewhat sounder condition than 24's English Electric one. Old 24 had an interesting after-life until 1959 as a showman's van with cut-down upper saloon.

Mr H W Snowball, who had been ill for more than a year, died on New Year's Day 1952 at the age of 63. He had served the undertaking for 25 years, although his spell of chief officership was relatively brief. Latterly he had represented Sunderland on the Northern Area PSV and Trolleybus Maintenance Committee and the Joint Electricity Distribution and Collection Committee of the Municipal Passenger Transport Association, and had sat on the Ministry of Transport PSV Area Maintenance and Repair Committee. His funeral on Friday 4 January was attended by 600

The stallholders have gone elsewhere and the bus station on the Empress Hotel site in Union Street, leased to the Corporation, has been open since 18 December 1951. This picture of it, taken soon afterwards, shows Cravens-bodied Crossley 20 in its revised red livery as worn also by fairly-new 8ft-wide, 27ft-long Roe-bodied Daimler 122, behind, that was used for centrifugal clutch experiments. Daimlers of this width used the standard 7ft 6in front axle which gave the wings their characteristic "overhanging" look as illustrated here, and the wheelbase was unchanged. The Daimler batch was numbered 116-127 and their bodies featured deeper windows. Two years were to elapse before passengers enjoyed the benefit of shelters and improved lighting at this location. (Copyright Sunderland Echo)

mourners and at the time of the service, all Corporation buses and trams were halted briefly as a mark of respect. Mr S Finkle, Deputy General Manager, took charge temporarily.

The regrettable discord between the SCT and NGT continued into 1952 and was by no means over. A further new council housing scheme was taking shape at Hylton Red House on the north side of the river. The Corporation applied for its Town - Marley Pots service to be extended into the new estate. NGT applied at the same time to operate an additional service. Each party opposed the other's application. Further wrangling followed and ultimately the Licensing Authority decided that SCT's application should stand and that NGT should operate to Red House from Park Lane via Alexandra Bridge, paralleling the North Hylton route as far as Washington Road/Castletown Road. NGT would enter Red House from the south, SCT from the east. Both services commenced on 21 January 1952 but neither operator was satisfied with this outcome. Each appealed to the Ministry of Transport and its findings were to uphold to Licensing Authority's decision. SCT's service was two-pronged, splitting as it entered the estate and terminating initially at Redcar Road (buses displaying "Red House South") or Ramsgate Road ("Red House North"). On 25 August 1952, both branches were extended so as to form a loop meeting at Redhill/Rhodesia Roads. NGT ran through the middle of the estate.

Returning to the disruption caused by the rebuilding of the Southwick Road railway bridge near the Wheat Sheaf, the tramway service could not have been restored in any event as the plans for the work on the bridge had not included the laying of the tram track. This meant it was virtually a case of tramway abandonment by default! Following six months of a two-mode service (Grangetown - Wheat Sheaf trams then Wheat Sheaf - Southwick shuttle buses), when the bridge works were finished the road was re-opened on 3 March 1952. A reorganisation of some bus services then took place as an interim measure pending rationalisation which brought about more economic working. The arrangements were these:

Old

bus	Villette Road - Ambleside Terrace
bus	Southwick shuttle service
tram	Grangetown - Wheat Sheaf

New

bus	Town - Ambleside Terrace
bus	Villette Road - Southwick
tram	Grangetown - Wheat Sheaf

The statistics for the year ending 31 March 1952 revealed an increase of more than ten per cent in operated bus mileage and passenger journeys. Both figures were now leaping ahead of those for the trams and this was to continue. The average number of bus passengers *per mile* was down by nearly two per cent. While traffic revenue per mile on the buses was up somewhat, working expenses per mile showed an even greater rise.

That recurring matter of bus garage accommodation came up again during the spring of 1952. The Transport Committee considered acquiring land adjoining the Wheat Sheaf tram depot, suitable for housing sixty buses. It was to be two years before anything further happened. One development that did take place during Mr Finkle's time in charge was the adoption of the Setright ticket machine. Originally forty examples were bought, the intention being to phase them in over a period of five years. They were so successful that this period was subsequently reduced to two years, 201 Setrights being employed on buses and trams by April 1954. The small number of machines needed for the jointly-operated North Hylton service differed from the others and had special green markings for identification.

The last day of April 1952 saw the withdrawal of the fleet's oldest two Daimlers, 26/27, after a commendable $17^{1}/_2$ years' service. Their fuel economy, mechanical reliability and the robust nature of their Roe centre-entrance bodywork added up to a good return on investment. As with all pre-war Roe double deck bodies in the fleet they had required virtually no major remedial work. Many operators large and small had to rebuild pre-war bodies drastically or replace them, particularly timber-framed ones, during the early post-war era. The only obvious modification carried out to SCT's pre-war Roe bodies on Daimler chassis was the replacement during early post-war years of the winding half-drop windows with top-sliding vents in order to reduce maintenance. Less obviously, some panels were replaced also. The teak framing was in sound condition other than for some localised deterioration of the pillars around where they were jointed to the lower saloon waistrail. New pillar sections replaced those areas affected by the decay. Between the levels of the seat rail and the cantrail, the lower saloon pillars were also braced with steel strapping 1in wide and $^{1}/_4$in thick, fixed to the inside. As was usually necessary the skirt rails were replaced, spray from the road wheels giving them frequent soakings in dirty water and clinging mud. The repair work ensured that those Roe bodies gave further service trouble-free.

1 July 1952 was a momentous day in the history of the Transport Department: Mr Norman Morton, B Com, M Inst T, MIRTE, took up his appointment as General Manager. During the Charles Hopkins era, the tramway system had been modernised,

The service to Prestbury Road at the western extremity of the large Pennywell estate commenced on 20 January 1951 and after the withdrawal of trams between Town and Grangetown on 30 November 1952 the two sections were linked by bus, although many journeys did not operate the full length of the route. Seen here soon after the revision and bearing evidence of mud and grit on the roads, Daimlers 107 and 122 (again), run eastbound and westbound respectively along Hylton Road near the Ford Hotel.

(Copyright Sunderland Echo)

renewed and extended, the buses playing a subservient role almost until his death. Then Harry Snowball had taken over the reins, working hard while fighting his own deteriorating health to see the Department though a difficult time of rapid expansion of bus services with scarce resources. Now the whole image, the appearance, the operations and many working practices were to be transformed within little more than two years. Norman Morton was firmly committed to municipal transport. He had clear, forthright ideas on efficiency and economy, anticipating and possibly setting trends. And as one employee put it many years later, "When he said jump, you jumped!"

Slightly younger than Mr Hopkins at the time of his appointment in 1929, Mr Morton was aged 42. He had begun his transport career in 1930 as a technical assistant with the Transport Department in his native Manchester, attaining the rank of major during his wartime service with the Royal Mechanical and Electrical Engineers. In 1941 and again in 1942 he won the silver medal of the Municipal Passenger Transport Association essay competition for technical and administrative staffs. Mr Morton was appointed Engineer and Deputy Manager of Southport Corporation Transport in 1943 and six years later was engaged by the Road Haulage Executive as District Engineer and Deputy District Manager of the Leicester/Northants District of British Road Services. Other interviewees for the Sunderland post were:

Municipal General Managers: Mr J Crawford (South Shields), Mr H Jones (Leigh, Lancs), Mr J C Wake (Burton- on-Trent) Deputy General Managers: Mr S Finkle (Sunderland) and Mr G A Singleton (Wolverhampton).

On 28 August 1952, the Transport Committee heard from Mr Morton that the tram track on the Grangetown section needed some £17,000 spending on it. He recommended that buses should replace the Grangetown trams, suggested some other simultaneous adjustments to bus services for greater efficiency, and requested permission to report on the future policy of the undertaking. The Committee agreed to all.

From 20 September 1952, trams were replaced by buses on football specials from Town. Buses were not so liable to be delayed by football traffic congestion and could complete the return journey in less time than the trams so that fewer, indeed often only half as many, were needed. With buses, the Department would estimate the attendance before each home match of the Sunderland first team and put on one vehicle from Town per 10,000 of the crowd (50,000 not being exceptional). Buses would do as many journeys as necessary or practicable. Five days after this change Mr Morton told the Committee that there were now about twenty bus services and it would assist identification if they were numbered. A numbering scheme was therefore to be devised and introduced. When the Committee met again five weeks later Mr Morton spoke about fleet livery. The Corporation's red and cream, he submitted, were similar to those of NGT buses and caused confusion among passengers. Members examined a specimen panel in the proposed new colours of mid-green and cream (Mr Morton clearly being aware of the power of visual aids!) and the Committee resolved to change the livery colours. The new shade, incidentally, was not unlike the Tilling green of Durham District Services which also operated into Sunderland!

The final bus to be repainted red and cream was the ex-Stockton unfrozen Leyland 25. Delicensed during July - October 1952 for overhaul, it emerged in a new format which had been devised as a prototype for the layout of the green and cream. There had been some experimenting in the paint shop, local parts of 25's Roe body being repainted with differing proportions of red

Delivered during Autumn 1952, soon after the arrival of Mr Norman Morton as General Manager, were twelve fine eight feet wide, four-bay Roe-bodied Guy 6LW Arabs of Mark III with a smart performance and distinctive crisp exhaust note, all but the final one having preselective gearboxes. The low bonnet and radiator permitted the fitting of a deeper windscreen and slightly lower bulkhead waistrail. Here the first of them, 128, enhanced by the polished front wheel nut guard ring, stands in Park Lane accompanied by a Northern Guy Arab III and a Sunderland District pre-war Leyland Tiger TS8. Note the difference in the "Shop at Binns" format compared with the twelve 1951 Daimlers. *(Copyright R Marshall)*

and cream until Mr Morton was satisfied. At that time 1947 AEC Regents 82-87 were due for repainting and on 1 December 1952 it was 86 that took a bow in a format broadly similar to that of Leyland 25, but with green in place of red. The characteristic front and rear advertisement was now to be standardised in one line as **"SHOP AT BINNS"** in an unserifed bold style in green on a cream background. Other than for a slight change to the style of lettering in 1953, this remained the standard until the mid-1960s. Illustrations will best clarify detail differences. However, at the rear only of 86 it was initially an experimental *gold leaf* on a green background and at the rear of second green bus 82 it was *red* on a cream background.

During October-November 1952 while the new livery was gestating, the twelve new and impressive Roe-bodied Guy 6LW Arab IIIs were delivered in red as 128-139, possibly SCT's finest post-war buses and the first in the fleet to break the £4,000 barrier. Their bodies, again of Roe's "Pullman" design, were four-bay and the stanchions were clad with distinctive cream-coloured Doverite "hygienic plastic covering". The original specification had been for 56 seats but Mr Morton had secured Committee agreement to increase it to 58. This was to be standard on new buses for two years and achieved by re-spacing the offside seats upstairs in order to fit an extra double one. Many existing buses were to be converted from 56-seaters to 58 by this means. Likewise, sanction had also been obtained for one bus to have a constant-mesh rather than preselective gearbox "for test purposes", 139 being the one concerned. With the standard Guy rear axle ratio of 5.6 to 1 and forward gear ratios just a little lower than the corresponding Daimler ones, in service these Guys generally had a slight edge on performance.

Another Guy event took place in 1952. Saloons 7/8 had their 6W engines replaced by 5LW units which were more appropriate to their weight. The 5LWs were not new ones and as they are not recorded as having the 'K' power setting it may be inferred that they were taken from the stock of spare Gardners, no engines from pre-war Daimlers being on hand. There is just a chance that they may have originated with two of the utility Guys, Massey 66 and Pickering 68, which some time previously had been converted from 5LW to 6LW, but it has not been possible to confirm this.

During October 1952 Mr Morton's report on the future of the undertaking was approved by the Transport Committee and then the full Council, the chief points being noted below. The target was to be achieved with a few days to spare.

1. During the previous five years an average of £37,000 had been spent annually on tram track maintenance.

2. With trams, the Department was prevented from making the best use of its buildings and as the number of trams required after the impending conversion of the Grangetown service would be only 39 it was plainly uneconomic to retain the separate organisation for operating them.

3. Running trams and buses along the same roads meant costly and unnecessary duplication.

4. Apart from platform staff, it required an average of 1.9 employees to operate each tram compared with 0.92 for each bus. Wages represented 65.5 per cent of operating costs for 1951/52, highlighting the the significance of this.

5. Buses should replace trams completely within two years.

One minor change that took place during the eventful autumn of 1952 was that the part-day operation of some journeys on the Seaburn Camp - Springwell service via Mount Road and Ettrick Grove was discontinued as from 22 October. Special school journeys now made it unnecessary. All journeys now ran via Barnes Park Road and Durham Road. Other service changes took effect on 1 December 1952. The last tram had run to Grangetown the previous night but the substitution of buses was not a straightforward one. Service reorganisation was as follows:

Old

Prestbury Rd - Town - Docks **a**
Seaburn - Park Ave - Town **c**
Helmsdale Rd - Town

New

Prestbury Rd **b** - Town - Ryhope Rd - Grangetown
Seaburn - Park Ave - Town - Ryhope Rd - Grangetown **c**
Helmsdale Rd - Town - Docks **a**
Town* - Durham Rd - North Moor Lane - Farringdon (Allendale Rd) **d**
Town* - Thornholme Rd - Durham Rd - Sacriston Av - Plains Fm (Pearl Rd) **d**

a to Docks via Boro' Rd, returning via High St
b some journeys from Hylton Lane
c peak periods only
d joint with NGT.

*Route through Town from west: Vine Pl - Crowtree Rd - Brougham St (terminus) - Waterloo Pl - Holmeside - Derwent St - Mary St

The joint services to Farringdon and Plains Farm were entirely new and the outer termini were 3.3 and 2.5 miles from Town respectively. Farringdon was yet another fledgling council housing estate, situated on the south side of Durham Road facing Thorney Close. As with Pennywell and Red House, the location of Farringdon and Plains Farm gave NGT a stake in the services. Following a census to ascertain the numbers of passengers using the trams and company buses respectively, both parties accepted a joint working ratio of 4:1 in favour of the Corporation. Plains Farm was a pre-war estate a little lower down Durham Road on the south side also, adjoining Humbledon and Springwell. The two new bus services were linked operationally so that each bus ran in this sequence: Town - Plains Farm - Town - Farringdon - Town. Sunderland District buses took over from NGT a few years later, the licence always having been a joint SCT-NGT-SDO one.

That period comprising the early to mid-1950s was an exciting one for observers of the local transport scene in Sunderland, with new and imaginative developments seeming to be take place regularly. 1953/54 were probably among the most significant years in the history of municipal bus operations in the town.

One alteration that could hardly be missed following Mr Morton's arrival was a change of livery from red and cream to green and cream, introduced in December 1952. First bus treated was AEC Regent 86, followed by others of its batch as depicted here in John Street by 84, with hand-painted "Binns" lettering and fleet numerals of the existing style. In April 1953 the new unserified fleet number font was introduced, followed by the neater style of transferred "Binns" lettering in July. The AECs kept their original destination apertures for another three years and then were altered to have the type fitted to rebuilt utility Guy 69, behind, which also carries the new "Binns" transfers. *(Copyright R Marshall)*

42

6 - Look, No Trams

Further work on the wartime utility bodies was now becoming necessary, Mr Morton describing the condition of some as "critical". Complete rebuilding of the utility bodies as well as mechanical overhaul was undertaken by the Department. The first one to emerge from the workshops, in February 1953, was Massey Daimler 61. This bus and its twin, 60, kept their original 56 leathercloth-covered seats but subsequent utility rebuilds had their 56 wooden-slatted seats replaced with 58 leathercloth-upholstered ones. Some of the replacement seats may have been taken from pre-war Daimlers numbered between 28 and 41 while others were undoubtedly acquired second-hand. Full details with dates are given in Appendix 1.

The method of rebuilding was to strip down the bodies completely, removing all panelling except for the dash and in the case of 60/61, the cab side panels. Re-panelling was done in aluminium alloy. It included the roof other than for the front and rear domes which were removed and sent out to be repaired locally. All rebuilds were given new, larger destination apertures at front and rear, the front also having a service number aperture. New steel staircases were put in and lower saloon flooring was replaced with new softwood. Most pillars and waistrails, of poorly-seasoned ash and beech, were replaced also. Initially beech or any other suitable hardwood was used but with the final few utilities and subsequent bodies to be rebuilt it was the versatile and robust keruing. Where not already done, original half-drop windows were replaced with top sliding vents, two per side upstairs and one per side downstairs. Rubber-mounted glazing was not used other than on three Guys: Masseys 62/65 and Pickering 68, where it was limited to the upper saloon front windows. Rebuilding was carried out to a very high standard and the completed vehicles looked smart and well-finished in the new green livery. New and neater styles of character for the fleet name, number and "Binns" advertisement appeared in turn on repainted or new green buses by June 1953.

Some of the utilities were delicensed for several months awaiting rebuilding. The work was carried out over a three-year period to March 1956, buses re-entering service at average intervals of about ten weeks. Six wartime buses were not rebuilt but rebodied, of which details later. Ex-Blackburn Guys 5/6 kept their original Pickering bodies which were neither rebuilt nor repainted green before they became driver trainers in 1955 and were withdrawn in 1957. Daimler 71 was fitted with a Gardner 5LW engine in place of its original AEC 7.7-litre unit in April 1954, eighteen months ahead of its body rebuild, and similar bus 72 received a 5LW when it underwent body rebuilding early in 1956. In January 1955, the third Daimler CWA6, 73, still with AEC engine and neither rebuilt nor repainted green, sustained serious collision damage and was delicensed immediately pending subsequent disposal.

The previously-mentioned economy measure that was to be applied to the running of the night service was its conversion to driver-only operation. 1939 Blagg-bodied Crossley saloon 22 was adapted for the purpose by the Department. The bulkhead was altered in such a way as to create a gap in the centre through which fare transactions could be conducted. A diagonally-positioned window was inserted between the cab nearside and the left side of the bulkhead. Mr William Watson, the inventive bus bodybuilding foreman, designed the door control which was situated above the cab nearside window. So well-balanced was the mechanism that only the slightest effort was needed to operate it. Some years previously he had made an excellent 1:16 scale model of Corporation "Ghost Tram" 86, now displayed at Monkwearmouth Station Museum. Re-seated from 32 to 34, Crossley 22 entered service in its new guise but still in red livery on 25 March 1953. Twin bus 23 was never altered. The Transport Department had obtained special permission from the licensing authority to use driver-only operation because, until the legislation was amended soon afterward, it was normally confined to single deckers with no more than 26 seats. A similar project had been commenced at the beginning of 1953 by the Huddersfield Joint Omnibus Committee using 43-seaters by special permission on a rural route and Mr Morton went to observe it. Clearly he formed some ideas that were to be seen later in Sunderland. Driver-only operation had been tried on Wearside more than once previously but now it had come to stay.

The Annual Report for the year ending 31 March 1953 was Mr Morton's first and showed that bus mileage operated was now more than double the tram figure. Bus passengers carried were nearly 54 million, 9 per cent above the 1952 total. Mr Morton paid tribute to all employees for their loyalty and support. "No manager could ask for a better staff," he remarked. A cause for concern again, though, was abuse of the 2d universal transfer facility. On 7 April 1953 it was abolished and replaced by a 5d universal return ticket. This was available up to 9am Monday to Saturday except bank and other public holidays, allowing one transfer of vehicle if required for immediate continuation of journey with bus and tram

National highlight of 1953 was the Coronation of Queen Elizabeth II on 2 June. Daimler 36, withdrawn some three months previously, was specially repainted and decorated for the event, touring the town. For the next six years it served as the depot snow plough at Fulwell and in 1960 was the final centre-entrance bus to be disposed of.

(Copyright Sunderland Echo)

43

Daimlers CVG5s 140-147, delivered during the summer of 1953, were the first new buses in green and introduced the new standard "Binns" style of lettering. They were 5LW-powered and reverted to the 7ft 6in width and 26ft length. Their Roe bodies, although teak-framed, incorporated some lightweight materials and with the help of such other weight-reducing measures as smaller tyres and a 12- rather than 24-volt electrical system, the result was an unladen weight of just under seven tons. This was a ton less than the eight feet wide Daimlers and Guys of the previous two years with consequent greater operating economy at a time when cost-consciousness was increasing markedly. 142 here loads in Union Street after the closure of the bus station. The fitting of chromed radiator shells to this batch improved appearance. All future forward-engined double deckers were to be 7ft 6in wide, 27ft long and 5LW-powered.

(Copyright holder not known)

interchangeability excepting buses on the North Hylton service. The return journey could be made at any time after 9am the same day under the same conditions. This facility still represented enormous value with up to 16 miles of travel for 5d and yet abuse still continued. Only four out of 94 municipalities still offered a transfer ticket. Some service revisions were carried out on 18 May 1953, including an extension of 0.8mile from Grangetown (via Ryhope Road) to Leechmere Road/Helvellyn Road. The Prestbury Road service was now virtually split into two overlapping sections at most times. Here is a summary of the changes:

Old

Seaburn - Park Ave - Town - Ryhope Rd - Grangetown **a**
Prestbury Rd **d** - Town - Ryhope Rd - Grangetown

New

b Seaburn - Park Ave - Town - Ryhope Rd - Grangetown- **c** Leechmere Rd
be Hylton La - Town - Ryhope Rd - Grangetown - **f** Leechmere Rd
e Prestbury Rd - Town

a peak periods only
b co-ordinated 5-min frequency Town - Grangetown
c alternate journeys only
d some journeys from Hylton La
e co-ordinated 5-min frequency Town - Hylton La
f some journeys

Only eight weeks later, on 13 July, alternate journeys to Seaburn via Park Avenue were extended to Seaburn Camp, summer only. Before then, however, Whit Monday 25 May saw the recommencement of tours of Whitburn and Sunderland, the first since before the war. Double deckers were used and the tours were operated over the Coronation period, 30 May - 7 June, then on Sundays 12/19 July and during the local shipyard holiday period of 26 July - 9 August inclusive. The route from Seaburn was:

Whitburn - Moor La - Shields Rd - Fulwell Mill - Marley Pots - Southwick - Alexandra Br - Pallion - Ford - Springwell - Humbledon - Alexandra Rd - Grangetown - Hendon - Docks - Wearmouth Br - Wheat Sheaf - Roker

The tours were considered successful, yielding some 27d per mile which was a little above the overall average. They were to continue as a seasonal feature. A further development involved pre-war Daimler 36, withdrawn from service in February 1953, which was given illuminated decorations as a Coronation feature and toured the town. After the limelight and glory came six years of mundaneness as a snowplough.

Roe Daimler 112 of 1950 had its picture in the *Sunderland Echo* one evening after overturning on an unsurfaced track at Durham while returning the Transport Department cricket team from a summer 1953 match. The edge of the track had crumbled under the nearside wheels. There were no serious injuries to Driver Tommy Stafford or any of the passengers, and as the bus had made a soft landing it was only slightly damaged. Drivers were then instructed not to take vehicles away from metalled roads. Mr Morton reported the matter to the Committee on 26 June 1953 but at the same meeting he also mentioned that three months previously, Manchester-style Crossley 11 had been fitted with a Gardner 5LW engine, as had Crossley 13 in 1950. He said that the two Gardner-powered Crossleys were giving $1^{1}/_{2}$mpg better fuel consumption, that the maintenance of a 5LW cost only half that of a Crossley engine and that if the other Crossley 'deckers were treated similarly the nett saving over the anticipated life of the vehicles would be £13,000. Committee approval was given and the conversions were to take place as detailed in Appendix 1. The Gardner fitted to No11 was probably a spare although the remainder were from pre-war Daimlers. Some other operators also replaced Crossley engines with units of other makes.

The bus-operating industry was becoming increasingly cost-conscious. Wages and salaries, over which there was virtually little control, formed the largest single item of revenue spending and in 1953 represented 52.5 per cent of SCT's bus operating costs. Second came vehicle fuel, representing 18.3 per cent, a rise from 8.9 per cent since 1946. The high level of tax on vehicle fuel was particularly resented. In 1950 it had been 9d per gallon, rising to 2s 6d by 1952. As the nett price was 1s 2d this meant that taxation amounted to 214 per cent! Operators realised that fuel could be saved if vehicle unladen weights were to be reduced to something nearer their pre-war levels. A typical late pre-war double decker weighed up to about seven tons but the 1952 Roe-bodied Guys weighed 8.0.0. Manufacturers responded with lightened versions of both chassis and bodywork and some examples had been on display at the 1952 Commercial Motor Show.

Eight Roe-bodied Daimlers ordered in autumn 1952 arrived in June/July 1953 as 140-147. They were CVG5 chassis although the original specification had called for *six*-cylinder engines, later amended. This was in keeping with the swing toward economy and they were much lighter than anything for eleven years, virtually a ton less than the 1951/52 buses. The driver had a view of the lower saloon and platform through a ceiling-mounted mirror in the cab positioned suitably in relation to a small window in the front bulkhead and there was a service number indicator at the rear as well as at the front, both generally to be standard on new and rebuilt non-utility double deckers. Although the Roe bodywork was teak-framed, weight-reducing measures included the following (1951/52 features in brackets; * denotes future double deck standard to 1958):

- 5LW engine* (6LW);
- 26ft length (27ft*), 7ft 6in width* (8ft);
- 30-gall fuel tank (35-gall);
- tyres - front 10.00 (11.00) x 20, rear 9.00 (10.00) x 20;
- 12-volt electrical system (24-volt).

Other features:

- seats with slimmer (and less comfortable) cushions and back squabs*
  (upholstered in light green leathercloth);
- pressed aluminium interior window finishers* (painted chromatic grey);
- smaller windows (glass being heavier than metal panelling of similar area).

Service numbers were introduced on 3 July 1953. There was no discernible sequence either historical or geographical in the scheme. The numbers were:

1	Town - Alexandra Rd	9	Helmsdale Rd - Docks
2/3	Town - Farringdon/Plains Farm	10/11	Grangetown - Pennywell/Ford
4/5	Town - Red House South/North	13	Villette Rd - Southwick
6	Town - Ambleside Terr	15	Thorney Close - Docks
7	Prestbury Rd - Leechmere Rd	18	Seaburn Camp - Springwell
8	Seaburn Camp - Leechmere Rd	48	S'land - N Hylton (NGT number)

Except in the case of service 48, journeys stopping short of the ultimate terminus on any route were denoted by the letter 'x' after the service number. The use of 'x' in this way was the practice in Manchester where Mr Morton had begun his career. Short workings to Fordham Road were 10x, although they were in fact more of a deviation from the Ford route which was 11. NGT and subsequently

SDO buses on joint services were meant to show the SCT service number preceded by the letter "S", although again it was not always done. They were unable to display the "x" suffix if it had been appropriate to any of their workings. Service number boxes were fitted under the nearside front canopy of other unrebuilt SCT buses, not including pre-1943 vehicles except Crossley 23 and Leyland 56.

Saturday 6 September 1953 was another record day. Arsenal were the Roker Park visitors in the afternoon, watched by a crowd of 60,000. A military tattoo was held at Seaburn during the evening, attracting 12,000. Then a further 10,000 were estimated to have seen the illuminations at Roker and Seaburn. The day's peak was not at the end of the football match but on the sea front at 10.30 - 11pm. Receipts on the buses and trams amounted to £2,744. There was still more demand for the night service and on 5 October 1953 it was extended westward from its Southwick Road terminus to Castletown Road Ends. Extra journeys were run at midnight and 4am from 14 December.

In 1953, to the west of the ruined Hylton Castle and north of Castletown, yet another new housing development was commenced, appropriately named Hylton Castle Estate. On 2 November a bus service from Town numbered 17 was started, the Licensing Authority ruling that it was to be operated equally between SCT and NGT. Originally the off-peak frequency was a 30-minute one but at peak periods it was *16* minutes. The frequencies became 20 and 12 minutes respectively on 15 February 1954. The route from Fawcett Street was as shown below, later amended. Then from 31 May buses on service 17, Town - Hylton Castle, took the route mentioned below

Twenty-five further Daimler CVG5s were delivered in winter 1953/54, differing from the previous eight in several ways. Twenty bodies, those of 148-167, were Roe-built as illustrated by 162 (right), rounding Ivanhoe Crescent soon after the abandonment of the Durham Road tramway section, the overhead wires already having been removed. 173-184 were Guy Arab 5LW Mark IV "new look" chassis with Crossley metal-framed bodies, arriving before most of the Daimlers and while they too contained some Park Royal-like features, notably the upper saloon emergency window as on 174 (left), they were easily distinguishable from the Roe Daimlers. The Roe side windows were slightly shallower than those of the Crossley bodies.
(Copyright Sunderland Echo)

within the estate. Frequencies were gradually increased to five minutes at weekday peaks on 21 March 1955.

From 2 Nov 53: Town - W Sheaf - Southwick Rd - N Hylton Rd - Washington Rd - Hylton Castle (Canterbury Rd/Cheadle Rd)
From 1 May 54, within the estate: Craigavon Rd - Cranleigh Rd - Cheadle Rd - Cardigan Rd (terminus)

Mention was made earlier of the fact that driver-only operation was to spread. During the autumn of 1953 preparations were made to reintroduce it on the Alexandra Road service. September/October respectively saw the two Guy Arab saloons of 1950, 7/8, altered by Roe to be like Crossley 22, but with electrically-operated door. Driver-only operation began on 16 November 1953 and of course regular passengers had seen it all before on the Guy Wolves. In order to speed up ticket transactions a flat fare of 2d for adults and 1d for children was introduced, the previous adult fares having been 1^1/2d-3d. Drivers also sold books of twelve 2d vouchers for 1s 9d which further reduced the overall time spent handling cash at stops. Universal fares were not available at first but were brought in by the end of year. The new form of operation saved more than 3d per mile. Early pioneers of driver-only operation had included Alf Bradwell, later an inspector, and Roland Wilson. On the driver-only night service there had been one regular man, Ralph Parnaby, from its inception but a small team of drivers who had volunteered now ran the Alexandra Road service, receiving enhanced pay as laid down in the Transport Agreement. They included Spencer Bradwell (brother of Alf and later to become an inspector also), Harry Hickman, John Precht, 'Spike' Hughes and Fred Taylor. Regrettably there was a degree ill-feeling on the part of some other platform staff toward the solo drivers. It was argued that they were helping to destroy employment. In the light of the severe staffing difficulties and economic considerations, it was inevitable that there should be a move to a more efficient working practice which in fact was not carried out at the expense of jobs. Staff shortages would continue to be a problem for the Department.

Over the years, Mr Morton experimented with various demonstration buses and two were operated during December 1953. Details of demonstrators are shown in Appendix 1. The Department was now eager to convert the Circle - Roker - Seaburn tram service to buses but this was dependent on the delivery of some of the 37 vehicles ordered during spring 1953, SCT's largest-ever requirement. They were specified to have Gardner 5LW engine and preselective gearbox. Their bodywork, to weigh not more than 55cwt, was to be metal-framed "for longer life" on Mr Morton's recommendation as was to become policy, with some exceptions. He had also advised that one tender for aluminium alloy-framed bodywork, probably from Saro of Anglesey, should not be accepted as this was a little-known form of construction, and that another concern should not be considered due to "unsatisfactory experience" of its products. Clearly this was Massey Bros although their existing bodies in the fleet were timber-framed and at that time they were about to concentrate on metal framing which previously had been optional. (When several decades later the writer asked a retired municipal transport manager what in his opinion was the most durable make of metal-framed bus body of the 1950s/60s, he replied without hesitation, *"Massey Brothers"!*). Mr Morton had also recommended the rejection of "a new type of lightweight construction" which had "not been proved", undoubtedly referring to the Metropolitan-Cammell-Weymann organisation's Orion body. The final decision had been to split the chassis and body orders as follows: 12 Guy chassis, Crossley-bodied; 25 Daimler chassis, 20 Roe-bodied and five with locally-built Associated Coachbuilders bodies. There had been pressure on the Council from the National Association of Vehicle Builders to support local industry but ACB, inexperienced in building double deckers, was given the business only because it would use framing provided by Metal Sections Ltd of Oldbury, Birmingham, the highly-regarded suppliers to both home and export markets of completely knocked down, fully fabricated, jig-built metal framework. Then at a very late stage it had come to

light that contrary to standing orders, the Transport Committee had not given its authority for Roe to sub-contract for the supply of metal framing from Park Royal! This was done in a seeming hurry only five weeks before the first delivery. Here is a summary of the whole batch:

148-167	Daimler CVG5	Roe H33/25R
168-172	Daimler CVG5	ACB H33/25R
173-184	Guy Arab IV 5LW	Crossley H32/25R*

See footnote 3 in Appendix 1, Table 1

During 23 December 1953 - 1 January 1954, the dozen Guys and three of the Roe Daimlers were delivered, the others arriving gradually until April. Enough were available for bus service 20 to take over the Circle - Roker -Seaburn tram service, comprising 5.62 route miles, on 4 January 1954. The buses ran as follows:

Seaburn - Roker - Wheat Sheaf - Town - Holmeside - Derwent St (westbound) or Vine Place (eastbound) - New Durham Rd - Western Hill - Chester Rd - Kayll Rd - Hylton Rd, then through Town via High St W - Crowtree Rd - Northumberland St - Union St (bus station) - return via High St W

The first of the ACB-bodied Daimlers, 168, was delivered on 20 January 1954 and ceremonially handed over by Mr L C Kitchener, General Manager of ACB, to the Chairman of the Transport Committee, Cllr T W Atkinson, with Mr Norman Morton in attendance. A picture of 168 appeared in the *Echo* as its body was the first double decker to be built in Sunderland. No more were built after SCT's 168-172 and ACB folded later in 1954. All 37 new buses were eye-catching in that they were fitted with the so-called tin front, concealing the radiator and conforming to what was regarded as the new look in double deck bus fashions. It was of a pattern first introduced by Birmingham Corporation on Crossley buses in 1950

Daimler CVG5s 168-172 had bodywork built on Wearside by Associated Coachbuilders using framework supplied by Metal Sections. The design incorporated under licence the Roe "safety" staircase with a triangular window as shown here as 168 undergoes its tilt test. Its body was 6cwt over the specified weight, the complete bus being 7.11.0 unladen, although the other four were pruned to 7.5.1. Note the "Binns" advertising, it now being SCT standard practice for this to be applied by the coachbuilder. Unlike the other buses entering service during Jan - Sep 54, the ACB-bodied Daimlers did not later receive the modified design of staircase or increased seating capacity.

(Copyright Sunderland Echo)

46

The first twelve Crossley-bodied Guys, 173-184, had recessed windows and, as with the contemporary Roe products, London RT-like interior window finishers. The windows of the Crossley bodies, however, were slightly deeper as comparison of photographs will reveal. Although the Crossley bodies also had the Roe "safety" staircase but no stair window, after their seating capacity was increased to 63 a visible clue from outside was the position of the bend in the stair-top handrail which as in this picture was nearer to the adjacent pillar than originally. A smart 180 is several years old in this scene and like the other tin-fronters has had its fog lamp removed and a later type of flashing direction indicator fitted, although the one shown here appears to have lost its amber cover. Mr Morton had recommended the metal-framed bodywork be standard all new buses and while he was against aluminium alloy for framing, the Crossley bodies on the fleet's Guy chassis did employ that material for the upper saloon frame with steel below.
(Copyright holder not known)

and obviously influenced by trends in motor car styling. The new Daimlers had the preselector lever set in a "gate" incorporated into a box on the left of the steering column, somewhat AEC-like. All three makes of body had the Roe "safety" staircase, built under licence by Crossley and ACB. Some of the features of the Roe bodies, and others on the Crossley bodies, were similar to those of the London RT family, 3,000 of which had been built by Park Royal. The Roe lower saloon panels were attached by screws but those of the upper saloon were riveted to the pillars and had no beadings between them except at the foremost main pillar. At the other pillars each panel was shaped at its rearward edge so as to overlap the next one. Unfortunately, the riveted panels worked loose and Roe sent someone to carry out emergency remedial work which included the fitting of beadings. All bodies had dark green leathercloth seating and matching interior trim. Although Mr Morton had expressed misgivings about the use of aluminium alloy for bus body framework, in the case of the Crossley bodies it was employed for the upper saloon.

With the closure of the Circle tram service and the immediate scrapping of twenty cars it was possible to use the Wheat Sheaf depot for all tramway accommodation and maintenance. Work then began on adapting Hylton Road car works to house buses. At about the same time, the Council approved the purchase by the Transport Department of 1,596 square yards of land (first discussed two years previously as has been indicated) next to the Wheat Sheaf depot as part of a long-term development policy. Later in 1954 the Council approved plans to alter and extend the Wheat Sheaf buildings too, using the acquired land, after the final stage of tramway conversion. The office block would be improved and modernised and the tram depot turned into the central repair works for buses.

Final tramway abandonment was now a priority and in February 1954 more orders for new buses were ratified by the Council. They comprised twelve Daimler and twelve Guy double deckers similar to the latest ones which would replace the last of the trams and most of the remaining centre-entrance buses. Four single deck Guys chassis, similar to a demonstrator tried three months previously, were ordered for further driver-only operation. It was possible for buses to replace trams on the Town - Durham Road section as from 29 March, other service changes taking place at the same time. Residents of upper Thorney Close then had a more direct route to the town centre with a $^1/2$d fare reduction, services 23 (5.61 route miles) and 24 (4.55 route miles) running at an integrated frequency of five minutes. The arrangements were:

Old

6   Ambleside Terr - Newcastle Rd - Town

15   Docks - Town - Ettrick Grove - Springwell - Thorney Close (Theme Rd)

Trams   Seaburn - Fulwell - Town - Durham Rd

New

6   *Withdrawn*

15   Docks - Town - Ettrick Gr - Springwell - Thorney Close (Telford Road) *(destination "Telford Rd")*

23   Ambleside Terr* - Newcastle Rd - Town - Durham Rd - Thorney Close (Theme Rd) *(destination "Thorney Close")* (*route within estate:* Thorney Close Rd - Thorndale Rd - Tilbury Rd - Thorne Rd - Tadcaster Rd) (*revised route north of Seaburn Station:* Alston Cres - Keswick Av - Dene La/Ambleside Terr (terminus) returning Ambleside Terr - Alston Cres, etc**; (previous terminus at Alston Cres/Ambleside Terr))

24   Fulwell (Blue Bell)* - Newcastle Rd - Town - Durham Rd (former tram terminus)

Trams   Seaburn - Fulwell - Fawcett St

All journeys extended to & from Seaburn (Dykelands Rd tram terminus) from 10am daily from 25 Jul - 8 Aug 1954 (shipyard holidays), except Sats

** Anti-clockwise circuit, altered to clockwise 14 Jun 54*

It is difficult to draw definite conclusions from some of the annual statistics for the year ending 31 March 1954 because of the large amount of changing over from trams to buses and the reorganisation of some bus services. There was a small increase in the combined total number of passenger journeys. This would have been greater had it not been for severe weather early in 1954 and, ominously, the effect of television which had been enhanced by the 1953 Coronation. Average bus passengers per mile and average working expenses per mile both showed a minute drop. The proportion of working expenses to traffic revenue was down some two per cent. Average traffic revenue per bus mile was up some two per cent but the bus mileage operated and total number of passengers carried both rose by at least 17 per cent. Stringent economies and the streamlining of administration had been implemented.

Work on the conversion of the Hylton Road building had gone ahead quickly and it became possible to make it an operational bus depot from 10 May 1954. To begin with, only services 10/11 (Grangetown - Pennywell/Ford) were run from Hylton Road using Daimler CVG5s 140-147 plus some of the 148-167 batch. Subsequently these services also were operated from Hylton Road with more buses as detailed:

June:

2/3*	Town - Farringdon/Plains Farm	15	Docks - Telford Rd
7	Leechmere Rd - Prestbury Rd	20**	Circle - Roker - Seaburn
9	Docks - Helmsdale Rd	48*	Sunderland - North Hylton
* Joint with NGT		** Shared with Fulwell Depot initially	

October:

8	Seaburn Camp - Leechmere Rd	18	Seaburn Camp - Springwell

Note. The services mentioned above were regular all-day operations; works and special services and duplicate journeys did not necessarily conform. Service 20 reverted entirely to Fulwell Depot from Oct

Hylton Road Depot bus allocation when fully operational

Daimler COG5	40/47	Daimler CVG5	140-169
Daimler CWG5	60/61	Crossley DD42/3	9-14, 19-21
Daimler CVG6	88-99, 106-115	Crossley DD42/7C	100-105

Hylton Road buses were distinguished by a letter "X" before the small fleet number on the bonnet side and over the fuel filler cap. Over the years there were to be changes and adjustments to the vehicle allocation and service operations of each depot. On the same day as Hylton Road Depot became operational, 10 May 1954, the services to Southwick and Red House were rationalised, eliminating overlap on the Town - Southwick section. Route mileages became 4.7 and 4.8 for services 4/5 respectively. The situations were:

Old

4/5	Town - Red House Sth/Nth **a**
13	Villette Rd - Southwick

New

4/5	Villette Rd - Red House Sth/Nth **b**
13	*withdrawn*

Route through Southwick:

a Sunderland Rd - Carley Rd - Collingwood St - Goschen St - Beaumont St (original Marley Pots route)

b Sunderland Rd (later re-named Southwick Rd) - The Green - Beaumont St

Another but less radical change occurred on 19 May 1954. The route of service 1 was shortened by about 150 yards west of The Cedars, buses now using Ashbrooke Range (previously unsuitable) instead of Glen Path.

A new "north side" tour was introduced on Whit Sunday 1954, supplementing the existing full town circular tour. Both then ran every Sunday during 11 July - 5 September and on each day of the shipyard holiday fortnight from 25 July. On 31 May, two part-day services were commenced for the benefit of workers. These operated during morning, mid-day and late afternoon works times only as detailed here:

12/13	Humbledon (Prospect Hotel) - Ford - St Luke's Rd - Pallion - Southwick - Fulwell (12) or Red House South (13)

Four weeks later the first of the expected 24 new double deckers arrived, delivery of all but one continuing until 27 September. 185-196 were Crossley-bodied Guys and 197-208 were Roe Daimlers, generally similar to the previous batches but with detail alterations on the Crossley bodies. The "missing" Daimler was special and will be mentioned shortly.

July 1954 was a record month for the transport undertaking when more passenger journeys were recorded than in any previous July. A total of 7.47M passengers were carried on buses and trams, an increase of some 165,000 over July 1953. The inevitable reduction in tram receipts was more than outweighed by the increase in bus receipts, the combined increase being £2,168. Busiest services were 10/11 (Grangetown - Pennywell/Ford, 1.023M) and 20 (Circle - Roker - Seaburn, just over 1M). It was also decided in 1954 to run illuminations tours again and they operated during 3 September - 3 October from Union Street at a shilling fare (children 6d). They were not perpetuated and after 1955 the illuminations were abandoned until 1986. Circular tours were still to remain a seasonal feature for some years, however.

The closure of the remaining tramway section, Town - Fulwell - Seaburn, took place on 1 October 1954. Hylton Road Depot was opened officially for buses on the same day. After the last service journey that night a valedictory procession took place, using "Ghost" car 86 as the ceremonial last tram. Buses took over the next day and the route length of service 24 became 5.45 miles. The particulars were:

The 185-196 Crossley-bodied Guy dozen had flush-fitting windows, distinguishing them from 173-184, and a different design of interior window finisher. In this scene at Pallion New Road/Watson Street during the late afternoon peak period the fact that 189 has been altered to seat 63 is revealed by the position of the upper saloon passengers as the offside front seat was further forward than the corresponding nearside one after modifications. Also in the picture is all-Crossley 11 (left of road) and rebodied Guy 81 (behind 189). Although Watson Street had been overbuilt to the left, it continued to be shown as a destination for the many extra journeys terminating there.
(Copyright Sunderland Echo)

48

Old

23	Ambleside Terr - Newcastle Rd - Town - Durham Rd - Thorney Close
24	Fulwell - Newcastle Rd - Town - Durham Rd
Trams	Seaburn - Fulwell - Fawcett St

New

23	As before
23x	Fulwell (Blue Bell) - Newcastle Rd - Town **a**
24	Seaburn - Fulwell Rd - Town - Durham Rd
24x	Fulwell (Blue Bell) - Fulwell Rd - Town **b**
Trams	*withdrawn*

a This was a deviation of the 23 route, following the original 24 route between Fulwell and Town and operated to maintain the existing 5-minute co-ordinated frequency with ser 23 between Seaburn station and Town.
b Operated to maintain a 5-minute frequency with ser 24 between Fulwell (Blue Bell) and Town.

The trams' final day also saw entry into service of 26, the first of the single deck Guy quartet, type LUF, 30ft long and 8ft wide, Nos27-29 entering service by 23 October. They were the Corporation's first underfloor-engined buses and the first with Burlingham bodies. Before the 1950s, most single deck and double deck chassis operated in Britain had the engine mounted vertically in a fore-and-aft position over the front axle. New designs of single decker then began to appear in which the engine was turned on its side in a horizontal position under the body floor. The front axle was set back several feet and generally the entrance was placed ahead of it in the overhanging part of the body. This layout enabled the body to have a more box-like shape which made better use of the available space and permitted a much increased seating capacity. When the maximum length for single deck buses was increased to 30ft during 1950 it was possible to accommodate up to 45 seated. As with all future SCT single deckers, 26-29 were designed specifically for driver-only operation and the seating capacity was kept to 42 by the provision of a centre exit, reducing the time spent loading and unloading. The ticketing and cash-handling equipment were to the driver's left on the cab nearside and this was a vast improvement ergonomically on the arrangement with Crossley 22 and Guys 7/8. Although H V Burlingham of Blackpool was better-known as a builder of stylish luxury coachwork, from its earliest days in 1928 the firm had built some bus bodies and during the mid-1950s was gaining orders for its

metal-framed single and double deck bus bodywork, jig-built in a spacious factory with modern facilities. Burlingham had submitted the lowest tender apart from one un-named builder which did not provide a specification.

Guy Motors had introduced the Arab UF ("underfloor") chassis at the 1950 Commercial Motor Show, with four- or five-speed constant-mesh or preselective gearbox and usually Gardner 6HLW engine. The 'H' in the engine designation signified "horizontal" position and indeed, it was Guy Motors that had first

In autumn 1954, four Guy Arab 5HLW LUF chassis with horizontal underfloor engines and metal-framed Burlingham 42-seat dual-door bodies, built for driver-only operation, entered service as 26-29. The seats were upholstered in patterned moquette with higher back squabs, just visible in this view, in contrast to the seating in he 1953/54 double deckers. Pictured here is 28, after its first repaint, the omission of the cream band at cantrail level perhaps detracting a little from the appearance. The elongated chromed wing motif at the front, in this case surmounting the Guy badge, was a Burlingham hallmark on buses as well as coaches at that period. *(Copyright holder not known)*

adapted a Gardner 6LW to be turned on to its side for underfloor mounting in mid-chassis. Gardner subsequently added the option to its range on the market. The Arab UF was among the "first generation" heavyweights of its type, competing with the market-leading AEC Regal Mark IV and Leyland Royal Tiger. Then following the trend, two years or so later, Guy brought out the Arab LUF ("lightweight underfloor") chassis. The attraction of the LUF for Sunderland Corporation was the availability of Gardner 5HLW power. Only Daimler and Atkinson were marketing underfloor-engined chassis with Gardners at that time and the Daimler was probably too heavy for the 5HLW. The new Guys went to work on service 1 and the night service. Crossley single deckers 22/23 were then withdrawn along with the remaining pair of Guy Wolves, 1/2.

Visitors to the 1954 Commercial Motor Show who went to the demonstration park may have seen two double deck buses with what was at that time the exceptionally high seating capacity of 65. Both were based on Daimler CVG5 chassis and one, a Roe-bodied

A further twelve Crossley-bodied Guy 5LW Arab IVs (185-196) and twelve Roe-bodied Daimler CVG5s (197-208) were to arrive during summer and early autumn 1954. Bob Hedley the signwriter here poses at Fulwell depot with a gleaming 202, fresh from its appearance as a Roe exhibit on the demonstration park at the 1954 Commercial Motor Show and without advertisements in this case but sporting cream-painted tyre rims (a typical Roe "Show" feature). 202 differed from the other new buses by having a modified design of "safety" staircase, windowless, that permitted increased seating capacity in both saloons, the total being 65 rather than 58. All other Roe-bodied Daimlers and Crossley-bodied Guys from No148 were to receive a 202-style modified design of staircase and more seats during 1954-56, although in their case the upper saloon capacity became 35 rather than 37, giving a total of 63. This became the standard for forward-engined double deckers, 202 remaining uniquely a 65-seater. Outside, modified buses could be identified from the position of the staircase handrail across the platform window which was one step-width more toward the nearside than with the original design. In the case of the Roe bodies a more obvious change was the removal of the staircase window. *(Copyright Sunderland Echo)*

Here the absence of the distinctive staircase window shows that Roe-bodied Daimler 206 has had its seating capacity increased from 58 to 63. That other clue, the precise position of the bend in the stair-top handrail (and accordingly the seat immediately ahead of it), may also be seen. The original type of flashing direction indicator is fitted.

(Copyright R Marshall)

example for Sunderland Corporation, was of course the "missing" 202 (the other was Northern Counties-bodied, for Walsall). 202 reached Wearside on Friday 8 October and entered service the day after delivery on a Football Ground - Cairns Road short working. Charlie Parnaby, brother of Ralph who drove on the all-night service, was at the helm and it seems that the intention was to see how the conductor would cope with full loads on a journey just under a mile long. The seating capacity of 65 could be achieved only by modifying the staircase design. As has been explained, the Roe "safety" staircase had always been of 2-5-1 format but now it became 3-4-1, reducing the amount of space occupied by the forward-ascending stairs and creating 10in more room for seating on the offside of the upper saloon. 65 was now the practical maximum for a double deck bus (37 up, 28 down) without a rearward-facing bench for five at the lower saloon front. 202 weighed slightly less than the other outwardly similar CVG5s, due in part to the use of synthetic foam in the upper saloon seats.

Higher seating capacities were an item on the agenda at the Transport Committee meeting held on 28 October 1954. Mr Morton obtained authority to have the seating capacity of buses with more than a 10-year life expectancy increased. He explained that the 65-seater (202) "did not entail discomfort to passengers" (although some may not have agreed). The Committee noted also that as the site of the Union Street bus station was due for redevelopment it would have to vacated in due course, although this was not to be until 20 August 1956. It was also agreed that one of the new Guy saloons would be loaned to Dundee Corporation for a week, Guy Motors paying the hiring fee. The one that journeyed from Wear to Tay was 29, looking at home among Dundee's similarly-coloured buses.

The day following that Committee meeting was a cold, breezy and very wet Friday that also saw a visit of HM the Queen to the north-east, including Sunderland. Some bus services were curtailed and the Transport Department conveyed more than 12,000 pupils from their schools to their allotted viewing points along the route through Seaburn, Roker, Monkwearmouth and the town centre taken by the royal procession, returning them afterward. The time of the visit overlapped normal works finishing times and this, coupled with the need for additional journeys for sightseers,

placed an enormous burden on the Department. Organisation was greatly assisted, however by the experimental use of Pye radio telephone equipment with which bus movements were co-ordinated successfully from a control point at the Wheat Sheaf offices. Mr Morton was delighted and the Committee agreed subsequently to the purchase for £553 of an installation comprising one fixed station with remote control, two mobile stations and one "walkie-talkie". This equipment was to prove invaluable for the control of seaside and football traffic, and in emergencies. After radio came the movie, for at its November meeting the Committee was shown a preview of the Department's film "Going Places", made at a cost of £742 and giving insights into the working of the Department. It included some scenes shot on the final day of tram operation. So popular did the film prove among local schools and other organisations nationwide that a second print was made.

Another housing estate was by now nearly complete. Situated on the south side of Chester Road opposite Pennywell and named Grindon Village, on 22 November 1954 it received a bus service, No16, again operated on a 50-50 basis with NGT. Initially it ran on a Monday - Saturday frequency of 30 minutes, hourly on Sundays, buses showing "Grindon Village". Hylton Road Depot ran SCT's share of the service and the route from the town centre (Brougham Street) was:

Union St and Holmeside (westbound) or Crowtree Rd (eastbound) - Chester Rd - Grindon Mill - Greenwood Rd - Gleneagles Rd

Returning to seating capacities, changes to the utility-bodied Guys and Daimlers have been documented already and although the Crossleys and Daimler CWD6s were not treated, the Department converted all other post-war 56-seaters to 58, with just one exception to be mentioned later. As to the "new look" buses, after only three weeks in service, during August 1954 Daimler 204 was rammed in the rear by tram 95 and badly damaged. It was then returned to Roe and came back on 9 December with the same style of 3-4-1 staircase as 65-seat Show bus 202. The seating capacity of No204 was increased, however, not to 65 but to 63 (35 up, 28 down). Except for ACB-bodied Daimlers 168-172, the other 58-seat Daimlers and Guys numbered 148-208 were to be altered similarly to 204 (see Appendix 1). The revised staircase design and 63-seat capacity was to become standard for SCT's new Roe bodies to 1958.

The arrival of a relatively large number of new buses during 1953/54 along with the fairly rapid repainting into the green livery and in some cases rebuilding of older buses led to a uniformity of appearance not previously seen in the fleet. Utility-rebuilding had begun with Daimler 61 in February 1953 and Guy 74, treated during spring 1954 and pictured only a month after re-entering service, here illustrates what a splendid job was carried out and how such features as the standard destination apertures and new styles of numeral and "Binns" lettering imparted a neater and more coherent image. Neither was it all superficial, as more efficient and economical maintenance procedures and other working practices were being implemented behind the scenes at this time, too. The rebuilt utilities did not have the service number at the rear but other alterations included the replacement of wooden-slatted seats with upholstered ones where applicable. Only ex-Blackburn Guys 5/6 and Daimler 73 were not rebuilt or repainted green. *(Copyright R Marshall)*

7 - What Size Bus?

Centre-entrance Guy 59 and utility Guys 63/67/78/79/81 were fitted with handsome new teak-framed Roe bodies late in 1954 and re-entered service in early January 1955. They had the revised 202-type staircase and 61 seats. Body weight was kept down and with a new unladen weight of 7.5.3 some of them were -practically half a ton lighter than originally. 63 is seen here at the Wheat Sheaf and incorrectly carries the bonnet side for a 6LW engine. All six rebodied Guys had five-cylinder units, 81 being re-engined from 6LW. *(Copyright holder not known)*

increase in mileage meant that passenger *volume* was up only marginally. During this period SCT buses were featured in trade advertisements again. Drummond-Asquith of Birmingham, manufacturers of Dawson vehicle washers, used a photograph of a line of Daimlers, headed by 167 having a shower and brush-up in the drive-through wash at Hylton Road Depot. The "Binns" advertisement was touched out! Fulwell Depot had portable drive-through Februat bus wash, acquired in 1954 and to be replaced in 1958 by a Dawson machine, incidentally. The underfloor-engined Guy saloons appeared in two Burlingham advertising features, the second of them drawing attention to their being driver-only operated.

The Transport Department wanted to commence a new driver-only Grangetown (Regent Cinema) - Southwick (The Green) service via

The rebuilding work on some of the wartime Guys could not be completed in the time available before their recertification dates. Rather than have the work done by outside firms at high cost it was a sounder proposition to have new bodies fitted. Six chassis were therefore sent to Roe late in 1954 for rebodying. These were 59, with non-utility centre-entrance Roe body, Masseys 63/78/79/81 and Pickering 67, all returning to service in the new year of 1955. No81 had also exchanged its 6LW engine for a 5LW. The new bodies were teak-framed, contrary to policy, and outwardly they resembled the bodies on 1953 Daimlers 140-147. Chief differences were the new style staircase and a seating capacity of 61.

On 14 March there was a 1d increase in the universal fare. The Corporation's wage bill was expected to rise by some £26,000 a year as a result of a pay award to platform staff and the modest fare rise would bring in an estimated £15,000 more revenue. Actual revenue from passengers for the current

The final utility to be rebuilt was Daimler CWA6 72, in March 1956, losing its upper saloon forward-facing window vents at the same time. It also had its AEC 7.7-litre engine replaced by a Gardner 5LW, altering its type designation to CWG5. Two years later it was to decapitate itself under a low bridge and subsequently replace 36, the surviving pre-war Daimler, as the depot yard snowplough at Fulwell. *(Copyright R Marshall)*

financial year was some £670,000. It was calculated that if SCT charged fares at the average for the country, the increase in annual revenue would be nearly £300,000 (assuming no loss of passengers, of course). This is how they compared at the beginning of 1955:

Fare 1½d	2d	2½d	3d	3½d	4d	4½d
SCT average distance						
1.17	1.78	2.26	2.71	3.26	3.73	4.29 miles
National municipal average distance						
0.68	1.14	1.56	2.01	2.44	3.03	3.41 miles

The Annual Report for the year ending 31 March 1955 recorded the final demise of the trams. Although there had been a large increase in the bus passenger total, an almost corresponding

Alexandra Road, Kayll Road, Pallion and Alexandra Bridge. Its introduction was delayed on account of a dispute with the National Union of General and Municipal Workers, which wanted there to be no stops on the Southwick - Barnes Park Road/Durham Road section because this was covered already by double deck service 18 (Seaburn Camp - Springwell). The Department wanted a limited number of stops at key points. In the interim, on 16 May 1955, a service with the disused number 6 was started between Grangetown and Durham Road/Barnes Park Road only, along the full 1½-mile length of Alexandra Road. Workings were linked with those of service 1 (Town - Grangetown via Hill View) so that buses did not operate on service 6 in isolation. Initially the basic frequency was 15 minutes between 11am-7pm, and 20 minutes outside those times and on Sundays. The service was to be extended, although not by the route originally intended, after the dispute had been resolved and from 14 November ran as shown below on a basic hourly frequency, increasing to half-hourly at peak periods and on Saturday afternoons. The route length was six miles, running partly the same way as service 18 and partly in the opposite direction to it. On 11 July 1955, service 18 had been extended by about 300 yards from Somerset Road/Grindon Lane to Grindon Lane/Gleneagles Road, catering for the lower end of Grindon Village although the destination shown was still "Springwell". Service 18 is included for comparison on account of its significance in the dispute (opposite-direction parts in *italics,* same-direction parts in **bold** type):

6   Grangetown - Alexandra Rd - *Durham Rd - Springwell Rd -* Holborn Rd - Front Rd - St Luke's Rd - **Pallion - Alexandra Bridge - Southwick.**

18   Springwell (Grindon La/Gleneagles Rd) - *Springwell Rd - Durham Rd -* Barnes Park Rd - Kayll Rd - **Pallion - Alexandra Bridge - Southwick -** Fulwell - Seaburn Camp.

On 16 May 1955, there were also other service revisions as given below. These were an attempt to resolve the problems of late running caused by peak time traffic congestion on the relatively short 23x/24x, where buses had little opportunity of regaining lost time.

Old

7*   Prestbury Rd - Town - Ryhope Rd - Grangetown - Leechmere Rd/Helvellyn Rd

8   Seaburn Camp - Park Ave - Town - Ryhope Rd - Grangetown - Leechmere Rd/Helvellyn Rd

23   Ambleside Terr - Newcastle Rd - Town - Durham Rd - Thorney Close

23x   Fulwell (Blue Bell) - Newcastle Rd - Town

24   Seaburn - Fulwell Rd - Town - Durham Rd

24x   Fulwell (Blue Bell) - Fulwell Rd - Town

       Two sections: Prestbury Rd - Town as 7, Hylton Lane - Grangetown as 7x with some journeys to Leechmere Rd as 7

New

7   Prestbury Rd - Town

8   Seaburn Camp - Park Ave - Town

21   Fulwell (Blue Bell) - Newcastle Rd - Town - Ryhope Rd - Grangetown - Leechmere Rd/Helvellyn Rd

22   Fulwell (Blue Bell)* - Fulwell Rd - Town - Ryhope Rd - Grangetown

23   as before

24   as before

23x/24x   withdrawn as regular scheduled journeys

*All journeys in 1955 extended to & from Seaburn (Dykelands Rd) at following times:

11am to finish of service on Sundays from Whitsun to end Sep, also Aug Bank Holiday Monday;

11am to 7pm daily from 25 July to 6 August (shipyard holidays).

Services 21-24: co-ordinated sections

21/23   Seaburn Station - Newcastle Rd - Town
21/22   Town - Ryhope Rd - Grangetown
22/24   Fulwell (Blue Bell) - Fulwell Rd - Town
23/24   Town - Durham Rd

In June 1955 Mr Morton prepared a confidential report on the financial position of the undertaking. In it he said that there had been no general fares increase since 1951 although costs and capital expenditure had risen greatly in recent years; many economies had been made; staffing was a constant problem; and Company operation was eroding passenger traffic. The report with its recommendations as to possible remedies is summarised in Appendix 4.

As to seating capacities, the conversion of 58-seaters to seat 63 was going ahead where practicable. March 1956 was the target for completion, although it was missed by two months. The conversion of 56-seaters to 58 was to take place over a longer period. Mr Morton calculated that by 1956 the average seating capacity of the fleet would have increased by some 40 per cent since 1939.

Regarding vehicle policy generally, SCT was somewhat against the trend during this period. While many operators were going in for lighter vehicles, a reversion to the earlier width of 7ft 6in after acquiring 8ft-wide buses was exceptional. Standardisation on 7.0-litre Gardner 5LW-engined double deckers other than for operation on relatively flat terrain was unusual, too, especially after so much experience with the 8.4-litre 6LW. Economically, Sunderland's policy of combining higher seating capacity with smaller engine made sense. The newest buses could carry more passengers and they consumed less fuel. Various documents produced during the mid- and late 1950s put their average fuel consumption at between 10.52 (quoted previously) and 10.78mpg, with 10.97 claimed by Mr Morton himself for five-cylinder Guys 173-196. These figures compared well with 9.74 to 10.0mpg for the 6LW-powered 8ft-wide buses in the fleet. The 6LW of course gave greater mileage between overhauls than the more heavily-stressed 5LW yet, notwithstanding the lower maintenance costs that this meant for the 6LW, the cheaper one overall was still the 5LW on account of its better fuel consumption. Leyland Motors' advertising at this time, incidentally, was making much of the *10.53*mpg being claimed for new 9.8-litre synchromesh PD2 Titans weighing only 6.12.0 in Edinburgh on normal city routes. In 1955, SCT operated a Daimler CVG6 demonstrator weighing only 6.18.2, but preference for the 5LW remained unaffected.

The Daimler CVG5s and Guy 5LW Arabs were, however, somewhat slow on hills and acceleration was only moderate, particularly when heavily-laden. As this tended to be at busy periods when additional time was taken up with boarding and alighting and there were more delays due to road traffic congestion, punctuality was affected. They were generally less comfortable than earlier buses, yet comfort may not have played a very important part in shaping passengers' attitudes to bus travel. During this period a survey was carried out at a local women's guild meeting attended by 67 members. They may not have been typical, but they rated their bus facilities in this order of priority:

1 - service frequency; 2 - level of fares; 3 - service reliability; 4 - platform staff conduct; 5 - comfort, condition and appearance of buses

The good organisation of the Corporation's transport system was still being hampered by platform staff shortage. An intensive advertising campaign had produced some response, mainly from young women, but it was anticipated that the summer of 1955 would see an exacerbation as staff took their holidays or went away to Territorial Army camps as some did, at a time when demand for services was high. Accordingly it was agreed by the Transport Committee in June that the Department should engage university students as conductors for the summer season. During this period concern was expressed about Fulwell Depot, which was still based

There can be no doubt that such vehicles as the 116-127 batch of Daimlers benefited from their repaint into green. Along with Guys 128-139 they kept their original large destination aperture and the added under-canopy number box. Only Daimlers 106-109 and 140-147 were delivered new with chromium-plated radiator shells but subsequently other individual buses received them and vice-versa, a case in point being 121 pictured here in Union Street bus station, showing the beautifying effect of the gleaming metal combined with black and green. *(Copyright R Marshall)*

The march of progress? Traces of tramways are gradually being erased as this 1955 picture reveals, looking east from the Gas Office Corner, and will be completed throughout the town by the 1959. Both buses are on sections where once trams had run. ACB-bodied Daimler 172 passes the museum, having come from Villette Road, and an unmodified Roe-bodied Daimler of the 148-167 group has emerged from John Street (left, beyond hoardings) and makes its way down Borough Road to the Docks. To the immediate left is Fawcett Street. *(Copyright Busways Travel Services)*

mainly on the original former rope works building and an old corrugated iron shed. The layout was inconvenient and the use of floor space uneconomical. Even though Hylton Road Depot was operating 70 buses, about 20 of the 105 vehicles allocated to Fulwell had to be parked in the open yard overnight. The Transport Committee did agree in principle to the acquisition of adjacent land for a new building but ultimately the project came to nothing.

Mr Morton's fares proposal in the June report was brought into operation on 19 September 1955. The minimum $1^1/2$d fare now applied to a distance of one mile, with $^1/2$d for each additional half-mile. Universal transfer returns went up by 2d to 8d and ordinary transfers were abolished. It was estimated, however, that up to 60 per cent of journeys would continue to be made at the same fares as in 1951. By the end of the 31 March 1956, traffic receipts were to go up by nearly £76,000, representing about 10 per cent. This increase was more than double the rise in working expenses.

The Massey bodies of Daimlers 88-99 were now giving cause for concern. Over a four-year period they were to be rebuilt similarly to the utilities. The first of them, 92, was the final bus to be refurbished at Fulwell Depot, re-entering service on 1 January 1956, having been treated before the last of the utilities, Duple Daimler 72. Future major repair work was to be carried out at the new Wheat Sheaf Central Workshop which came into part-use from that date. All mechanical, electrical and body overhauls, repairs and painting were gradually transferred from Fulwell until the new Wheat Sheaf works became fully operational on 5 March 1956. Only steam cleaning (for

the whole bus fleet) continued to be carried out at Fulwell. 97 was delicensed for two years before re-appearing in December 1959. In the meantime 98, which had been overhauled in May 1958, received serious nearside frontal chassis damage in a collision on 22 February 1959 and was withdrawn immediately. The body of 98 was hardly affected and ultimately it was decided to transfer this body to the chassis of 96 (the exception that was mentioned near the end of the previous chapter), the only bus of the batch still untreated. Having been delicensed since March 1958, 96 returned with its transplanted body 1 January 1961 and the chassis of 98 with the original body of 96 were scrapped.

Services linking the town centre with Roker, Fulwell and Seaburn were rationalised to eliminate overlap on 9 January 1956. Some residents of Featherstone Street objected to buses running past their houses and the upshot was a public enquiry by the Traffic Commissioners. The route was then revised, all details being as follows:

Old

8   Town - Park Ave - Seaburn **a** - Seaburn Camp (some journeys terminating at Seaburn as 8x)

20   Circle - Town - Roker - Seaburn **b** (alternate journeys terminating at Roker as 20x)

22   Grangetown - Ryhope Rd - Town - Fulwell Rd - Fulwell

24   Durham Rd - Town - Fulwell Rd - Fulwell - Seaburn **c**

Note. Seaburn termini: **a** - Seaburn Terr/Whitburn Rd; **b** - Whitburn Rd/Seaburn Terr; **c** - Dykelands Rd

53

New

8 *withdrawn*

19 journeys previously Circle - Roker 20x now as follows, replacing 8 except along Roker Baths Rd:
Circle - Roker - Park Av - Seaburn - Seaburn Camp (some journeys terminating at Seaburn as 19x)
(Route through Roker - <u>to Seaburn Camp</u>: via Harbour View - Roker Terr - St George's Terr - Park Parade;
<u>from Seaburn Camp</u>: via Park Parade - Featherstone St - Harbour View)

20/22/24 *as before*

Revised 31 Aug 56

19 Route through Roker, <u>both directions</u>: Harbour View - Roker Terr - St George's Terr - Park Parade

Other changes early in 1955, on 13 February, affected services 15 and 18. Both had a common section along parts of Durham Road and Springwell Road. They were now split at Springwell Road/Sunningdale Road so that alternate journeys on each ran to Springwell and Telford Road in turn, without any change to service numbers. Service 15 had never been commercially viable. While the peaks were heavy other times were extremely slack and from 27 August 1956, frequencies were adjusted accordingly. The running of services 15/18 to alternate termini was to be abandoned from 21 January 1957.

No new buses were obtained in 1955 and only one, a single decker numbered 30, in 1956. Unusually it comprised an Atkinson lorry-derived chassis powered by a forward-mounted vertical Gardner 4LW engine and metal-framed Roe body of standard Park Royal group appearance. The doorway was of dual width, the forward half being the entrance and the rearward half the exit. Fourteen months later a similar specimen was placed in service as 31, seen here in Holmeside. Both pottered about on the driver-only operated services although like the converted 1950 forward-engined Guys, 7/8, they were of questionable suitability for their purpose due to the need for fare transactions to take place to the rear left of the driver rather than at right angles as with Guys 26-29. At 5.6.0 unladen, the Atkinsons were slightly heavier than some underfloor-engined types. They were slow, noisy, and juddered when starting from rest but were extremely reliable and economical. *(Copyright C W Routh)*

Improvements to services 2/3 were implemented during the late 1950s as detailed below. By 1959, SDO was running the joint operator's mileage at weekends.

27 Feb 56

2 Farringdon terminus moved 400 yards from Allendale Road/Ashdown Road to Ashdown Road/Arundel Road.

26 Nov 56

3 extended by 1.3 miles from Plains Farm via Durham Road - North Moor Lane to Farringdon (Allendale Rd/Avonmouth Rd), co-ordinated with service 2 to provide an additional Farringdon - Town link

6 April 1959

2 Farringdon terminus moved 0.2mile to Atlantis Road/Antwerp Road

A driver taking a bus out of the depot was not normally news, but it warranted a report and photograph in the *Echo* on 20 March

1956 because the driver was the General Manager himself, pictured at the wheel of Crossley 12 emerging from Hylton Road Depot. Mr Morton had decided to do the job for a week to gain first-hand experience of conditions both on the road and on the job. Even if his adventures did include taking a packed 5LW-engined bus up Stoney Lane (where a drop down to first gear was often required with a heavy load), it did not alter his attitude to five-cylinder power! However, other events did, eventually.

For the year ending 31 March 1956 the traffic revenue and working expenses figures per mile were encouraging. Passenger journeys also rose slightly more than the operated mileage in percentage terms. Mr Morton said that the results were reasonably satisfactory. By this time, too, in the light of experience with Guy Arab LUF saloons 26 -29, he had developed reservations about engine accessibility, uneven tyre wear and the inevitable high floor line. This was no criticism of the Guy LUF model as such, which was up to Guy's usual standard of robustness and reliability: it applied to virtually all underfloor-engined single deck models. Mr Morton would have preferred a single decker with the characteristics of the Daimler and Guy double deckers. He approached Guy Motors about producing a "one-off" model suitable for 30ft x 8ft fully-fronted bodywork and light enough to be powered by a vertical forward Gardner 4LW engine. Guy expressed interest and SCT ordered one chassis. However, Guy backed out and subsequently the order went to the highly-respected Atkinson Vehicles Ltd of Walton-le-Dale, near Preston, a commercial vehicle chassis builder since 1915 that had entered the PSV field as recently as 1950 and had built only a relatively small number of bus chassis.

A second Atkinson was ordered subsequently and the two Roe-bodied saloons, 30/31, were delivered in 1956/57 respectively. Atkinson modified a lorry chassis design to produce the type, designated L644LW, and it had a straight frame (with a correspondingly high floor level), the body being mounted on outriggers. Transmission was through a David Brown four-speed synchromesh gearbox, there being no type of epicyclic unit suitable for this chassis. Park Royal metal framing was used for the Roe 41-seat bodywork which featured a double-width doorway immediately aft of the front axle. As with Guys 26-29, seating was moquette-covered with leathercloth trimmings. Engine noise within the saloon was probably too great and to some degree they reminded one of Bristol L5G saloons in other fleets. Driver John Precht enjoyed taking the reins of an Atkinson and he could always handle one with ease. From an economy standpoint these two Atkinsons were a success, giving 15 per cent better fuel economy than Guys 26-29. No other Atkinsons of this type were built for the home market although they would have proved suitable in some rural areas.

The Union Street bus station had to be vacated on 20 August 1956 and buses then set down and picked up on the streets. This necessitated a re-routeing through the town centre of the services affected, although there were to be subsequent changes and adjustments.

A perpetual headache for SCT and similar operators lay in the sudden heavy peaking in demand for buses up to about 9am and then again late in the afternoon, exacerbated by some overlap in the needs of schoolchildren and workpeople. SCT's normal service requirements on weekdays were for 93 buses over a period of about 17 hours in the day. At peak times the need was for a further *60* buses which worked for only up to *four* hours a day. On the joint SCT - NGT Hylton Castle 17 service, for example, with a five-minute peak frequency there were five normal departures to Town between 8.20 and 8.40am and often no less than six extra journeys within the same period. Eight fully-laden buses would usually leave the estate in succession. However, over 350 schoolchildren would have alighted from the buses at the Wheat Sheaf or before. Then at Watson Street, the busiest Pallion works loading point during the late afternoon peak, on three days a week the main finishing times were 5.20, 5.30

Eight further Daimler CVG5s with 63-seat Roe bodies were acquired in 1957 and numbered 209-216, the last having semi-automatic transmission as an experiment which was not to be repeated on any forward-engined bus in the fleet. Heading south along Ryhope Road, 210 here portrays the more upright frontal profile of the PRV group's metal-framed products during this period, clearly derived from the outline of London's Routemaster in the development of which Park Royal was involved. Roe's "safety" staircase was fitted and the windows were deeper than those of the previous Roe metal-framed bodies. Weighing 6.17.3 unladen, 209-215 were the lightest post-war double deckers in the fleet. All except 213 and 216 were to survive into PTE days. *(Copyright holder not known)*

and 6pm. It was impracticable for most buses to complete their journeys with the 5.20 workers and get back in time for the 5.30 loads. On Fridays there was severe congestion as all the works finished at 5pm! The Department argued for staggered starting and finishing times for works and schools. It made strong representations to employers and unions but it was not until 8 April 1957 that staggered hours affecting some 17,000 workers were introduced, permitting better organisation with reduced waiting. Shipyards and engineering works were treated separately, finishing times varying only by up to ten minutes on Monday to Thursday and in the case of the engineers, 15 minutes on Friday.

At the end of 1956, Massey Daimler 61 became the first utility to be withdrawn. Some service frequencies were reduced temporarily from 31 December due to fuel rationing as a result of a crisis in the Middle East. This arose following the forcible nationalisation by Egypt's President Nasser of the Suez Canal, precipitating a military attack by Britain, France and Israel in an attempt to regain international control. General details were:

Reduced frequencies	5min to 6; 10min to 12
Withdrawn:	Sunday morning Docks journeys
Reduced:	Football specials; private hires

These measures cut bus mileage by five per cent. Extra passenger traffic was generated by vehicle fuel rationing, however, as it caused the number of private car journeys to fall. The situation brought about an increase in the cost of fuels because oil companies added 6d to the price of a gallon of fuel oil and the Government put 1s 0d on the tax (already at 2s 6d). All fares were therefore increased

by a halfpenny on Saturdays and Sundays from 12 January 1957. After the fuel problems abated, normal services and fares were resumed on 8 April 1957. Regarding vehicles, the two remaining centre-entrance examples, Daimler 47 and Leyland 25, were withdrawn on 28 February and 30 April 1957 respectively. Rear-entrance Leyland 58 ran until 27 May, after which there was nothing of pre-war appearance in the fleet.

Traffic revenue and working expenses rose by about six and seven per cent respectively in the year to 31 March 1957. Mileage was down by 1.6 per cent, reflecting the Suez crisis reductions. The overall number of passengers carried, practically 88 million, was up only marginally and had it not been for the crisis it would probably have been reduced. It was, however, to remain the highest ever for Sunderland Corporation buses.

Eight new Roe-bodied Daimler CVG5s were delivered as 209-216 in May 1957, believed to have aluminium alloy framing for the upper saloon. Although outwardly all were identical, 216 was different underneath. Instead of the usual preselective gearbox and fluid flywheel it had a direct-acting semi-automatic 'box with electro-hydraulic control and a combined fluid flywheel and centrifugal clutch, possibly the first Daimler so equipped. Gear-changing was carried out by moving a miniature gear lever that actuated electrical contacts, protruding upward from a control box on the left of the steering column and similar to that used over the following decades on thousands of Daimler and other makes of bus with semi-automatic transmission. There was no clutch or gear-change pedal. When new, 216 carried a typewritten notice in the cab instructing drivers to make *upward* gear changes without releasing the accelerator but to release it when changing *down*. One of the theoretical advantages of this type of gearbox was that upward changes of ratio could be made while torque was still being applied. In practice, however, a gear-change made in this way induced 216 to make a huge kangaroo-leap forward, causing most drivers therefore to change gear as they would with a layshaft 'box. This somewhat defeated the object of adopting the more modern mechanism. Within months, 216 was fitted with a normal fluid flywheel as the fluid flywheel-clutch was not entirely satisfactory. The gearbox was manufactured by Self Changing Gears Ltd (usually known as SCG) of Coventry which since the previous year had been a Leyland subsidiary, although supplying Leyland's competitors. Other similar trials are covered in Appendix 1.

The 'box for 216 was purchased by SCT and sent to Daimler for fitting to the chassis. Daimler then delivered to the Corporation the original preselective 'box specified. 216 also differed from 209-215 by being fitted with 24-volt instead of 12-volt electrical equipment as this might not have coped adequately with the additional task of gear control on 216. The weight penalty for 216's differences was almost 4cwt. Although 12-volt apparatus had been standard since 1953, future forward-engined SCT buses reverted to 24 volts even though they had spring-operated preselective gearboxes. Pictured in the *Echo* when newly delivered, 216 was described as being "child's play" to drive. It is thought that all eight new buses and future Daimler CVG5s delivered to the fleet had the 5.75 to 1 rear axle ratio which under most conditions gave them better acceleration than CVG5s with the 5.17 version.

There were now changes to driver-only operated service 1, the destination "Alexandra Road via Hill View" having been dropped in favour of "Hill View via Alexandra Road" although the outer terminus was still at Grangetown (Regent Cinema). There were also changes during 1957/58 to both ends of services 21/22 affecting the Grangetown and Fulwell areas, all serving new private housing developments and described below.

20 May 57

1 Town - Alexandra Rd - Sea View Rd W - Hill View Rd - Hereford Rd - Westheath Av - Grangetown - unchanged but alternate journeys now 1x

1x Town - Alexandra Rd - Sea View Rd W - Leechmere Rd/Greystoke Ave (basic co-ordinated frequency to/from Town increased from 20 to 15min)

1 July 57

1 all journeys to/from Town now this service - route as previously

1x altered to shuttle service: Grangetown - Greystoke Av

21 Fulwell (Blue Bell) - Newcastle Rd - Town - Ryhope Rd - Grangetown - Leechmere Rd/Helvellyn Rd - alternate journeys extended to Leechmere Rd/Greystoke Av

4 Nov 1957

21 Leechmere Rd (those journeys terminating at junc/Greystoke Ave now extended to junc/Tunstall Rd) - Grangetown - Ryhope Rd - Town - Newcastle Rd - Fulwell (Blue Bell) (basic 10min frequency along Leechmere Rd to junc/Helvellyn Rd and 20min to junc/Tunstall Rd)

10 Mar 1958

22 Grangetown - Ryhope Rd - Town - Fulwell Rd - Fulwell (B Bell) - alternate jnys extended via Dene La to *Dene Estate (basic 10min frequency to Fulwell (Blue Bell) and 20min to *Dene Estate)

14 Jul 1958

21 All journeys along Leechmere Rd now operating to junc Tunstall Rd (basic 10min frequency)

1 Dec 1958

22 All journeys now operating to *Dene Estate, returning as 21 via Fulwell (Blue Bell) - Newcastle Rd etc to Tunstall Rd

21 All journeys from Tunstall Rd to Fulwell (B Bell) via Newcastle Rd, returning as 22 via Fulwell Rd etc to Grangetown

Terminus: Dovedale Rd. Full title Seaburn Dene Estate, but 'Seaburn' not used on destination blinds for this location

An 850-house extension to the Red House council housing estate was begun during 1957 and services 4/5 to Red House South/North from Villette Road were altered twice as the population grew. The existing terminus of both was at Redhill/Rhodesia Roads. Rotherfield Road, a new thoroughfare, linked the original part of the estate and the extension. The changes were:

1 Jul 1957

4 (South) extended - Rotherfield Rd - Ravenswood Rd/Ramillies Rd* - returning as 5 via Ramillies Rd - Rotherfield Rd (circular)

5 (North) extended - Rotherfield Rd - Ramillies Rd/Ravenswood Rd* - returning as 4 via Ravenswood Rd - R'field Rd (circular)

1 Dec 58

4 (South) extended - Raeburn Rd - Ravenscourt Rd (southern part) - Rhondda Rd/Rennie Rd** - returning as 5 via Ravenna Rd - Ravenscourt Rd (northern part) - Raeburn Rd

5 (North) extended - Raeburn Rd - Ravenscourt Rd (northern part) - Ravenna Rd/Rennie Rd** - returning as 4 via Rhondda Rd - Ravenscourt Rd (southern part) - Raeburn Rd

*increase of 0.6mile **increase of c500yds*

At the Transport Committee meeting held on 10 July 1957, the Chairman, Cllr T W Atkinson, commented that passengers were describing the upper saloons of buses as "gas chambers". He was responding to a point raised by Cllr Mrs M Burlinson about poor ventilation. She stated that many sliding windows either would not open or would not shut, and asked that different types of ventilating windows should be considered for new buses. The Chairman assured her that they would be. There was to be curious development following this exchange. Soon afterward, late-night drunken revellers seemed to discover that in the case of Widney Famco double-sliding aluminium-framed vents as fitted to all SCT double deckers since 1953, if the forward half were slid its full extent

rearward it could be pushed right out of the frame and on to the road. Great fun perhaps, but the Transport Department soon put a stop to it by securing the forward half of each vent in the closed position and cutting off its handle. In effect this reduced already poor ventilation and the atmosphere during the evening peak in a fully-laden 63-seater carrying 35 upstairs with all those cigarettes, pipes and home-bound bodies hardly bears imagining. One of the town's best-known conductors would call out, *"Seats upstairs in the gas chamber!"* (see Appendix 3). Regarding conductors, incidentally, the situation was again becoming acute. A further intensive advertising campaign was carried out in August 1957, baiting potential applicants with a promise of £9 0s 0d for a basic week.

Just as the trams had finally given way to buses in 1954, so on 12 August 1957, buses took over from another but more ancient form of transport, withdrawn two weeks previously. That was the 7th-century ferry crossing between the East End and Monkwearmouth, known as "the ha'penny ferry" and operated by the River Wear Commissioners. In latter decades they used steam vessels named after two of them, *Sir Walter Raine* and *W F Vint*. The two double deckers on the "experimental" un-numbered bus service ran non-stop over the 1.3-mile route described below, initially in both directions during the morning, mid-day and late afternoon peak periods. On 9 September, the service was altered to run from south to north in the morning and mid-day peaks only, and from north to south during the mid-day and late afternoon peaks only.

High St E & W - W'mouth Bridge - Wheat Sheaf - Roker Ave - Church St N - Hallgarth Sq

Following the serving upon Sunderland Corporation by the Traffic Commissioners of an order to abolish the 8d universal return fare, the Corporation lodged an objection and a public hearing was held on 30 October 1957. The Commissioners' decision was then to raise the universal fare to 10d for three months, and then to 1s 0d. The first rise coincided with a general increase in fares on 2 December 1957, the basis then being:

$1^1/2$ d: 0.84mile   2d: 1.34 miles $2^1/2$ d: 1.84 miles
3d: 2.34 miles, then $1/2$d for each additional 0.5mile

By the autumn of 1957 there was a growing demand for workers' special buses to operate into the Docks premises rather than to terminate near the entrance gates in Barrack Street which was the regular Docks service terminus. From just inside the harbour entrance at the mouth of the river, the South Docks complex stretched for practically a mile parallel to the sea shore, separated from it by a narrow strip of land. The area comprised the Tidal Basin; the ship repairing yard of T W Greenwell & Sons with two graving dry docks; the Half Tide Basin and a small single dock; the large Hudson Dock North; the North Eastern Marine Engineering Co's premises; the shipyard of Bartram & Sons from which the ships were launched directly into the sea; and Hudson Dock South and the Hendon Dock. More than 2,000 people were employed in this zone and some had to walk about half a mile for their buses. The River Wear Commissioners opposed a bus service on the grounds of hazards such as tight curves, narrow bridges, overhead obstructions, the risk of grounding and unprotected railway traffic movements. Following discussions, on 14 November 1957 a demonstration was arranged in which Guy 136 carried representatives of all parties concerned on a tour within the docks premises. This led to the commencement of late afternoon peak time special journeys on 18 August 1958. Buses entered the docks by Barrack Street Bank, picking up near the works canteen west of the Hudson Dock North/Half Tide Basin swing bridge, leaving by Pottery Buildings Bank. At a later date, buses returned via Barrack Street Bank and from 18 January 1960 were to cross the swing bridge to pick up at Bartram's entrance.

Between late 1957 and May 1958, further inroads were made into the utility stock and only Pickering Guy 68, Massey Guys 65/69 and Duple Daimlers 71/72 remained. Massey Guys 64/74 became driver-training vehicles following withdrawal and the similar 62/70/75-77 became 37-41 in the fleet of the Grimsby & Cleethorpes

The ordering of eight metal-framed five-bay Northern Counties bodies for Daimler CVG5 chassis was a surprise, that Wigan concern never previously and never again receiving SCT's custom. They entered service in March 1958 as 217-224 and were of attractive, neat outline, sporting push-open vents at the front of both saloons. The first new buses since 1949 to have normal staircases, they had upper saloon framing of aluminium alloy.
(Copyright holder not known)

being acquired in 1961 by Jaguar Cars Ltd which only in mid-1960 had also acquired the Daimler car and bus-building concerns. Both Guy and Daimler production of bus chassis was to continue but most of Guy's single deck output would go for export.

As well as six new Guys, there were two Daimler orders pending. The first was delivered during February-March 1958 as 217-224, CVG5s once more but surprisingly with bodywork by the Northern Counties Motor & Engineering Co Ltd of Wigan (NCME). This concern had received orders from Middlesbrough and Stockton but never previously from Sunderland Corporation. These functionally attractive bodies were well-finished, did not have Roe-type staircases and sported *forward-facing push-open* ventilators at the front of both saloons. Those Committee Room remarks about stuffiness appear to have made some impact! They were only marginally heavier than Roe Daimlers 209-215, even though 217-224 had 24-volt electrical equipment. Allocated to Hylton Road Depot, their arrival enabled 1946 Massey Daimlers 15-18 to be withdrawn, eliminating another minority-make engine, Daimler, from the fleet. A single deck AEC Reliance demonstrator was on loan during March 1958 and in view of developments several years ahead, this was a significant event.

In the 1958 Annual Report Mr Morton referred to the nationwide Asian 'flu epidemic and said it had cost the Department £6,000 through loss of passengers, high sickness payments and additional overtime working. Attracting new employees had proved unusually difficult the previous summer and then at one point during the 'flu outbreak there had been a record number of 99 platform staff (15 per cent) absent. The recruitment position had eased by early 1958, Mr Morton said, assisted by union agreement to the direct engagement of a limited number of drivers (that is, allowing them to by-pass the usual procedure of becoming conductors first). Regarding passenger totals, the Corporation's 1958 figure was only some 300,000 less than that for 1952 (including trams) whereas the national municipal average *loss* was some 12 per cent greater. In this respect Sunderland had been fortunate. SCT's fares still compared well with those many other undertakings, too.

During March - May 1958, the final dozen forward-engined Daimler and Guy double deckers, also the last with five-cylinder

Joint Transport Board, lasting until 1961/62. The G&CJTB General Manager, Mr John Rostron, had been with SCT during 1950-55, latterly as Deputy General Manager and regularly as centre-half for the Transport Department football team! Obviously Mr Rostron knew of the high standard to which the Guys had been rebuilt (62 as recently as summer 1955) and his Board was getting value for money at £200 per bus. A Gardner-engined bus would probably have a scrap value of about £100.

There was a mishap at Pallion on the afternoon of 1 December 1957 when 86, an air-braked AEC with only crew aboard, ran out of control from the Watson Street loading point, down the steep Woodbine Terrace, overturning on to its offside. It was not seriously damaged but some windows were broken and fuel oil escaped from the filler pipe. Luckily the crew escaped unhurt. It is believed that the driver was new and had mistaken the low air pressure audible warning for something else. After righting, 86 was found capable of moving under its own power. Following repairs, with the other five AECs it carried a typewritten notice in the cab: *"When buzzer operates, rev engine to build up air."* A few weeks later, Daimler 119 made an inauspicious start to 1958 by being involved in a scrape with two trees and a lamp standard in Park Avenue on New Year's Day. Minor injuries were sustained by the driver and two passengers. Later in January Mr Morton was short-listed for the General Manager's post at Huddersfield but the appointment was not offered to him and he was to remain in charge at Sunderland for almost another ten years.

Changes were made to services 10/11 on 13 January 1958. On Monday to Friday all regular journeys were operated between Grangetown and Pennywell as service 10 on a six-minute frequency. This meant that as the previous co-ordinated frequency had been five minutes, on weekdays the section between Ford and Pennywell now had a bus every six minutes instead of every ten. During the same month a single deck Guy Warrior demonstrator bus was on loan but there were to be no further orders for Guy following one for six 'deckers already in the pipeline. Indeed, during 1960 Guy Motors Ltd was to go bankrupt (due largely to the cost of developing the revolutionary but unsuccessful Wulfrunian double deck chassis),

Only weeks after the entry into service of 217-224, a further twelve Roe-bodied vehicles arrived, the chassis order being split equally between Daimler (225-230, type CVG5) and Guy (231-236, Arab IV 5LW). Daimler 230 here carries a goodly load at the Wheat Sheaf. The twelve 1958 Roe bodies, well-finished and stylish, had teak framing for the lower saloon and aluminium alloy for the upper but all future new buses were to have steel-framed bodies. All the Daimlers and one of the Guys (231) lasted into the PTE era. *(Copyright holder not known)*

In 1958, rebuilt Pickering-bodied utility Guy 68 was converted to open-top for use on sea-front tours. In a livery of two-tone blue, it is seen trundling along at Seaburn while something on the landward side attracts the attention of the children upstairs. The bus kept its 6LW engine (a replacement for its original 5LW some years previously) and in 1960 was to be illuminated and decorated for the undertaking's diamond jubilee. Ironically it was only some a few weeks after 68's alteration that Daimler 72 was similarly converted, by accident. *(Copyright holder not known)*

Fleet age analysis (by year of entry into service)

1943	7*	1949	6	1954	65
1944	3*	1950	12	1956	1
1946	3	1951	12	1957	9
1947	12	1952	12	1958	20
1948	12	1953	8		

*3 rebodied (total 6), re-entered service 1955

A historic demonstrator was operated by SCT in October/November 1958. Registered VKV 99, it was the first Daimler CVG built to the new length of 30ft for two-axle double deckers, legalised on 1 July 1956, and the first bus to be powered by an example of the then newly-introduced Gardner 6LX engine, although fitted originally with a 6LW. Further details are contained in Appendix 1, but it is mentioned here because at that time Mr Morton was notably against operating 30ft-long double deck buses with seats for 70-plus. In a trade press article entitled, *What Size Bus Do You Take?*, he argued that they offered no appreciable advantage over 27-ft long buses with 63 seats. He believed that the answer for many services lay in smaller buses, one-man operated, on better frequencies and with cheap fares. That was a significant observation in view of what was to follow during the next decade.

engines, were placed in service as 225-230 and 231-236 respectively. All had handsome Roe bodywork of traditional "Roe" outline, employing teak framing for the lower saloon and aluminium alloy for the upper, a Roe option since about 1955. They also had forward-facing window vents at the front of each saloon. A unique feature of 231-236 among British-operated Guys was that their preselector lever was not of the usual gear-stick type but set in a left-hand quadrant below the steering wheel as with ten six-wheel Arabs supplied to Johannesburg. The body of 236 also incorporated some experimental plastics materials for the upper saloon ceiling panels and some seat backs. Daimler 229 was fitted with fluorescent lights in the lower saloon, a form of lighting to become almost universal on PSVs. 225-228 were allocated to Hylton Road Depot and 229-236 to Fulwell.

There were two developments involving utilities during the summer. Pickering Guy 68 emerged on 1 July as an open-topper in two-tone blue, for use on a 6d four-mile sea front Roker - Whitburn tour at weekends and during the local holiday period, weather permitting. Objections from Anderson and Wilson of the Economic Bus Service had been overruled. Ironically, only the following month, Duple-bodied Daimler 72 also became an open-topper when it was *decapitated* under Wellington Lane railway bridge at Deptford (which was never on a bus route). Rumour had it that the General Manager was hopping mad, and no wonder. 72 replaced pre-war Daimler 36 as snowplough in 1959 and held that role for some years.

At this point the fleet had reached a watershed. No further forward-engined buses were to enter service and the future was to see some radical changes of attitude and practice.

Fleet summary, 31 Aug 1958

8 single deck:	2 Atkinson 4LW, 2 Guy 5LW, 4 Guy 5HLW
174 double deck:	6 AEC 9.6-litre, 15 Crossley 5LW, 68 Daimler 5LW, 34 Daimler 6LW, 40 Guy 5LW, 13 Guy 6LW
Fleet total:182,	not including Massey Guys 64/74 (used for training) and Duple Daimler 72 (out of service).

In April 1959, unique constant-mesh Roe Guy 139 took a holiday in Wigan where it was fitted with a Cave-Browne-Cave heating and ventilating equipment at the Northern Counties works. This picture shows the frontal intake apertures, later partially blanked off, and the side louvres necessary with this system. 139 was to remain unique in this respect too and outlived the other eleven Guys of its batch, ultimately surviving into preservation. *(Copyright holder not known)*

There were changes to town centre routeings in autumn 1958, as listed here:

previously, from various earlier dates

4/5 (Villette Rd), 9 (Docks via Boro' Rd), 10/11 (Grangetown via Hendon) - south along John Street

19/20 (Circle), 21/22 (Tunstall Rd/Grangetown via Ryhope Rd), 23/24 (Thorney Close/Durham Rd) - south along Fawcett St

from 10 Nov 58

4/5 - south along Fawcett St; 21/22 - south along John St

In March 1959, 86 was the first AEC to be withdrawn, the others following by autumn 1960. November 1959 was to see the withdrawal of Duple Daimler 71, leaving Massey Guys 65/69 as the only utilities in normal service, open-top 68 running seasonally. For the year ending 31 March 1959 there was a small rise in passenger journeys but during the final three months a fall had occurred. *The downward trend in this figure was about to begin.* By 1967 the total would fall more than 22 per cent and the average number per mile by

One of the many demonstrators loaned to SCT was this low-height, integrally-constructed AEC-Park Royal Bridgemaster, used in May 1959 and pictured in Durham Road approaching Thorney Close. Compared with the Department's own buses of elegant Park Royal outline this was an ungainly-looking thing, lacking the grace normally associated with that coachbuilder's products, although the green of its Liverpool livery was not unlike that of the SCT fleet. It featured coil-spring suspension, bouncy at the rear and independent at the front. *(Copyright A B Cross)*

15 per cent. This tendency had commenced in London from 1949 and in many other towns and cities by the mid-1950s. Sunderland differed somewhat in that the downward spiral began so late. It may be that the combination of low fares and frequent services had helped a little to hold back the tide, but the inexorable rise in the popularity of the motor car and the effect of other social changes could not be kept in check for any longer.

The summer of 1959 was sunny and warm. On 12 July a seasonal Docks Tour was introduced from Seaburn, taking in the East End of the town for a fare of 9d (children 6d). It was a failure and therefore not repeated. Promenade Tours with open-top Guy 68 did somewhat better although still taking below-average receipts. On 15 August, joint service 48 journeys terminating at Castletown (Primary School) were extended by some 400 yards via Hylton Castle Road to The Briars.

A minor fall in passenger traffic over most of the day, more marked in the evenings, on Sunday mornings and on Saturdays before 8.30am, led to the following changes from 23 November 1959:

Frequency reduced from 5 to 6mins (co-ordinated) or from 10 to 12mins (single)

Mon-Fri after 7pm, all day Sun

4/5   Villette Rd - Red House South/North

21/22   Dene Estate - Grangetown - Tunstall Rd

23/24*   Ambleside Ter/Seaburn* - Thorney Close/Durham Rd

Now extended to/from Seaburn Camp (see service 19, below)

All day Sun-Fri

19*/20+ Circle - Seaburn Camp* via Park Ave/Seaburn via Roker+

All journeys now to/from Seaburn only (see service 24, above)

+Sun morning journeys via Park Ave as 19*

The late 1950s comprised a period when double deck bus design was being turned from back to front. Leyland Motors had developed the 30ft-long 78-seat Atlantean model in which the engine was mounted transversely at the rear under a bustle-shaped cover. With a set-back front axle the Atlantean had its entrance at the extreme front where, it was claimed, the driver could oversee loading and unloading. Although as stated earlier Mr Morton was by no means convinced of the value of larger double deckers, SCT did have an Atlantean demonstrator on loan from Leyland during September 1959. The local press quoted a transport spokesman as

saying that the new bus was too big for the town. Clearly this referred to the seating capacity, which tied in with the Mr Morton's attitude. Even that, however, was to change in due course.

On 3 October 1959, the Omnibus Society, of which Mr Morton was President for the year, visited Sunderland Corporation Transport Department. The Northern Branch Secretary of the Society was Dr R P Doig and he complimented Sunderland on being "a go-ahead bus town". Two further services for workpeople were introduced during 1959, although it has not proved possible to ascertain precisely when. Both operated to and from Doxford's shipyard at the south end of Alexandra Bridge at works starting and finishing times only. They were:

14   Doxford's - St Luke's Rd - Portsm'th Rd - Grindon La - Sunningdale Rd - Springwell Rd - Humbledon (Prospect)

Unnumbered
    Doxford's - St Luke's Rd - Ford - Holborn Rd - Prospect - Durham Rd - Thorney Close (non-stop Doxford's - Prospect, minimum fare 4d; experimental, no known details of withdrawal)

SCT received trade press coverage again on 9 December 1959 when new and futuristic-looking bus stop signs were introduced in Fawcett Street. They were shaped like a tall mushroom with a shiny stainless steel pole as the stem and a large flat sign displaying the number, route and destination of the relevant services at the top (although omitting the words "bus stop"), capped by a shallow dome with powerful lighting. So the 1950s ended. At their beginning it had been clear that the trams could not last for much longer and would have to go. All the associated upheaval had taken place before 1955. Now, as the 1960s were about to come in, it was plain to the far-sighted General Manager that the bus-operating industry was to face challenges which it would need to be prepared and equipped to meet. That would mean more upheaval and, in Sunderland at least, of a most radical nature too.

It's a warm 1959 day in Union Street, the railway station is still bomb-scarred and the conductor prevents Daimler 110 from toppling over. The bus illustrates the effect of the standard indicator arrangements on its appearance. This was the one that was altered and had its seating capacity increased to 58 in 1955 but ran until 1957 licensed as a 56-seater. The radiator shell fluting has been painted gold, a short-lived practice carried out only spasmodically during the late 1950s, Western SMT being another operator favouring it. Terminal points reverted to the highway following the vacating of the bus station site (off picture, left) on 19 August 1956. *(Copyright R Marshall)*

8 - Far-reaching Proposals

At the beginning of the 1960s, the Sunderland Corporation route network was vastly greater than in 1939. As well as covering all the former tram routes, buses now served housing areas on what had been rural land at Hill View, Farringdon, Springwell, Thorney Close, Grindon Village, Pennywell, Hylton Castle, Red House and Seaburn Dene. Here is a list of the bus services as at January 1960 which the relevant map will illustrate:

Driver-only services

1	Town - Alexandra Rd - Hill View - Grangetown
6	Grangetown - Humbledon - Ford - Pallion - Southwick

Crew-operated services

2**	Town - Farringdon (Antwerp/Atlantis Rds)
3**	Town - Plains Farm - Farringdon (Allendale/Avonmouth Rds)
4/5	Villette Rd - Town - Red House Sth/Nth
7	Town - Prestbury Rd
9	Docks - Town - Helmsdale Rd
10/11	Grangetown - Hendon - Town - Pennywell/Ford
10x	Town - Fordham Rd *(peak time deviation of 10)*
15	Docks - Town - Telford Rd
16*	Town - Grindon Village (Gleneagles Rd or Glencoe Rd) or Pennywell Shops
17*	Town - Hylton Castle
18	Seaburn Camp - Southwick - Pallion - Humbledon - Springwell
19/20	Circle - Town - Roker - Park Ave (19 only) - Seaburn
21/22	Tunstall Rd/Grangetown - Town - Newcastle Rd - Fulwell/Dene Est *(see map for clarification)*
23	Ambleside Terr - Newcastle Rd - Town - Thorney Close
24	Seaburn - Fulwell Rd - Town - Durham Rd
48*	Sunderland - Castletown or North Hylton

* Joint with NGT
**Joint with NGT & SDO

Peak time services (crew-operated)

12/13+	Humbledon - Ford - Pallion - Southwick - Fulwell (B Bell)/Red House (Ramillies Rd)
14+	Humbledon - Grindon La - Pennywell - Pallion - Doxford's

+ At unknown future dates, service 13 was split at Southwick, some journeys then operating via N Hylton Rd to Hylton Castle (Clacton Rd); service 14 was extended from Doxford's, via Alexandra Bridge and Southwick to Fulwell (Blue Bell)

Other services (night, peak times or as required)

c = crew-operated   d = driver-only operated

Fordham Rd or St Luke's Cross - Football Ground **c**
Town - Football Ground **c**
Ferry Service (Hallgarth Sq - High St E) **c**
Night Service (Castletown Rd Ends - Town - Humbledon) **d**

Tours, school and additional special services not included

Note. *Some services had regular or peak time short workings with 'x' suffix to service number*

1960 was also the Transport Department's diamond jubilee year and a commemorative brochure was produced. It reviewed the Department's achievements, pointing out that 15 per cent more mileage was being operated with 15 per cent fewer vehicles than seven years previously. Open-top Guy 68 was decorated and illuminated suitably, proclaiming "60 years of public service" on the sides. Power for its illuminations was provided by a generator driven from the transmission shaft.

The figures for the year ending 31 March 1960 were reasonably encouraging. It will be seen from Appendix 2 that continued economic operation had resulted in a slight drop in working expenses per mile and that operated mileage was down for the first time in 26 years. Despite the fall in working expenses per mile, the general trend in costs was to remain upward, accelerated by a staff pay award and improved working conditions early in the fiscal year 1960/61. Average gross weekly earnings of waged employees then became £12 3s 8d, an increase of nearly eleven per cent. Consequently, fares were raised on 27 June 1960. Those with $1/2$d denominations were abolished, apart from the $1^1/2$d minimum. Despite these rises, SCT fares were still appreciably below the national average. The new structure was:

$1^1/2$d - 0.6mile; 2d - 1.1 miles; 3d - 2.2 miles etc, up to 6d - 5.5 miles and over

A new driver-only operated service was introduced on 4 July 1960 catering for a private housing development at High Barnes, west of Ettrick Grove. At the same time, other services were revised for greater operating economy. Co-ordinated services 19/20 (Seaburn - Circle) were now split at Chester Road/Kayll Road/Ormonde Street, and lower Cleveland Road had no service running along it. Details are given below.

Old

7	Town - Prestbury Rd
15	Docks - Town - Telford Rd
19	Seaburn - Park Ave - Town - Circle

New

7	Docks - Prestbury Rd (see 15 below)
8	Town - High Barnes, via Holmeside - New Durham Rd - Eden House Rd - Hunter's Hall Rd - Mount Rd - Woodville Cres - Oatlands Rd *(one way)* - Woodland Drive* *(one way, terminus)* - returning via Wavendon Cres *(one way)* - Woodville Cres etc.*(not Sun; Mon-Fri until 8pm only)*
15	*Withdrawn.* Town - Docks section covered by 7. Town - Telford Rd section partially covered by 19
19	Seaburn, then as before to Chester Rd, then Ormonde St - Cleveland Rd and as former 15 to Telford Rd

*To be extended 25 Mar 63 by about 250yd to Wavendon Cres/Melbourne Pl

Returning to engines, Mr Morton's eagerness to standardise on the reliable and economical Gardner was no secret. After the elimination of Crossley, Leyland, Daimler and 7.7-litre AEC engines by 1957, the last of the AEC 9.6-litre units went at the end of October 1960 when 82 was withdrawn. The fleet was now all Gardner-powered, but only until January 1961 when three AEC Reliance saloons arrived as 32-34. Their chassis designation, 2MU3RV, meant series 2, *Medium-weight, Underfloor-engine, 3 = five-speed synchromesh gearbox, Right-hand drive, Vacuum brakes.*

No new buses were purchased in 1959 and 1960, but three AEC Reliances with synchromesh gearboxes entered service early in 1961 as 32-34. They introduced a revised and pleasing single deck livery comprising a cream lower half with decorative polished mouldings as shown here by 32, although it has undergone a little front-end modification. In 1969/70 they were to be repainted with the an area of cream sandwiched between green panels and roof. The attractively-proportioned 41-seat bodywork was by Roe with the now-standard Park Royal outline and the interior furnished to a high standard. New single deckers were to outnumber double deckers for the remainder of the undertaking's history. *(Copyright R Marshall)*

They had the AEC type AV470 engine, marketed as the 7.75-litre unit. Semi-automatic transmission had been specified but synchro-'boxes were accepted for quicker delivery. On the home market there was no single decker to fit SCT's Gardner specification except the heavy and expensive Daimler Freeline.

The Corporation's policy was now to introduce new buses offering greater comfort and so the 41-seat dual-door Roe bodywork was finished to a high specification. All future bodies for SCT were now to be based on metal framing which in this case was supplied by Park Royal, and single deckers were to have dual doors. Features included:

- Seats with higher back squabs and deeper cushioning, upholstered in London Routemaster-pattern moquette of red, black and yellow with tartan-like effect, used by permission.
- Interior lining panels trimmed with red leathercloth.
- Ceiling panels of Darvic plastics material, colour-impregnated pastel blue (not needing to be repainted) with darker blue beadings.
- Window finishers stove-enamelled in primrose.
- Heaters and fluorescent lighting fitted.
- Blue Cronapress continuous strip bell-push above windows on each side.
- Luggage pen positioned immediately aft of the centre exit.
- Chassis frame dropped ahead of front axle, allowing a two-step entrance up to the fare-paying point, with a further step to the saloon floor.

The reorganisation of traffic movement through the town centre was implemented on 20 March 1961, based on one-way flows northbound/southbound along Fawcett/John Streets respectively. Buses had begun to operate on that principle a week previously which reduced problems on the day of the change. The new scheme did relieve congestion and help bus operation but of course it was only a palliative. Traffic volume kept increasing and before the end of 1963, the number of vehicles registered in Sunderland was to exceed 21,000, more than double the 1954 figure. Meanwhile, the Department continued to be beset by spiralling costs, reducing passenger figures and recruitment difficulties among other problems. In the year to 31 March 1961, working expenses per mile had risen almost seven per cent. Nevertheless, excellent results were being shown on the engineering side. Although craftsmen were earning an average of 72 per cent more than in 1952, maintenance costs had not increased over the same period. Vehicle condition was not suffering, however, as the number of breakdowns in the year was the lowest

ever recorded. Overall fuel consumption of 10.23mpg was also a record figure, never to bettered. Passenger journeys regrettably fell by more than four per cent. Concerning platform staff, out of 142 applicants sent by the Ministry of Labour, only 33 were considered suitable to employ and eighteen of those left within three months. When the Corporation applied to raise the minimum fare from 1^1/2d to 2d (leaving other fares unchanged), to be implemented on 24 July, the Chairman of the Licensing Authority said the increase was "too modest". The distance of 1.1 miles allowed for 2d was twice the national average and only four others out of 94 operating municipalities had managed to keep a three-halfpenny fare for so long.

A further new council development of some 1,700 houses at Town End Farm, north of Washington Road and facing Hylton Castle estate, began to receive a service on 10 April 1961. Numbered 28, it also was an equal joint SCT-NGT operation and the route was initially:

Town (Fawcett Street) - Wheat Sheaf - Southwick - Washington Road - Town End Farm (Blackwood Road/Bayswater Avenue)

In an internal report, Mr Morton had expressed interest in rear-engined double deckers of 30ft length. The rear-engined Leyland Atlantean has been mentioned, but Daimler's broadly similar Fleetline had gone into production in 1960 and what attracted Mr Morton to the it was its availability with Gardner engine. A Fleetline demonstrator was loaned to Sunderland during May 1961, although this example was then powered by the refined 8.6-litre turbocharged Daimler CD6 unit.

Operating economies were the aim again when the General Manager proposed some major changes to bus services for summer 1961. The threat of unofficial strike action on the part of some crews resulted in the declaration of a dispute between the General and Municipal Workers' Union and the Corporation. The main points of objection were *(a)* the proposed extension of driver-only operation to parts of crew-operated services (along Newcastle Road to Dene Estate and from Ettrick Grove to Docks), *(b)* the reduction of some frequencies, and *(c)* the cutting of some running times. The matter was referred to the National Joint Council for the Municipal Road Passenger Transport Industry for arbitration. Following its decision in October, a modified version of the original proposals was to be introduced early in 1962.

A further seven AEC Reliances had been ordered in December 1960, along with one Daimler Fleetline. The Reliances were 35-41, delivered July 1961 - January 1962, similar to 32-34 internally but differing in having AEC Monocontrol semi-automatic gearboxes, air brakes and 41-seat bodywork by Willowbrook, a make new to SCT. Significantly, in July 1961 the bare chassis of the Fleetline ordered eight months previously was exhibited on vacant land off Union Street. During two weeks of that month, too, a Gibson ticket machine was borrowed from London Transport, issuing LT tickets! It was used as a quick way of collating information about the distances travelled by passengers. Unlike SCT's Setright machines, the Gibson recorded the numbers of each denomination of ticket issued.

Again the Department's chronic and serious staffing problems were highlighted following an unfortunate accident at 8am on 25 November 1961. A bus collided with a private car, seriously injuring the

The brighter livery and embellishments were applied to the four Guy LUFs when they were repainted. 26, followed along Holmeside by an Alexander-bodied Leyland Atlantean of Sunderland District, is an example. *(Copyright R Marshall)*

Further AEC Reliances followed in 1961/62 but these had 41-seat Willowbrook bodies, again attractively proportioned and with high interior appointment. There were two orders, the first (35-41) with semi-automatic gearboxes and the second (42-45) with synchromesh. The basic design of the bodies was as specified by the British Electric Traction Federation as its standard, adapted in this case to SCT's requirements, Willowbrook being one of several coachbuilders that produced BET basic standard bodies for various operators. They are represented by 42 carrying a fair load from Dene Estate on 28 March 1968.

(Copyright R Marshall)

occupants who included a pregnant woman. The bus driver had worked his rest day the previous day and finished at 11.39pm, starting his next shift at 5.15 on the morning of the accident. He stated that he had fallen asleep at the wheel due to fatigue. But for the collision he would have gone on to work a double shift that day. As a result of this regrettable event, traffic staff were instructed to arrange duties strictly in accordance with regulations. Consequently, on the following day, a Sunday, no fewer than ten late-shift driving duties could not be covered and the journeys that they would have operated did not run. Five days later, Mr Morton caused some raised eyebrows at the Transport Committee meeting by referring to the accident and suggesting that municipal bus workers should have higher pay. The figures he put forward were a basic rate of £12 10s 0d for drivers, compared with the actual rate of £10 3s 6d

which was enhanced to an average of £14 0s 0d with overtime. Further ideas were a 40-hour five-day week instead of the existing 84-hour eleven-day fortnight. Transport work was unattractive because of its irregular, unsocial hours and low basic wages. Only by improving basic pay and conditions, Mr Morton submitted, could the transport industry hope to attract enough people of the right calibre to eliminate the need for excessive overtime working. In return for improvements there would have to be more efficient practices, including wider acceptance of driver-only operation. Mr Morton's proposals would of course have required a change of attitude throughout the industry and probably some amendments to the negotiating mechanism for pay and conditions.

The amended service revisions were implemented on 15 January 1962 and may be summarised as follows:

Old		New	
1 **d**	Town - Alexandra Rd - Hill View - Grangetown	1 **d**	Dene Est - Newcastle Rd - Town - Alexandra Rd - Hill V - G'town
8 **d**	Town - High Barnes	8 **d**	Dene Est - Newcastle Rd - Town - High Barnes
7	Prestbury Rd - Town - Docks	7	(see 7/9 , 20, 21, below)
9	Helmsdale Rd - Town - Docks	7/9	Helmsdale Rd - Town - Docks via High St/Boro' Rd **a**
		15 **d**	Ettrick Gr - Cleveland Rd - Chester Rd - Infirmary - Town - Newcastle Rd - Dene Estate
16*	Town - Grindon Vill (Gleneagles Rd or Glencoe Rd) or P'well Shops	16*	Grindon Village - Pennywell Shops journeys withdrawn, Mon-Fri
19	Seaburn - Park Ave - Town - Telford Rd	19	Seaburn - Park Ave - Town - Chester Rd c (see 24, below)
20	Seaburn - Roker - Town - Circle	20	Prestbury Rd - Hylton Rd - Town - Chester Rd
21/22	Dene Est/Fulwell - Ryhope Rd - Town - Grangetown/Tunstall Rd	21	Prestbury Rd - Hylton Rd - Town - Ryhope Rd - Grangetown
		22	Seaburn - Roker - Town - Ryhope Rd - Tunstall Rd
23	Ambsde Terr - Nwcstle Rd - Town - Thorney C	23	Fulwell (Blue Bell) - Fulwell Rd - Town - Thorney Close
24	Seaburn Camp - Fulwell - Town - Durham Rd	24	Seaburn Camp - Fulwell Rd - Town - Telford Rd (see 19, above)
28*	Town - Town End Farm (Blackwood Rd/ Bayswater Ave)	28*	Town - Town End Farm (Blackwood/Brunswick Rds)
		29*	Town - Town End Farm (Brunswick/Blackwd Rds via Hylton La**)

a *Docks Circle - 7 via High St & Boro' Rd, 9 via Boro' Rd & High St*   * *Joint with NGT*

c *Buses went along Kayll Rd and turned at its junction with Henderson Rd but showed "Chester Rd" as destination*

d *Driver-only-operated*   ** *ie Hylton La off Washington Rd (not off Hylton Rd)*

Note. After going along Newcastle Road and Charlton Road, the driver-only single deck services now penetrating Dene Estate ran initially as shown in '**a**' below. When Alston Crescent had been extended into Dene Estate and curved to meet Dovedale Road, buses went either way around the one-way circuit shown below in '**b**':

a   Station Rd - Alston Cres - Ambleside Terr (northbound)/Keswick Av (s'bound) - Dovedale Rd - Dene Estate terminus

b   Station Rd - Alston Cres - Dene Estate terminus - Dovedale Rd - Dene Lane - Fulwell (Blue Bell) - Station Rd
and vice versa. Service 1 approached the terminus via Alston Crescent and services 8/15 via Dovedale Road. They did not turn around at the terminus but continued, service 1 buses changing to 8 or 15 and and vice versa. Co-ordinated frequency Dene Estate - Newcastle Rd - Town: 5min.

The pioneering Daimler Fleetline was 250, entering service in April 1962. It broke new ground in several ways, introducing the rear-engined concept, a brighter livery of cream and green in a somewhat Birmingham-like format, decorative polished mouldings. There were also distinctive peaked roof domes at front and rear which were part of SCT's specification and helped to reduced the blandness of the outline. The 70-seat bodywork was Roe-built to Park Royal design, attractive and comfortable inside even if the external aesthetic appeal was debatable. In this Brougham Street scene, 250 shows the final version of "Binns" lettering as introduced in 1966, using the group's own "in-house" style which made the slogan look more like advertising and less like part of the bus's livery. *(Copyright R Marshall)*

The revisions were designed to achieve maximum operational efficiency and to offset some of the loss of passenger traffic. In a local press article published three days before their introduction, Mr Morton had called the changes a "new deal" for 1962. He pointed to the need for greater economy and for adaptation to changing travel patterns. There was in fact a two per cent saving in mileage run which would have been greater but for the Town End Farm extension and increased frequencies. Fuel tax, however, was to rise by 3d to 2s 9d per gallon on 28 July 1961. By the financial year-end there were indications that the fall in passenger traffic had slowed.

One change that created a widespread adverse reaction from passengers was the withdrawal of the Circle service dating back to the early tramway days of 1901. There were protests, petitions and letters to the editor of the *Echo*. People contacted their councillors. They said they wanted to travel direct from Hylton Road to Chester Road and the Royal Infirmary (New Durham Road). Mr Morton replied that they still could: in the opposite direction, clockwise via Town on the revised service 20 instead of anti-clockwise via Kayll Road However, the furore did not die down and eventually something was done about it, of which more in due course.

The Daimler Fleetline chassis that had been displayed in the town during the previous July, a CRG6LX model, was delivered on 10 March 1962 as 250, with amply-powered Gardner 6LX engine, *Daimatic* semi-automatic four-speed gearbox and Park Royal-framed Roe bodywork, all to be standard to SCT's future Fleetlines (except for three with the 6LW engine). Mr Morton had originally recommended the purchase of three rear-engined double deckers but

the Committee would agree only to one. A new numbering series had now commenced, the existing highest double deck bus number being 236. There were several notable features about the Fleetline 250, as noted below.

- Peaked roof domes at front and rear, incorporated to create a distinctive appearance.
- Straight staircase, ascending rearward.
- Seating capacity kept to 70 for greater comfort (Fleetlines delivered from 1963 had 77 seats).
- Seating trim dark red leathercloth edged with blue upstairs and dark green downstairs.
- Downstairs ceiling panels aluminium, stove-enamelled cream; upstairs light blue Formica laminated plastics material.
- Heaters and fluorescent lighting fitted (to become standard).
- Additional destination indicator positioned above the fourth nearside lower saloon window, the next fourteen Fleetlines having this feature, subsequently removed.

A new livery format was used, comprising green lower saloon panels and cream waistrail, with mostly cream above. While the bus indeed was eye-catching, the body styling comprised merely superficial changes to a basically insipid and unexciting design. Just as it had been displayed as a chassis before bodying, the now-complete 250 was displayed before entering service on the same site alongside 1949 Crossley 103 and 1954 Daimler 154, illustrating how bus design had developed over the previous thirteen years. The Fleetline started running initially from Fulwell Depot on services 23/24.

From 9 to 15 April 1962 there was a regrettable unofficial strike of bus crews, condemned by the Union. Again, they had grievances over plans for further driver-only operation and schedule changes. It had a most adverse impact on passenger traffic and may only have served to accelerate the existing decline. During the first six months of the financial year a loss of £24,000 was incurred by the Department

There were further developments with single deckers during that spring and summer. The two Roe Guy saloons, 7/8, withdrawn the previous autumn, were put back into service during May 1962. Then over the following two months 42-45, further AEC Reliances, were delivered. Their Willowbrook bodies were similar to those of 35-41 and their chassis to 32-34, that is, with five-speed synchromesh gearboxes. The return to "stick-change" transmission was made to secure better delivery dates from AEC. Within about eighteen months, fourteen Reliances had entered the fleet. Their standards of comfort were high and their acceleration outstanding but they suffered from mechanical problems such as cylinder head gasket failures. The engine vibrated excessively when idling and the mountings had to be modified. Fuel consumption was no better than that of the Fleetlines which were about three tons heavier.

Yet more service revisions took place on 9 July 1962. Here is a summary of them:

Old

7/9	Helmsdale Rd - Town - Docks via High St/Boro' Rda
19	Seaburn - Park Ave - Town - Chester Rd
28•	Town - Town End Farm (Blackwood Rd/Bayswater Ave)
29•	Town - Town End Farm (Brunswick/Blackwood Rds)

New

7*	Ettrick Grove - Cleveland Rd - Town - High St - Docks - Boro' Rd - Town - Newcastle Rd - Dene Estate
9	Helmsdale Rd - Town
19	Seaburn - Park Ave - Town - Circle°
28•	Extended via Bexhill Rd to new terminus at junc Baxter/Berwick Rds
29•	Extended via Baxter Rd to new terminus at junc Baxter/Berwick Rds

* Driver-only operated
° Restored Chester Rd - Kayll Rd - Hylton Rd link
• Joint with NGT

Note. There were some increases and some reductions in certain service frequencies implemented on the same date. Subsequently, perhaps during 1963 (there is no mention of it in records), service 7 appears to have ceased running between Town and Ettrick Gr, leaving that section to service 15.

Four driver-only services now went through Dene Estate on a circular course with a co-ordinated five-minute frequency to/from Town, changing service at the terminus, as follows:

Service	Into Dene Est	Out of Dene Est	Service
1	via Dovedale Rd	via Alston Cres	8
7	via Dovedale Rd	via Alston Cres	15
8	via Alston Cres	via Dovedale Rd	1
15	via Alston Cres	via Dovedale Rd	7

There were more Daimler Fleetlines in the offing and the first, 251, was exhibited on the Roe stand at the Commercial Motor Show in September 1962, remarkable for being displayed *bearing advertising* in the form of the legendary "Binns" exhortation. 251 entered service the following month and four more (252-255) arrived in November. All five differed from 250 in having 4in-deeper upper saloon windows which did improve the appearance somewhat, helping to reduce still further the top-heavy appearance already mitigated by the lower overall height. In February 1964, 255 was to receive a short parcels rack in the lower saloon and two extractor fans positioned at the rear of the upper saloon. The parcels rack was to become part of the future specification for Fleetlines but not the extractors. Later, the rack was to be removed from all buses when passengers complained of bumped heads. Old buses withdrawn during 1962 were driving school Guy 64, the first few of the Crossleys and more Massey Daimlers. Crossleys 13/100 became mobile polling booths with the General Purposes Committee until 1972 when they were acquired by a Bolton dealer, subsequently being preserved (see Appendix 1). Several service developments took place toward the end of 1962 as summarised here:

3 Nov 62

Weekends and public holidays: adult fares increased by 1d, children's by 1/2 d (estimated to yield an additional £60,000 p/a)

11 Nov 62

Sers 4/5, 10/11 re-routed southbound from John St to reach Boro' Rd via Athenaeum St & Foyle St

26 Nov 62

Sers 17, 28/29 (Town - Hylton Castle and Town End Farm respectively) co-ordinated and until 11 Feb 63, alternate buses to Hylton Castle again entering the estate via Canterbury Road. (There was to be minor re-routeing within Town End Farm from 19 Oct 64, allowing better co-ordination from Blackwood Rd)

1 & 12 Dec 62

Express services to Football Ground introduced from Prestbury Road and Red House respectively as required

Succeeding 70-seat Fleetlines 251-255 and 77-seat 256-288, all Roe-bodied, had slightly deeper upper saloon windows than 250 as photo comparisons show. This helped the appearance somewhat. Here 260 of 1963 has a leisurely rest in John Street, plainly on a Sunday.
(Copyright holder not known)

Early in 1963 the Transport Committee, after rejecting the idea of a new bus garage for the whole fleet at Camden Street, Southwick, decided to extend the Wheat Sheaf works to house all buses instead. The plan turned out to be a very long-term one. Although the office block at the Wheat Sheaf was to be rebuilt in 1967, the buses remained at their existing garages until well after the Corporation Transport undertaking had ceased to exist. It was decided also that single deck buses without rear service number boxes should be fitted with them. Underfloor-engined Guys 26-29 had had them from new and only the AECs were now treated, the additional aperture being positioned to the nearside of the rear registration number with the blind operated by an *exterior* handle. Future single deck buses were to have the aperture situated centrally above the rear window, operated from inside. Additional Sunday morning journeys for churchgoers were started from 11 February 1963 on these services: single deck 1/7/8/15; double deck 3, 4/5, 10/11, 16, 17/28/29. Two days later, the Town Council considered whether the whole bus fleet should be fitted with heaters. At that time only about 11 per cent of buses had them and although the idea was rejected on the grounds of cost, it was decided that all future buses should be equipped with them. (By this period heaters were generally becoming a standard fitment nationally.) At the same time, the Council approved the purchase of three *Atkinson* single deckers, the reasons for which will be discussed later.

For the year ending 31 March 1963 there was an alarming drop of 5.6M (seven per cent) in passenger journeys, the largest so far and the highest proportion since 1934. It was estimated that the 1962 strike was responsible for nearly a quarter of the reduction but a poor summer in 1962, some of the severest weather on record early in 1963 and a sharp rise in local unemployment had made the situation worse. Mr Morton expressed disappointment at the number of collisions during the year which had risen from 344 to 428. A significant proportion was of a relatively minor nature and the rise was attributed to the inexperience of drivers with the new forward-entrance type of bus. By now, the wisdom of having 12 per cent of mileage driver-only operated was now showing clearly. As at 31 March 1963, although the overall average traffic revenue was 33.19d per mile, that for the driver-only services was only 22.2d, emphasising the need for economical operation. By May 1963, utility Guy 65 and Massey Daimler 99 had been withdrawn. The only remaining Crossley was 21 which had been the first post-war one delivered. In that month, nine new Fleetlines were delivered as 256-264, similar to the previous ones other than for having 77 seats (43/34). Although later in the year a further Fleetline and an Atlantean were to visit as demonstrators, only Fleetlines were to be acquired for future double deck needs. Following a national pay award in April which added some £56,000 to the Department's wage bill, cross-town fares were increased on 29 July 1963. They became a summation of the previous separate fares into Town and beyond the Town fare stage. The usual weekend surcharge of 1d (^{1}/2d for children) was added to normal fares in this new structure:

2d: 1.1 miles; 3d: 2.2 miles; 4d: 3.3 miles and so on up to 9d: 8.8 miles

The Promenade and Circular Tours had not run in 1962 but were restored in 1963. It was a poor summer, however, and the Promenade Tour operated only 96 miles and took only some £5 in receipts. Although starting off favourably in 1958 when receipts had been £82, subsequent years saw only £45, £24 and £15 taken before the 1962 break. The service was not continued after the 1963 season and the open-top Guy 68 was to be officially withdrawn on 30 June 1964. Circular Tours continued at least until 1967 but it has not proved possible to trace precisely when they ceased to run. At

Whitsun and during the 1963 shipyard holiday fortnight a special direct service was operated between Red House Estate and Seaburn. It continued for several years although again, further details do not appear to be extant.

In September 1963, starting with 254, the Fleetlines began to be fitted with service number blinds at the rear. The blind was housed in a protruding box mounted next to the lower saloon nearside rear window in the cut-away section, with operation from the inside. Then at the end of September 1963 a landmark in the fleet history was passed. Massey Guy 69, the last remaining wartime utility bus still with its original body (not including open-topper 68), was

It was a surprise when three 45-seat Marshall-bodied Atkinson underfloor-engined single deckers were acquired in 1963/64, numbered 46-48, after Atkinson had ceased home-market bus production. The attraction with these was the availability of Gardner power, in this case 6HLW. 46 had a constant mesh gearbox originally and the gear lever can be seen in this shot. After seven months it exchanged this 'box for a semi-automatic unit, much more suitable and with which 47 and 48 were fitted from new. *(Copyright R Marshall)*

withdrawn. Another three months would have made it twenty years from the date of 69's first being registered. Two factors were remarkable here. One was that when the utilities were built during the war it could hardly have been envisaged that any of them would last so long. The other was that similar Guy 65, withdrawn five months previously, had been the penultimate of the sixteen utilities to have its body rebuilt, in May 1955, but 69 had been among the earliest, indeed only the fourth, in July 1953. Even after withdrawal it was retained for driver-training until being sold in October 1964. (Some utilities elsewhere lasted even longer, however.)

On 7 October 1963, services 10/11 (Pennywell/Ford - Grangetown via Hendon) were altered. Since 1958 all Monday - Friday journeys (except for some peak time ones) had been on service 10 and now all Saturday journeys were made the same on a revised frequency. The same month also saw the beginning of a somewhat drawn-out wrangle between the Transport Department and local bus and coach operator W H Jolly of South Hylton. Jolly's had run a South Hylton - Hylton Road/Kayll Road service for 40 years, using single deckers and originally connecting with the Circle trams. They then applied to extend their service to Town. The Corporation made its own application to run a service to South Hylton and each operator opposed the other's application. Ford Parish Council and its higher tier, Sunderland Rural District Council, supported Jolly and objected to SCT at the hearing before the Chairman of the Licensing Authority. Thirty villagers from South Hylton also gave evidence in Jolly's favour. The Corporation had monitored Jolly's buses from the kerbside and provided information as to loadings and travel patterns between South Hylton and Town. A suggestion by the Corporation that the service should be operated jointly was not acceptable to Jolly. The Chairman granted Jolly's application and their service was extended to Town via St Mark's Road and the Royal Infirmary, not picking up locally east of Kayll Road corner. The Corporation lodged an appeal and this was heard before a Ministry of Transport Inspector at Newcastle in July 1964. A report was then sent to the Minister of Transport, Mr Ernest Marples, stating that the Licensing Authority had not given sufficient weight to all the evidence put by the Corporation. The Labour Party won the general election in October 1964 and the Minister of Transport then became Mr Tom Fraser. He dismissed the appeal in April 1965 and SCT buses never were to run to South Hylton.

The first of the ordered Gardner 6HLW-engined Atkinson 45-seat single deckers entered service on 21 December 1963, the other two following in January 1964. There had been a change to the regulations in 1961 when the maximum permissible length and width of PSVs in Britain had been increased respectively from 30ft to 36ft and from 8ft to 8ft $2^{1}/2$in. The new Atkinsons, 46-48, were of the greater width and an intermediate length of 33ft 8in, permitting increased seating capacity. Another new make bodywork was introduced, Marshall of Cambridge, at that time a regular supplier to the BET Federation. The bodies for Sunderland Corporation were of basic contemporary BET specification with curved glazing at front and rear, although detail design was to SCT requirements and interior finish was comparable with that of the AEC Reliances. The floor level was somewhat high and the steps uncomfortably deep for less agile passengers. 46 differed from 47/48 when new because it was fitted with a David Brown *constant mesh* five-speed gearbox (nothing so advanced as synchromesh, which itself was hardly suitable). Other than for Guy 139, the last new buses with constant mesh gearboxes had been 1947 Crossleys 9-14, all of which were now withdrawn. It seems clear that Mr Morton had entertained second thoughts about this detail and although it was too late to stop 46, the other two were modified before completion to incorporate a Self Changing Gears semi-automatic four-speed 'box with full pneumatic operation. The gear selection lever was housed in a floor-mounted pedestal identical to that used by Leyland on forward- and underfloor-engined models, and an automatic lock-up fluid clutch was fitted. 46 was modified to have the same gearbox and transmission in July 1964. Two of this unusual trio, 46/48, survive in preservation at the time of writing.

The choice of Atkinson arose from SCT's unhappy experience of the AEC Reliance, referred to previously. A Gardner-powered chassis would have been the obvious preference but at that time there was no such underfloor-engined model on the open market. SCT made a tentative approach to the Jaguar group to see whether Daimler or Guy could produce one. Although only three such buses were then required the Department was prepared to order six-off if this would have been a more suitable number for the manufacturer. The enquiry came to nothing and apparently only Atkinson was able to fill the bill, even though that firm had not produced any home-market bus chassis since 1958. As it happened, the three for Sunderland were the final ones to be built by that firm whose total then came to a mere 116 for British operators over the thirteen year span that Atkinson had been building PSV chassis.

A Government document published in November 1963 under the chairmanship of Professor Colin Buchanan, an adviser to the Minister of Transport, caught the attention of the operating industry and authorities. Required as a possible basis for future transport policy formulation and entitled *Traffic in Towns*, among its chief conclusions were:

- The scope and urgency of the traffic problem were great; and it would become much worse.
- Public transport had a future role and should be cheap; there would be a need for some limits on private car use in busy areas; but the Report placed no strong emphasis on the potential of the bus in minimising the scale of future difficulties.
- The cost and size of new developments would be enormous; and while accommodating the increase in motor vehicles would necessitate vast expenditure, it would promise large new revenues.

The Committee then asked the General Manager to prepare a document on the current problems of the Department and the future role of municipal transport in the town. Mr Morton's illustrated report, *People and Transport: the Future of Public Transport in Sunderland*, was published in February 1964 after only three months. During that time, some 10,000 people had been interviewed any many studies undertaken. The subjects surveyed were: passenger trends; shopping; works travel; housing development; football traffic; road traffic conditions current and future; the case for a central bus station; bus design; the importance of staff; and the future financial position. There were eight tables and 23 diagrams in the report. While the Buchanan Report did acknowledge that public transport did have a role in shaping future traffic and travel patterns, to some extent it bowed to the inevitable growth of motor vehicles. Mr Morton, however, insisted that buses had a key part to play and that they should be accorded special facilities. His other main conclusions were:

1 - Better (possibly subsidised) public transport may prove cheaper than the cost of accommodating traffic growth.

2 - A flat fare of (say) 3d might attract longer-distance local riders (the principle of the postage stamp: one rate for any distance).

3 - New buses should have greater comfort, better facilities and good acceleration.

4 - Services should be regular and reliable, with bus-segregation in busy traffic zones.

5 - A central bus station would provide greater passenger convenience.

6 - Bus staff pay and conditions needed improvement in order to attract quality personnel in the quantities needed.

7 - The 1930 Road Traffic Act had consistently favoured company operators and was overdue for amendment.

8 - Private cars were uneconomical in their use of road space compared with buses (in terms of traveller-usage).

9 - The River Wear needed two new bridges in Sunderland and the Wheat Sheaf junction needed major attention.

10 - The football ground may have to be moved to a point west of the town centre.

11 - Meetings of the Joint Traffic Sub-Committee should be held every two months and a Traffic Investigation Unit created.

Three thousand copies were circulated locally, nationally and abroad. To say that it was years ahead of its time would hardly be correct. It was a document for the 1960s, anticipating the future. Rather, it could be argued that Governments, planners and others influencing policy have long been years *behind* the times as these words are written. Some of the Morton proposals were to be implemented but others only gathered dust.

In the Annual Report for 1964, passenger journeys showed a reduction and operated mileage a rise, both marginal. There had been a drop in the number of platform accidents from 226 to 185, attributable to more buses fitted with platform doors. Over the same period, the number of collisions had risen from 428 to 530, most of them again minor and involving front-entrance buses. At its meeting on 15 April the Town Council decided that the balance of £4,393 from the Reserve and Renewals Fund should be set against the nett deficit and the remaining sum of £20,629 transferred to the General Rate Fund. It would mean a rise in the rates charge of $2^{1}/2$d in the £. An opposition amendment to raise fares rather than allow the deficit to fall on the rates was defeated. Mr Morton reported to the Council that there had been charges of inefficiency levelled against the Transport Department. (These were from members of the public and a prospective councillor, using the correspondence columns of the local newspaper.) However, as the General Manager pointed out, of the 94 transport-operating local authorities in the country, Sunderland had the *sixth lowest* running costs per mile. The Transport Committee Chairman, Councillor J W Jamieson, told the Council that the Department was there "primarily to serve people and not to serve profit." In the face of criticism about subsidising fares from the rates, he added that this concept was not revolutionary but was already being practised by fifteen municipal undertakings. (In effect, the Council was adopting the Buchanan principle that public transport should be cheap.)

A further operating economies were effected on 11 May 1964, as noted below.

Old

9	Helmsdale Rd - Hylton Rd - Town
20	Prestbury Rd - Hylton Rd - Town - Chester Rd

New

9	Helmsdale Rd - Hylton Rd - Kayll Rd - Chester Rd - Town
	9 then continued as 20 (below) and vice versa
20	Town - Hylton Rd - Prestbury Rd

The Helmsdale Rd - Hylton Rd - Town section was now withdrawn

16	Frequencies increased, except Sun, Town - Grindon Village but Pennywell Shops journeys withdrawn

The 9/20 change eliminated an overlap along Hylton Road between Town - Hylton Road/Kayll Road. Objections came from Hylton Lane Estate residents who had again lost their link with Millfield. An elderly disabled widow organised a 2,000-signature petition but the Helmsdale Road - Town service via Millfield was not to be restored for two years. At this time, further Massey and now Roe Daimler CVG6s were withdrawn, and rebodied Guys 79/81 were transferred to the driving school.

Another dozen Daimler Fleetlines arrived during July/August 1964 as 265-276. Although all were delivered with the XGR registrations, 271-276 were re-registered with ABR-B year-suffix marks before entering service. These twelve buses were the first new ones to have intermediate points on the destination blind printed in lower-case lettering, although subsequent fitting of older blinds meant a reversion to capitals in some instances. 269 was involved in an serious accident on 24 August 1964 while going to Prestbury Road. Leaving the town centre, in Silksworth Row it mounted the kerb, knocked down a lamp post, collided with a stationary car and then embedded itself in a shop front. Twenty-eight passengers and the crew suffered various injuries. There was an alarming aspect to the collision and it was to be repeated to some extent on 8 June 1967 when Fleetline 253 mounted the footpath in John Street and collided with the concrete canopy of Jopling's store. In both cases there was serious distortion of the upper saloon frontal framing, and the frameless dome and panelling below it were bent like thin card. This was in contrast to what was to happen in 1968 when 1954 Roe Daimler 203 collided with an overhead gantry at the Docks. Frontal damage in that case was much more localised toward the centre of the dome area which had traditional metal framing. The inference here is that the damage to the Fleetlines would have been more restricted and the passengers better protected had there been framing above waistrail level at the front.

269 was delicensed for repairs until 20 March 1965 and then sported two new features. One was a single-piece flat windscreen, slightly recessed, in place of the original two of which the offside one was recessed. This new detail was to be incorporated in the future specification for Fleetline bodies. 269's other novelty was a centre-exit door, claimed to speed up loading and unloading. As it was only of single width and in practice, 269 was to remain unique in this respect, many passengers tended not to use the exit door. The door itself had a sensitised edge and would open to touch, eliminating the possibility of trapping people or articles accidentally. Two years later, following an unfortunate event in which an elderly woman died after being trapped in an exit door and dragged along, it was decided that all the driver-only buses should have sensitised exit-door edges plus an audible and visual warning to the driver when doors were not fully closed and an interlock to prevent gear-engagement until warnings had been cancelled manually. 269's lower saloon seating capacity was now reduced from 34 to 30. Not many weeks after repairs, 269 had another mishap on a late-night journey when it mounted the footpath at the Hudson Road/Borough Road fork and crashed into the Seamen's Mission. There were no passengers aboard and no-one was hurt but 269 then needed further front-end rebuilding.

By mid-1964 another development of 511 council houses was springing up at Carley Hill to the north of High Southwick. A half-hourly driver-only service was commenced from Town (Fawcett Street) via a circuitous 2.7-mile route. Later, a further works service was also started and there were complex changes to services 4/5, 10/11, saving two buses. Details are given here:

17 Aug 64

25	Town - Newcastle Rd - Thompson Rd - Ridley St - Shakespeare St - Carley Hill (Emsworth Rd/nr Exmouth Sq) *To be altered 5 July 1965 , Sun only - Ser 1 from Grangetown diverted from Dene Estate to Carley Hill*

26 Oct 64

Works service (unnumbered)

	Prestbury Rd - Hylton Rd - St Luke's Rd - Westmoor Rd (n'bound)/ St Luke's Rd (southbound) - Alexandra Br - Southwick, *altered soon afterward -* northbound buses kept to St Luke's Road, with some journeys in both directions via Pallion Trading Estate.
4/5	previously Red House South/North - Town - Tatham St - Villette Road;
10/11	previously Pennywell/Ford - Town - Hendon - Grangetown (11, Sun only): 4/5, 10/11 altered and co-ordinated south of Town and alternate Mon - Sat Pennywell journeys truncated at Ford. Journeys from Red House S on ser 4 now via Hendon to Blue House Hotel (at Commercial Rd/Corporation Rd)*. Journeys from Ford now as ser 11 via Tatham Street and Corporation Road to Blue House** *Destinations shown:* * 4 - Blue House via Hendon; ** 11 - Corporation Rd & Villette Rd (although buses turned into Corporation Rd immediately before reaching Villette Rd).

The complete circuit for a bus (using Grangetown as a starting-point for example) then became:

From Grangetown as **10** to Ford - then from Ford as **11** to Corporation Rd - then from Corporation Rd (ie Blue House) as **4** to Red House S - then return via Red House N as **5** to Villette Rd - then return as **5** to Red House N - then return as **4** via Red House S to Blue House - then from Blue House (ie Corporation Rd) as **11** to Pennywell - then return as **10** to Grangetown

During collision repairs in 1964 the opportunity was taken to fit the new 269 with a centre exit, although it was not entirely a success, and a single-piece flat windscreen. The position of the staircase was unchanged but seating capacity was reduced from 77 to 73. No other double deck buses had dual doorways but Fleetlines 277-288 arrived with the single windscreen. A lady who has obviously just alighted from 269 at the front waits to cross Leechmere Road. *(Copyright R Marshall)*

1964 Fleetline 276 joins the rear of a convoy picking up in Fawcett Street, some passengers probably having heeded the advice of the buses and shopped at Binns (left of street). This picture illustrates the rear end of the standard Sunderland Corporation Fleetline, in this case complete with service number box. Other buses are (from nearest) a Leyland Panther, Crossley-bodied Guy 189, and a Northern Routemaster and Alexander-bodied Atlantean. *(Copyright "Oubeck")*

In the wake of his report on the future of public transport in the town published six months previously, in August 1964 Mr Morton submitted a detailed internal report entitled *Project for a New Bus Station,* accepted by the Transport Committee and subsequently, the Town Council. The Central Bus Station then began its gestation. Four months later, the Transport Department began to place advertisements in the Friday edition of the *Echo* each week, detailing service changes, publicising the use of its buses for private hire, inviting ideas and suggestions, and generally giving helpful transport information. The advertisements were worded and phrased in a simple and friendly manner, and clearly were of enormous value.

There were still serious difficulties arising from the high turnover of platform staff. During 1964, out of a total of 662 such employees, 194 conductors and 51 drivers left. The recruiting age for conductors had been lowered to 18 years in April 1964 and indeed, one third of those engaged since then had been under the age of 20. It was hoped that a bonus scheme, which was then at the planning stage and eventually to be implemented on 18 January 1966, would help to retrieve the situation somewhat.

1965 was a year of significant decisions. On 10 February the Town Council approved a contribution from the rates toward the expected deficit. At the same time, it accepted that the distance covered by the 2d minimum fare should be reduced from 1.1 miles to 0.6, to be implemented on 29 March. The Council was split on this matter, the Labour majority winning out against the Conservatives and Progressives who supported an amendment to raise the fares by a penny on weekdays (they were still raised at weekends) as well as to shorten the distance of the minimum fare. The opposition parties plainly believed that transport should be paid for by the people who used it. Labour believed it should be subsidised by those who *benefited* from it, representing a larger section of the community than mere users. The whole issue was in fact a time bomb, already ticking.

A further report, entitled *A Modern Transport System for Sunderland,* was published in March 1965. From its far-reaching proposals there was to be created a new and revolutionary form of running buses in the town. Driver-only operation was already well-established and the report envisaged all services being run with driver-only single deckers ultimately as a means of keeping fares low, frequencies high and of slowing the decline in passenger usage. However, the most radical of the proposals was the introduction of a flat-fare system (although this had been mentioned by Mr Morton in an internal report dated 21 January 1965). Payment of fares would not be only by cash but by metal tokens which the passenger would insert into a ticket-issuing machine. It was expected that as tokens would be cheaper than a cash fare, most passengers would use them. This would speed-up loading as transactions involving the driver would be greatly reduced. The document also analysed passenger loadings and trends, gave the specification of new vehicles which would be 36ft long with a passenger capacity of 66, anticipated substantial improvements in staff pay and conditions, discussed financing, and examined the effect on bus operations of traffic conditions.

The Annual Report for 31 March 1965 recorded that the rate of passenger-loss had slowed to 93,000, about 0.12 per cent. Mileage and receipts were both up a little but regrettably the gap between working expenses and traffic revenue had narrowed uncomfortably. The nett deficit of £52,418 was transferred to the General Rate Fund as decided by the Council. Boarding and alighting accidents had gone up by seven to 192 but collisions had reached 561, a "disappointing" increase of 31. Mr Morton referred to the "far-reaching" proposals in *A Modern Transport System for Sunderland* and said they were being investigated by the Committee. (Sunderland's system was still relatively efficient. Of 82 municipalities for which data is available, as at 31 March 1965 only nine had lower running costs per mile.)

Daimler Fleetline demonstrator 7000 HP returned to Sunderland on loan during May 1965, now fitted with a Cummins

68

The first of relatively many rear-engined single deckers comprised a trio of Leyland Panther Cubs new in 1965 and numbered 49-51. Marshall built the 45-seat bodywork, broadly similar in many respects to that on Atkinsons 46-48 and Panther Cub 49 captured at Ettrick Grove exhibits the curved rear windows popular on single deckers during that era.
(Copyright holder not known)

engine. This make was to feature again later in conjunction with the Daimler name, of which more in due course. Also in May 1965, another new type of engine came to the fleet. It was the Leyland O.400 of 6.5 litres swept volume, powering the Leyland Panther Cub PSURC1/1R chassis of which three examples entered service as 49-51. The Panther Cub was the 33ft 5in-long version of the 36ft and more powerful Panther, the engine being mounted horizontally and longitudinally behind the rear axle in both cases. Transmission was through the now-standard four-speed direct-acting semi-automatic epicyclic gearbox. Leyland's version of this, originating with SCG, was marketed as the *Pneumocyclic*. As its name implied, it was air-operated, in this case and indeed as with all future SCT buses having electrically-actuated control. The Panther Cubs were an improvement on earlier driver-only single deckers in that the floor level was significantly lower, although they were not truly a "low-floor" type as there were three steps from ground level to the saloon. When the Panther Cubs arrived, Guy saloons 7/8 were withdrawn for the final time.

12 June 1965 was the day of an unusual departure from Sunderland. It was not of a bus but of a delegation to Denmark comprising Cllr J W Jamieson (Transport Committee Chairman) along with Alderman R Wilkinson (Mayor and Vice-Chairman), two other elected members, Mr Morton and two senior officers, accompanied by two union officials. The five-day visit was made in order to observe the Copenhagen bus undertaking with its driver-only operated flat-fare token-payment system. Copenhagen's method was to be the model for future developments in Sunderland.

The following month saw a significant vehicle loan to the Corporation. It involved a Bristol RELL6G chassis (meaning Rear-Engined, 36ft-Long, Low-frame, 6-cylinder Gardner (HLX) engine) with Eastern Coachworks 54-seat bodywork. What was significant was the fact that only in July had Bristol and ECW products returned to the open market after nearly two decades of supplying solely to the State-owned operating sector. Clearly the attraction to Mr Morton was the availability of a Gardner engine in a suitable single deck chassis from a builder with a long reputation for producing robust, reliable and economical models. Subsequently an order was placed with Bristol.

It was on 14 July 1965 that the Council approved the conversion of all bus services to driver-only operation with a flat-fare system and the use of automatic token machines. The Transport Department then got to work on shaping the numerous details in preparation for the first phase of the scheme, to be implemented in a little more than a year. On 6 December there was a minor service change when the Town terminus of service 16 to Grindon Village was altered from John Street to Union Street.

To this point the 1960s had been one in which for practically all operators, particularly those in industrial areas, continually rising costs and falling passenger numbers were a constant source of anxiety. Passenger-loss was generally accelerated by increased fares and reduced frequencies. Endemic platform staff shortages and increasing road traffic congestion were creating havoc with what were usually well-organised and otherwise reliable services. In Sunderland most of these issues were about to be tackled radically, but ideology would apply a firm brake before long.

69

9 - Sooner Them Than Us

1966 was to prove historic, seeing the start of the radical action to which reference has been made. The year started modestly with a diversion of service 4 to reach the new Downhill estate on 4 January, later service changes also being outlined below.

Old			New	
4 Jan 66				
4	Blue House - Red House S		4	Altered beyond Ravenswood Rd via Kingsway Rd to Downhill
				(Kidd Sq) - <u>returning as 5</u> via Red House N to Villette Rd
2 Mar 66				
8	Town - Infirmary - Mount Rd - High Barnes		8	Withdrawn except for some peak time journeys
15	Dene Est - Newcastle Rd - Town - Infirmary -		15	Alternate journeys beyond Cleveland Rd to High Barnes
	Chester Rd - Cleveland Rd - Ettrick Gr			or Ettrick Grove (shops)

Note. Although it is not recorded, it may be that service 7 ceased operating to Ettrick Grove at this time and was confined to the Dene Estate - Docks section only.

11 Jul 66				
23/24	Thorney Close/Telford Road - Fulwell		23	All jnys to Fulwell extended to Seaburn until 8pm daily
	(Blue Bell)/Seaburn Camp		24	All 24x jnys to Seaburn extd as 24 to Seaburn Camp until 8pm daily.

The nett deficit for the year ending 31 March 1966 was £80,871, the Council already having decided to transfer the slightly greater anticipated sum to the General Rate Fund, equivalent to a 3d rate. Collisions were down slightly to 552 and platform accidents to passengers down by 73 to 119, exactly half the figure for 1961/62. The 4.3 per cent decline in passenger journeys was attributed to a poor summer and prolonged winter along with the fares increase taking effect on 29 March 1965.

Twelve new Fleetlines, 277-288, had been delivered during February/March. 277-279 were 6LW-powered and 277/278 were registered out of sequence. They were the final new double deckers to be bought by SCT. More sensationally, in July, new bus 53 arrived, the first of three dozen Copenhagen-inspired 36ft-long rear-engined single deckers comprising two orders, one for 33 Leyland Panthers (52-84) and the other for three Daimler Roadliners (85-87). Although the standard wheelbase of both types was 18ft 6in long, on SCT's Panthers it was shortened to 17ft 6in by moving the front axle rearward, leaving more room for the double-width entrance doors and platform. All had eye-catching Strachans bodywork and were intended for the first phase of conversion to total driver-only operation. The numbering sequence of the new buses encroached on that of the remaining wartime vehicles which were therefore renumbered (see Appendix 1 for all details). The choice of bodybuilder was a surprise. Strachans (Coachbuilders) Ltd of Hamble, Hants, previously London-based and not historically a major manufacturer (but at that time building 15 single deck bodies for London Transport), submitted the lowest tender, possibly because other concerns saw that the unusual specification would disturb their production methods and therefore quoted much higher. Sunderland's Panther 53 had been taken from Strachans to London on 22 July 1966 and inspected at the Ministry of Transport headquarters. On arrival in Sunderland it was exhibited in the town centre for a fortnight. Then Roadliner 87 called at London in September to be a Daimler exhibit at the Commercial Motor Show. At the conception stage, a plywood full-scale mock-up of the forward part of the saloon and cab had been built in the Wheat Sheaf works, enabling the Department to obtain a clear picture of various body specification details. Major bodywork features are summarised here:

In a blaze of publicity the innovative flat-fare token-operated system was introduced on 5 September 1966. The conversion of some services to driver-only operation could be implemented only in part due to late completion of the delivery of 33 Leyland Panthers (52-84) and three Daimler Roadliners (85-87), all with Strachans 47-seat bodywork with provision for 19 standing. Built to SCT specification, the body design was visually a most striking one, incorporating forward-sloping pillars at window level and a flat windscreen. In this scene at the Ministry of Transport office in London the first to be completed, Panther 53, is inspected by officials and reporters before delivery to Sunderland. *(Copyright Busways Travel Services)*

70

Strachans standard steel-framed, alloy-trussed, corrosion-resistant construction *(although in later years the framework did suffer from some rusting)*.

Roof domes, front & rear waist to skirt panels of glass-reinforced plastics.

Single-piece windscreen and forward-raked side window pillars.

Double-width front entrance and centre exit to reduce loading and unloading times.

Interlocking to prevent doors being opened while bus in motion.

Two 9-in platform steps from platform to saloon, with gently ramped floor from front to rear. No steps or footstools in saloon.

Public address system with two internal speakers plus an external one for driver to address intending passengers.

All doors flush-fitting to improve appearance and facilitate cleaning.

Side windows of standard dimensions to facilitate replacement.

Seat top rails of SCT design spray-covered with red nylon. Upholstery red PVC material.

Smoking in rear half only. Two extractor fans at rear end.

Interior window frames cream plastics finish with azure blue Warerite fillers between.

Ceiling panels cream Darvic with light blue mouldings.

Ticketing equipment. In cab: change-giver*; quick-action token dispenser*; twin-roll Ultimate ticket machine**.

On right of entrance: Autoslot token machine**.

*Supplied by Sporrong & Co, Stockholm
**Supplied by Bell Punch Co, Uxbridge

The Panther was Leyland's maximum-length rear-engined single deck chassis, powered by a horizontal Leyland 9.8-litre O.600 engine, a well-established type, and with four-speed semi-automatic Pneumocyclic gearbox having electro-pneumatic control. The chassis frame was stepped, that is, low at the front, slightly lower within the wheelbase then upswept over the rear axle and the gearbox and engine, and ramped gently to the rear. Daimler's Roadliner differed in that while the chassis frame rose over the rear axle, it was dropped to low height again toward the rear. The Roadliner also had air suspension and its engine was mounted vertically at the extreme rear of the frame, a position made possible by its being the compact 9.63-litre Cummins V6-200 unit of American origin with V-formation cylinders. It was "over-square"

LEAVE BUS BY CENTRAL DOOR

At the London event the Joint Parliamentary Secretary to the Minister of Transport, Mr Stephen Swingler (left), is shown by Mr Norman Morton (right) how to place a token in the Autoslot machine which will then issue a ticket. Looking on (centre) aboard No53 is Mr Gordon Bagier MP, representative for Sunderland North constituency. *(Copyright Busways Travel Services)*

(the cylinder bore was greater than the piston stroke) and had the then relatively high governed speed of 2,100rpm.

The target-date of 5 September 1966 was met for the introduction of the flat-fare and token scheme to the whole of SCT's bus network and the attention of the transport industry was on Sunderland. Some transport managers viewed innovation with caution and a widely-held attitude clearly was "sooner them than us"! 2.5 million tokens had been minted by Imperial Metal Industries Ltd at a cost of £5,531 and the principles of the system were:

Any journey other than cross-town or certain works journeys - one token or cash fare 4d.

Tokens, 2s 9d for ten (discount of 0.7d on cash fare) - obtainable from driver or conductor on bus, or from Transport Dept offices at Union St and Watson St, Wheat Sheaf head office or Jopling's department store.

Cross-town and some works journeys - 4d cash fare.

On new driver-only buses

Passengers with tokens - to board by rearward half of entrance, place token in Autoslot machine on right, obtain ticket from machine without involving driver.

Passengers paying cash fare or buying tokens from driver - to board by forward half of entrance.

When paying 2s 9d on bus - choice of either 10 tokens for future journeys or 9 tokens plus ticket for that journey.

Children - either 2d cash fare or two could travel for one token (although initially only about 10 per cent of them did).

Elderly concessionary pass-holders - 2d cash (no tokens).

On jointly-operated services

Tokens not accepted by NGT but 12-journey ticket available for 3s 4d, equivalent to the same price per journey as tokens.

There were problems with cross-town and works journeys and so after two weeks, following consultation with the Traffic Commissioners, tokens were accepted for these. On the new buses, the main door-operating control was a sixth position in the gear-change "gate". This kept the bus in neutral and so prevented it from being started while any door was open. Additionally, the driver could not only operate the exit and entrance separately but could control each leaf of the entrance door independently in the event of failure of the Autoslot. In that case, the rearward leaf would be kept closed and all passengers would board by the forward half and tender cash or tokens to the driver.

On the day that the scheme was implemented, some services were altered and it was planned to convert others to driver-only operation. Unfortunately, only six of the new Panthers (52-57) had arrived instead of the seventeen promised by Strachans, which had a serious effect on arrangements. This is how the sequence went:

Original plan for conversion to driver-only operation, 5 Sep 66

9	Town - Chester Rd - Kayll Rd - Helmsdale Rd
19	Seaburn - Park Ave - Town - Circle
20	Prestbury Rd - Hylton Rd - Town - Chester Rd
21/22	Prestbury Rd (via Hylton Rd)/Seaburn (via Roker) - Town - Ryhope Rd - Grangetown/Tunstall Rd

Modified plan

19/22	to be run with new buses initially but due to shortage, were run with mixture single deckers and crew-operated double deckers, if available, until 20 Sep
9/20/21/26	to be converted 3 Oct, but no single deckers available until 24 Oct and then mixed buses used until 21 Nov

Existing services altered, 5 Sep 66

6	Grangetown - Southwick extended via Carley Hill to Witherwack (driver-only)
25	Town - Carley Hill extended to Witherwack (driver-only)
48	Sunderland - N Hylton (crew-operated) - now run by NGT only but SCT buses to be reintroduced 11 Oct 69

New driver-only service, 5 Sep 66

26	Town - Hylton Rd - Helmsdale Rd

31 Oct 66

7	Dene Estate - Docks - now via Boro' Rd, returning via High St (see 25)
25	Witherwack - Town, extended - High St - Docks, returning via Boro' Rd

Witherwack was a relatively small new housing development half a mile west of Carley Hill, buses terminating at Wiltshire Road. The 26 service was virtually a restoration of the

With token journeys now at 3.3d and the cash fare 4d, this meant a rise for passengers travelling up to 2.2 miles and a reduction for those travelling up to 3.3 miles (if tokens were used) or more (as against cash or tokens) on weekdays. Due to the 1d weekend surcharge that had been applied previously, the majority of passengers had not in fact experienced an increase in the average cost of their travel. Mr Morton said that early observations showed no rise in the number of longer journeys even though they were now significantly cheaper. As to the new buses, they were popular with the public and drivers. Their acceleration was good and they were manoeuvrable despite their length. One of the few criticisms about them was the high exit steps. Mr Morton said that it was hoped to improve this on future new buses. Council approval subsequently was given to spending £1,840 on modifying the design of 20 buses then on order so that the entrance steps would be 7in high instead of 9in and the exit steps 8^1/$_2$in instead of 10in.

At the end of the year the token system was awarded the "accolade for enterprise" by the local government trades union, NALGO. It was indeed a bold attempt to assist the move toward full driver-only operation as a possible means of arresting the decline in passenger journeys by reducing working expenses and so keeping average fares relatively low and service frequencies relatively high. It did, of course, also tackle the perpetual difficulty with platform staff shortage and in effect anticipated some of the aims of the Transport Act, 1968. In December 1966 a further unprecedented shift was made when two women conductors were trained as drivers. There had been two wartime female tram drivers but Joyce Beaumont and Pat Entwhistle made history on the buses.

The flat-fare and token system was officially opened by the then Minister of Transport, Mrs Barbara Castle PC MP (later to be Baroness Castle), on 6 January 1967. At a special meeting of the Town Council followed by a commemorative dinner hosted by the Mayor, Mrs Castle praised the town's pace-setting transport system. During the afternoon she had been taken on a short tour of the town on one of the new single deckers, Driver Harry Hickman, a veteran of driver-only operation, showing her how to use the Autoslot token machine. Before coming to Sunderland that day, the Minister had

previous service 9 linking Helmsdale Road with Millfield. Driver-only conversion problems were exacerbated by the fact that although there was a no-redundancy agreement, in anticipation of the changes the number of conductors had been reduced through natural wastage without engagement other than of recruits who undertook to be trained as drivers. Over the main summer period the Department had coped by using students seasonally but these were leaving by early September. As a result, while awaiting delivery of the new single deckers, a huge amount of mileage was lost over the whole network due to the shortage of conductors. On one Saturday, 173 journeys could not be operated. The remaining new buses entered service to 22 December, enabling older Daimlers, Guys and Atkinsons 30/31 to be withdrawn

On 21 November 1966, Mr Morton reported that the changes had shown that driver-only operation could be applied successfully to services running through densely-populated areas so long as the vehicles, equipment and fare structure were specially designed for the purpose. Four out of five passengers were potential token-users but of that group, only about 40 per cent were using tokens, which was disappointing. More passengers used tokens on the driver-only buses than on the double deckers, and five out of six people bought their tokens on-bus. Before 5 September 1966 the average fare paid had been 3.1d.

This picture of the driving cab of 53 shows the change and token dispensers (left). The switches on the left of the fascia are for the wipers, interior and exterior lights while those on the right are for the auxiliary equipment, including master door switches. It may be observed that the gear selector is in the neutral "doors open" position, this form of control ensuring that a gear be engaged only with the doors closed. *(Copyright Busways Travel Services)*

Much thought went into the detail of the body specification for the 1966 single deckers and a full scale mock-up of the front end, shown here, had been erected in the Wheat Sheaf works. *(Copyright Busways Travel Services)*

talked to members of the Tyneside authorities about a possible future single authority to be responsible for public transport in the area (and other conurbations).

When the Transport Committee met on 30 January 1967 it heard from Mr Morton that spiralling costs, almost entirely outside the Department's control, were outstripping all efforts to economise.

A decision was then made to apply a 3d rate levy and to increase the token and cash fares later in the calendar year. The minority of Conservatives on the Committee were adamant that the ratepayers should not have to bear any greater burden for the town's transport. In the light of developments only months away, their point bore great significance. Seemingly, however, they failed to grasp the concept of what came to be termed "non-user benefits".

A minor alteration was made to the routeing of service 15 at High Barnes on 20 February 1967. Then on 13 March service 16 (Town - Grindon Village) was converted to driver-only operation and also extended to the west end of Gartland Road. NGT buses then ceased to run on this service, the joint mileage being balanced by SCT's withdrawal from service 48 from 5 September 1966 and by adjustments to other joint services.

The 1967 results showed regrettable falls in passenger and revenue figures. The nett deficit of £195,895 was nearly two and a half times greater than the previous year's total. There were 793 employees compared with 951 in 1959 and 855 in 1966. The extension of driver-only operation the previous autumn had cut the requirement for conductors by 80 but the implementation of a 40-hour week and other factors had adjusted the nett staff reduction to 62. Even so, a full year of the pay award

The then Mrs Barbara Castle PC MP (later Baroness Castle), Minister of Transport, officially opened the new fare system of 6 January 1967 and is seen here holding the ticket that the Autoslot machine (right) has just issued to her, watched by Driver Harry Hickman, a veteran of the driver-only operated services. The microphone (above driver's left hand) enabled him to address the crowds at bus stops. *(Copyright Busways Travel Services)*

made during 1965/66 and further wage and salary increases during 1966/67 had brought about most of the rise in expenses.

The County Borough boundary was extended on 1 April 1967, embracing the former Rural District of Sunderland which comprised the villages of Ryhope, New Silksworth, East and Middle Herrington, Offerton, South Hylton, North Hylton and Castletown. The South Bents estate in Whitburn, part of Boldon Urban District, was also included. 30,000 people were added to Sunderland's population, bringing it to 220,000, but as almost all the new additions lived outside the Corporation's bus-operating territory they did not benefit from the flat fare scheme although they supported it through their rates. The Chairman of the Transport Committee acknowledged the problem and said it would take many months to sort it out. It was to be achieved by operating the necessary services jointly. At this time, too, a further council housing development was being built, at Gilley Law between Farringdon and New Silksworth. On 3 July 1967 it began to receive a bus service from Town via Durham Road and North Moor Lane, terminating in Aldenham Road and numbered 30. The licence was held jointly with SDO although only SCT operated it initially.

Ten more new Strachans-bodied Panthers entered service during July/August 1967 as 88-97. They were generally similar to the earlier ones and their arrival enabled services 23/24 (Thorney Close/Telford Road - Seaburn/Seaburn Camp) to be converted to driver-only operation *in part* on 24 July 1967, summer frequencies being introduced at the same time. The late delivery of ten further buses, coupled with a pay dispute, delayed the full conversion of these services. Two more service changes took place on 4 September when all but school journeys were withdrawn on Town - High Barnes (8), and Town - Helmsdale Road (26) ceased to operate on Sundays and after 7pm on other days.

Reference was made previously to events "only months away". The precipitating circumstance was a change in political control of the Council in May 1967 when it passed from Labour to Conservative. The Chairman of the Transport Committee became Alderman R B Spain and it was clear that he disapproved of the flat fare scheme and the rates subsidy to the transport system. The Corporation was already geared up to raising the fare and this took effect on 14 August, tokens becoming 2s 0d for six (previously 2s 9d for 10) with a 5d cash fare (previously 4d). A warhead exploded at the Transport Committee meeting on 28 September, however, when the Chairman sought approval to set up a joint advisory committee with the local companies in order to co-ordinate services and create a common fare structure throughout the town. This, of course, would mean the scrapping of the flat fare system replacing it with what Alderman Spain described as a zonal scheme. The Committee gave its approval in principle.

This was anathema to Norman Morton and on 9 October 1967 he tendered his resignation. Although he did not go so far as to suggest that there may have been secret negotiations between the companies and the Chairman, in a statement he did state plainly that the companies had been trying for years to break the Corporation's low fares policy and now they were going to succeed. Indeed, he continued, at the July hearing on the raising of the cash and token fare they had *demanded* a change in the municipality's fare structure. Abandonment of the flat fare scheme of itself had not even been

discussed in Committee, he said, and manifestly he resented what he saw as the alignment of the Committee and indeed also the *Sunderland Echo* with the Traffic Commissioners and the NGT in seeking to destroy the town's existing transport policies. Mr Morton defended the flat fare system in some detail, emphasising also that the Department's deficit was demonstrably not the result of driver-only operation but would have been much greater without it. He concluded by saying that he could not be identified with policies in which he did not believe and which he thought were neither wise nor necessary. One of the final things that Mr Morton did before quitting

Daimler Roadliners 85-87 were also Strachans-bodied and represented here by 86, and keen observers could distinguish them from the Leyland Panthers by the chassis maker's badge on the front grille, the cream steering wheel and the 1ft-longer longer wheelbase which brought the nearside front wheel closer to the entrance. The bus is seen at the foot of Newcastle Road in the revised livery with black fleet numerals introduced during late 1969. *(Copyright R Marshall)*

was to pay tribute to his staff in a personal message to them, saying he would never forget the "lads and lasses" of the Transport Department. Subsequently he was to obtain a post at Newcastle University and died in 1972, aged 62.

Mr Alan H Wright, BSc (Tech), C Eng, MI Mech E, MCIT, who had been Mr Morton's deputy since 10 January 1966, became Acting General Manager pending the appointment of a successor. Among other developments, on 30 November 1967 the Mayor, Alderman N Waters, officially opened new Transport Department offices at the Wheat Sheaf. Saturday 9 December saw a national one-day strike of municipal bus employees, followed by a week's working to rule. On 11 December, the Central Bus Station came into partial operation, services 2/3, 16, 30 using it. The front entrance and exit of the station were in Crowtree Road and there was a side exit to the re-aligned Brougham Street. Finally, Mr Richard E Bottrill, M Inst T, was selected as the new General Manager on 13 December and took up the post on 1 March 1968. A Liverpudlian aged 49, he had worked in public transport since 1936. Prior to his Sunderland appointment Mr Bottrill had been General Manager at South Shields and previously at West Hartlepool. Old buses continued to be withdrawn during the year.

Sunderland was complimented on its bus system in a report on public transport by the Prices and Incomes Board published in December 1967. It stated that the main hope for a reduction in staffing costs lay in further driver-only operation. The town had 35 per cent of services driver-only and among other medium and large operators only Reading warranted mention on this score. The report recommended purpose-built buses with separate entrance and exit, specialised equipment such as slot machines and simplified fare structures. In other words, the system pioneered by Sunderland was held up as a model! A news item on this report in the *Echo*, however,

When Bristols 98-107 arrived they were even more easy to distinguish from the other makes. Although the wheelbase was the same as that of the Roadliners, the windscreen was positioned several inches higher because of the front-mounted radiator, causing the green band (later cream) at the side to be shallower. Bodywork in this case was by Metropolitan-Cammell and a well-filled 98 loads at the Wheat Sheaf. *(Copyright R Marshall)*

did not mention any of the references to the local system by the Prices and Incomes Board.

The delayed new buses, Bristols of type RELL6G, arrived during January 1968 as 98-107. Their chassis was broadly similar to that of the Leyland Panther except that the Bristol's gearbox was positioned *ahead* of the rear axle. As with the Daimler Roadliners, the wheelbase was not shortened from its standard length of 18ft 6in. The bodywork was supplied by Metropolitan-Cammell-Weymann Ltd, the sales organisation for the Metropolitan-Cammell Carriage & Wagon Co Ltd of Elmdon, Birmingham, the builders (and also until its closure in 1966, Weymann's Ltd of Addlestone, Surrey). Metro-Cammell was to have built the ten bodies on Panthers 88-97 but poor delivery promises led to the Corporation's transferring that order to Strachans. The arrival of the Bristols enabled services 23/24 to be fully driver-only operational. Mr Morton had wanted a Gardner rear-engined model, in this case 6HLX unit, but he was no longer with the undertaking to see how it functioned.

When the Town Council met on 17 January 1968, the Transport Committee Chairman, Alderman Spain, asked for support to oppose the setting up of regional passenger transport authorities (mentioned by Mrs Castle during her visit), under which undertakings like Sunderland's might disappear. Some twenty years previously there had been resistance, even from Labour-controlled councils, to a Labour Government idea of a similar but larger area transport organisation. PTAs were also a Labour concept and in Alderman Spain's terms they represented "socialist dogma.....economics of the madhouse.....pie in the sky.....". His motion was carried, but the wheel was to be on the other axle five years later.

Other events of early 1968 included a raising of the cash fare on to 6d (previously 5d) and the price of tokens to 3s 0d for eight (previously 2s 0d for six) on 6 February and the extending of service 16 from Grindon Village (Gartland Road) to Hastings Hill (Sevenoaks Drive), a new private development, on 11 March. A nett deficit £159,738 was recorded for 1967/68 and met by the General Rate Fund, some £36,000 less than the previous year. December's industrial action by the bus employees was partly responsible for the 6.67 per cent passenger loss. The increase in traffic revenue per mile, however, was nearly three time the increase in working expenses. 1968's Annual Report was the last to be produced, the Committee

abolishing them "for economy reasons". Regrettably this means that some details for subsequent years are not available.

During the spring of 1968, Panther 55 was repainted in a revised livery of green with cream for the roof and the deep waistband and 71 received a new garb of green with cream for the window surrounds and the deep waistband. New buses received 71's version, and existing 36-footers were repainted in it by September 1970. Shorter saloons received completely green panelling below a cream waistband and window surrounds. AEC Reliance 43 was not repainted because on 12 July 1968 it sustained severe fire damage while on a private hire near Durham and was then withdrawn.

Alderman Spain addressed the Town Council again on 12 June 1968 and said that a flat fare of 6d by token and 8d by cash would be necessary to make the bus system self-supporting, *unless a zonal fare scheme were to be adopted.* The undertaking was not being run inefficiently, he claimed, for while it had almost the lowest working costs per mile of any municipality, the revenue per mile was substantially less than most. He referred to the flat fare scheme as "a great social experiment" that had failed. Clearly, this reference highlighted the difference in attitude between the two major Council groups, Labour believing that public transport should be a service for the community, perhaps like libraries and education, with rates support. The Conservatives wanted it ultimately to be a free-standing business. Despite Labour opposition, the Council approved in principle the motion to adopt zonal fares, which were to come into operation early in 1969. The ruling group knew they had the support of the Chairman of the Traffic Commissioners who had said regarding Sunderland, "The travelling public.....must pay an economic amount for their transport."

A cause of some excitement among operators at this time was the provision in the Transport Bill then going through the Parliamentary process for the payment of 25 per cent grants to encourage bus operators to replace their fleets quickly with modern vehicles suitable for driver-only operation. The Ministry of Transport notified the industry that subject to the passing of the Bill, grants should be payable on all eligible buses becoming available for use as from 1 September 1968. Buses would be eligible if ordered before 8 July 1968 and conforming to general design requirements, and if ordered after 8 July and conforming with more detailed specification. SCT had 34 buses on order at that time but only 26 of them would be eligible as the first eight were to enter service before 1 September. The grant for those eligible was worth about £45,000.

There were two batches, comprising 24 Leyland Panthers (108-131) and ten AEC Swifts (132-141), all with standard Strachans bodywork. The Swifts, representing AEC's rear-engined single deck chassis, had their wheelbase shortened by one foot to 17ft 6in like that of the Panthers and they were powered by the 8.2-litre AEC type AH505 engine developed from the AH470. Metro-Cammell-Weymann tendered for all 34 bodies at £3,505 each and was awarded the contract for the ten Swift bodies. However, MCW then wanted to increase the price per body by £110 because of the reduced quantity. The Town Council would not hear of it and gave the order for the whole lot to Strachans.

75

Within a little over two years, 90 new rear-engined 36ft-long single deck buses comprising four chassis makes had entered service. Single deckers averaged only 8mpg compared with the overall double deck figure of 9.3 and the Gardner 5LW consumption of 10-11mpg, although the newest buses were heavier and more powerful. Other running expenses were considerably greater, too, partly because of the more advanced specification but also because the newer buses were less reliable and routine servicing and repairs were more costly. The chief factors leading to increased maintenance costs of the long single deckers were:

- Remoteness of the rear engine, causing drivers to be less sensitive to audible signs of components beginning to fail, etc.
- Transmission development falling behind engine development, making components relatively less robust and more susceptible to abuse.
- Regular maintenance required for doors.
- Compressed air systems not being developed in line with requirements of modern buses.
- Unreliable heating and ventilating systems.
- Increased length and greater traffic volume leading to more collisions.

Some operators who had only a small proportion of rear-engined saloons disposed of them early but in Sunderland at the end of 1968 they represented about half the fleet. The undertaking persisted with them as virtually it had no choice and ultimately seemed to overcome many of the difficulties that brought about their premature withdrawal elsewhere. Most troublesome of all were Daimler Roadliners 85-87. They had the heaviest fuel consumption, the air compressor was unreliable and was positioned at the forward end of the Cummins engine where accessibility was difficult. Usually pressure would be lost overnight (normal on any make) and, as well as there not being any pressure for gear-engagement and brakes, the bellows of the air suspension would be empty. A few minutes' idling (or in cases of urgency only, fast revving!) would put things right but if the compressor failed, rectifying it took so long that the bus would not be able to go out on time. If the Roadliners were subjected to over-fast cornering the bellows would come loose from their mountings. Frequently, compressor gaskets would blow. There were problems with the steering drag links. And, lamented retired depot foreman George Laidler many years later, "We didn't have the proper tools for the job!"

Driving staff disliked the Roadliners for their poor handling on wet roads and the unusual characteristics of the short-stroke engine. Seemingly the Bristol REs were "a disappointment", not living up to their promise of accomplished performance in daily service. They were nevertheless comparatively reliable and economical. Clearly, drivers loved the Leyland Panthers which performed and handled well under all conditions, and also the AEC Swifts which they regarded as being fast with good brakes. Many operators found that with rear-engined single deck chassis the weight of the engine and gearbox behind the rear axle caused bending stresses on the chassis frame and these in turn were transferred to the body, causing structural problems. In the case of Bristols 98-107 these manifested themselves in the roof, resulting in loose framework joints and split panels. All ten buses were returned to Metro-Cammell for rectification under warranty in mid-1969. This problem never occured with the Strachans bodies as they did not have mountings at the extreme rear of the chassis frame. Some of Sunderland's Panthers did suffer other kinds of damage during their early years, though. On 25

September 1969, the body of Panther 83 was partly destroyed by fire and it was not returned to service until May 1972. On 10 April 1970, Panther 91 had its rear-end damaged when it was rammed by a double decker (possibly Roe Daimler 216) in snow. Two months later on 16 June, Panther 115 followed the 1965 example of Fleetline 269 by running off the road in Silksworth Row and embedding itself in a car showroom front, sustaining severe damage. In this incident nine passengers were hurt, one seriously, and Inspector Alf Bradwell was treated for cuts and a back injury.

Back in the autumn of 1968, two services were revised, although it has not been possible to confirm the precise date. They were:

23   Journeys from Thorney Close terminating at Fulwell (Blue Bell) extended via Dovedale Rd to Dene Estate, returning via Alston Cres to Blue Bell

15   **Old:** High Barnes or Humbledon (Ettrick Grove) - Cleveland Rd - Town - Newcastle Rd - Dene Estate

     New: High Barnes - Cleveland Rd - Town

On 13 October 1968, part of Union Street was closed to vehicular traffic in connection with a gyratory system using Holmeside, Crowtree Road, Brougham Street and Waterloo Place. Bus services 10/11, 19, 20/21, 26 then used the Central Bus Station, although it did not become fully operational until 23 November 1969. By the end of 1968, most of the 1954 buses had been withdrawn.

As mentioned previously, the zonal fare system replaced the flat fare on 6 January 1969. The fares were 4d cash or one token (3d each, sold eight for 2s) for any zone (or part of one). The children's fare was 4d and the concessionary fare 3d any distance. Zone 1 was the area within 0.75 mile radius of the Town Hall, zone 2 was between 0.75 and two miles radius and zone 3 was outside the two-mile radius. Different arrangements were made for services that did not pass through the centre of town. Zonal boundaries are tabulated in Appendix 5, and it should be noted that the list may include some service alterations not previously documented due to the unavailability of some records. Virtually all the research and hard work in preparation for the zonal scheme had been carried out under Mr Wright's direction while he was temporarily in charge before the appointment of Mr Bottrill.

On joint services, NGT now sold twelve-journey tickets at 3s, 6s and 9s. One aspect of the zonal system that some passengers found irksome was that, for example, a journey from the stop before a zone boundary to the stop after it cost 8d cash or two tokens, despite probably being only a few hundred yards long. While the flat fare system had been criticised for virtually penalising the short-distance rider, in those circumstances the zonal system was no better.

During 1968, experiments with a revised livery format using green as the lowermost colour were carried out because dirt on the original cream had a more adverse affect on appearance. 1966 Panthers 55/71 were the guinea pigs and the style applied to 71 was adopted. 55 here stands in Kayll Road exhibiting its unique layout. *(Copyright R Marshall)*

During that period there continued to be changes and adjustments to services. Alterations taking place on 10 March 1969 may be summarised as follows:

Old		New	
4	Villette Rd - Tatham St - Town - Downhill Downhill - Town - Hendon - Blue House	4	Villette Rd - Tatham St - Town - Downhill Downhill - Town - Tatham St - Corporation Rd*
5	Blue House - Hendon - Town - Red House N Red House N - Town - Tatham St - Villette Rd	5	Corporation Rd - Tatham St - Town - Red House N Red House N - Town - Tatham St - Villette Rd
10	Pennywell - Ford - Town - Hendon - Grangetown Grangetown - Hendon - Town - Ford	10	Grangetown - Hendon - Town - Ford - Pennywell**
11	Ford - Town - Tatham St - Corporation Rd Blue House - Hendon - Town - Ford - Pennywell	11	Blue House - Hendon - Town - Ford - Pennywell**

   * Ser 4:   Destination shown: "Corporation Rd & Villette Rd"

  ** Ser 10:   route from Ford to Pennywell via Front Rd & Fordfield Rd, destination "Pennywell via Ford", returning via St Luke's Rd

      Ser 11:   route from Ford to Pennywell via St Luke's Rd, destination "Pennywell via St Luke's Rd", returning via Fordfield Rd & Front Rd

Other changes

19	Seaburn - Circle: all journeys now via Park Ave
22	Seaburn - Tunstall Rd: all journeys now via Whitburn Rd
21/22	services along Ryhope Rd: ser 21 journeys replaced by 22, evenings and all day Sun

The nett deficit for the year ending 31 March 1969 was £79,514, about half the previous year's amount. Mr Bottrill had gone to manage Portsmouth's undertaking, being succeeded on 3 April 1969 by his deputy, Mr Alan H Wright, who at 41 was the youngest to be appointed since 1904. Mr Wright, a native of Wigan, had begun his transport career with Leyland Motors in 1951, serving with Manchester Corporation for ten years before coming to Sunderland in 1966.

A limited-stop half-hourly single deck service was commenced 2 September 1969, joint with SDO and numbered 112 (in NGT/SDO series), Town - Doxford Park (Mill Hill) via Durham Road and Farringdon. It catered for a private development at the western end of Silksworth and was Corporation-operated initially. Normal stops were observed between Doxford Park and the zonal 4/3 boundary at the Farringdon service 3 terminus, east of which the zonal 3/2 boundary at the Prospect Hotel was the only stop. An additional stop was to be made at Barnes Park Road as from December 1972. It was the first Corporation limited-stop service, the first new Corporation bus service to any part of the 1967 boundary extension "added areas" and the only one outside zone 3. At the same time, service 30 (Town - Gilley Law) was renumbered 113.

Staff shortages were still plaguing the Department in 1969. Despite inducements such as bonuses, the undertaking was unable to attract suitable personnel from the relatively high level of unemployed workers in the town. Buses were often missing due to the unavailability of a driver. This caused particular difficulty on low-frequency services. For mileage-balancing purposes NGT buses again operated some journeys on service 16 (Town - Hastings Hill) from 11 October 1969. Regarding vehicles, during 1969 a start was made on brightening up the final dozen forward-engined buses, Daimlers and Guys 225-230, 231-236 by repainting them in the Fleetline-style livery. Rebodied wartime stalwarts, Guys 240/241 (previously 79/81), were withdrawn during the year.

On 24 January 1970 there were further adjustments to some services from the town centre to the "added areas". SDO began to share services 112 to Doxford Park and 113 to Gilley Law. At the same time, joint operation also began on service 133 (originally 51)

to Silksworth (Vicarage Estate), Sunday excepted. This busy service had been exclusive to SDO, SCT now generally operating alternate journeys.

For the Transport Committee, the financial results at the 31 March 1970 year end were encouraging. The nett deficit was down to £20,800. This was only slightly more than ten per cent of the 1967 figure and the lowest since 1962. Operations were nevertheless efficient. Mr Wright, the General Manager, told the Committee on 29 June 1970 that of 75 municipal undertakings, only eleven had lower running costs per mile than Sunderland. Of those, ten were much smaller concerns. Sunderland was also seventh from top in terms of passengers per mile. Alderman W S Martin, who was also Chairman of the Finance Committee, wanted to see the town's system even higher in the tables even if it meant cutting one in five or six buses at off-peak times. The Committee decided to raise fares by 1d to 5d per zone, increasing the price of tokens from eight for 2s to nine for 3s. Silksworth representative Councillor Flacker Norman failed in a move to help Doxford Park residents by having tokens reduced to seven for 2s and the fourth zone eliminated.

The increases took effect on 24 August 1970. Children now paid 4d per journey but the concession remained 3d. By this time there had been more service changes, some possibly on the day of the fares revision (it has not proved possible to confirm). Some involved complex workings but this was by no means unusual! These are the details:

Owing to an industrial dispute, on 14 September 1970 the Union of General & Municipal Workers imposed bans on overtime and on the carrying of standing passengers, normal working being resumed on 16 November. The Department's experiences with rear-engined saloons were now causing management to look overseas for possible future vehicles and in October 1970, a Swedo-British Metro-Scania single deck demonstrator was borrowed, built by Metropolitan-Cammell-Weymann using Scania mechanical units. SCT was not to order any examples. However, nine new British buses delivered the same month were Marshall-bodied Leyland Panthers 142-150. The bodywork somewhat resembled that on Atkinsons 46-48 and although of SCT's standard layout, was built to

Old		New	
4	Villette Rd - Tatham St - Town - Downhill Downhill - Town - Tatham St - Corporation Rd	4	Villette Rd - Tatham St - Town - Downhill Downhill - Town - Hendon - Blue House
5	Corporation Rd - Tatham St - Town - Red House N Red House N - Town - Tatham St - Villette Rd	5	Blue House - Hendon - Town - Red House N Red House N - Town - Tatham St - Villette Rd
10	Grangetown - Hendon - Town - Pennywell	10	unchanged
11	Blue House - Hendon - Town - Pennywell	11	Corporation Rd - Tatham St - Town - Pennywell
12	Fulwell - Southwick - Pallion - Ford - Humbledon*	12	extended from Humbledon to Grangetown*
15	High Barnes - Cleveland Rd - Town	15	Docks - Boro' Rd - Town - Cleveland Rd - H Barnes Witherwack - Town - Cleveland Rd - High Barnes
25	Witherwack - Town - High St - Docks	25	Witherwack - Town - High St - Docks High Barnes - Cleveland Rd - Town - Witherwack

    peak times only

1968 Strachans-bodied Leyland Panthers 108-131 and AEC Swifts 132-141 were the first new buses adorned in the modified layout. The camera catches 133, five months old and taking a breath of sea air at Seaburn. It was considerate of the driver to reveal details of the entrance and exit step layout by leaving the doors open! *(Copyright R Marshall)*

Marshall's own conventional design based on BET specification and adopted by the National Bus Company (formed on 28 November 1968). The introduction of these buses enabled services 10/11 (Grangetown/ Corporation Road - Ford - Pennywell) to be converted to driver-only operation on 16 November 1970. A week before that, however, an experimental new single deck part-day service numbered 30, intended for shoppers and visitors to the new Civic Centre, had been introduced (although something similar using 14-seat minibuses had been visualised by Mr Morton in 1959). Regrettably it was a flop, being withdrawn on 31 December. Its route was:

Central Bus Stn - Brougham St - Waterloo Pl - Holmeside - Fawcett St - Bridge St - W Wear St - Bedford St - John St - Boro' Rd - Holmeside - Park Lane - Cowan Terr - Stockton Rd - Mary St - Vine Pl - Crowtree Rd - Central Bus Stn

When an application was made to extend the service 16 further into the Hastings Hill estate in an anti-clockwise circular route along Sevenoaks Drive, some residents objected on the grounds that buses *(but not private cars!)* posed a threat to children's safety. Following a public enquiry, the Traffic Commissioners allowed the application and said, "The bus is the safest vehicle on the road today." The extended service commenced on 14 December 1970. On the same day for the first time dogs were allowed to be carried on SCT buses. Another "first" took place on Christmas Day 1970 when services were operated by volunteer staff. Nine 1957/58 buses had been withdrawn during the year.

Preparations were now being made for the conversion to decimal currency and it had been realised that the new penny coin would be the same size as the Sunderland's bus token. A new set of slightly larger tokens was therefore minted, the inscription including the term "1 token" instead of "1 journey". New tokens were exchanged for old ones and the alteration took place on 18 January 1971, four weeks ahead of the currency change. Just four days before decimalisation, an imprest system was introduced for conductors and the drivers of single deckers. They were issued with tickets and tokens to a value of £47.99 and £46.66 respectively and it was their responsibility to replenish their stocks as necessary. When decimalisation took place on 15 February the fares became:

adults:	2p (4.8d, previously 5d) or one token per zone
children:	2p (previously 4d) or one token any distance
concessions:	1p (2.4d, previously 3d) any distance
tokens:	9 for 15p (previously 3s; no price change)

For the year ending 31 March 1971 there was a much larger deficit, amounting to £127,186. The total passenger figure had fallen by some 42 per cent since its peak of nearly 88 million in 1957 but

The Fleetline-style livery was applied to the 1958 Roe-bodied Daimlers and Guys from late 1969, considerably enlivening their appearance. 235, the penultimate Guy numerically, here uses a background of Central Bus Station gloom as if to emphasise the point. The light upperworks of the bus harked back to the mid-1930s period! *(Copyright holder not known)*

the mileage figure had dropped by only 16 per cent since its peak of nearly seven million in 1959. Concern was now felt because the only suitable double decker for training new drivers was Guy 242 (previously 139) with constant-mesh gearbox, then nineteen years old. A further 'decker was therefore acquired for training only and numbered 243. Surprisingly this was of a type never operated by SCT, a lightweight 1954 Metro-Cammell *Orion-bodied* Leyland Titan PD2/20 with synchromesh 'box, bought from Edinburgh Corporation. From the same source and for the same purpose two Alexander-bodied constant-mesh 6LW Mark IV Guy Arabs were to be obtained in 1972 and given replacement numbers 241 and 242. As an experiment, from 28 June 1971 smoking was prohibited on all buses before 1900hrs (the 24-hour clock having now been adopted). The ban was made permanent on 6 September 1971 and extended to the whole day in December 1972.

The batches of Daimler, Bristol and AEC rear-engined single deck chassis alternated with those of Leyland and the final group of all were of this make. Numbered 142-150, they were new on October 1970 and had Marshall bodywork with pillars and windows of normal shape. Represented here by 143, there was room for "Binns" advertising at both front and rear. Despite unfortunate experiences of the Leyland Panther elsewhere, after early problems Sunderland Corporation came to appreciate its qualities and this final batch have been described authoritatively as "lovely buses". *(Copyright R Marshall)*

Other changes took place on 6 September 1971 also. Hylton Road Depot became entirely driver-only and so all single deck buses were based there, with all double deckers now shedded at Fulwell. Service alterations also were carried out, occasioned by the 20 per cent platform staff shortage and saving nineteen buses, as summarised here:

Reduced frequencies

All services to or through town centre, particularly after 1900hrs, except for:

4/5	Downhill/Red House N - Villette Rd/Blue House
28/29	Town - Town End Farm

Altered services

7	Docks - Town - Dene Est, Grangetown - Town - Docks: Docks section withdrawn
25	Witherwack - Town - High St - Docks, H Barnes - Cleveland Rd - Town - Witherwack: W'wack - Docks section renumbered 7
11	Corporation Rd - Tatham St - Town - Pennywell: Corp'n Rd - Town section withdrawn, except for some peak time journeys
19	Seaburn - Park Ave - Town - Circle: Circle section withdrawn after 1900hrs and all day Sunday
26	Town - Helmsdale Rd (via Hylton Rd): withdrawn, except for some peak time journeys

On 21 November a one-way scheme was commenced, fully implemented on 6 December as the Wheat Sheaf gyratory system. The increased running times necessitated three additional buses and all traffic moved clockwise around this rectangle:

Roker Ave (easterly) - Church St N (southerly) - Dame Dorothy St (westerly) - Bridge Street N (northerly)

A cause for concern during this period was Reliance *reliability!* The AEC engines were troublesome and it was not unusual for four of these thirteen buses to be off the road together for repairs. Mr Wright recommended their early withdrawal and in fact two were taken out of service during the year along with five 1958 Guys. As to new buses, January 1972 saw orders placed for eighteen more Marshall-bodied AEC Swifts. The bus grant had now been doubled to 50 per cent as part of Government policy further to encourage operators to renew their fleets. These Swifts were to be the final buses ordered although not delivered until after the Tyneside Passenger Transport Executive had taken over SCT operations.

The nett deficit for the year ending 31 March 1972 came to £167,315 and the passenger total was now barely more than *half* its 1957 peak. As from 1 April 1972 the Transport Committee ceased to exist and its functions were taken over by the new Environment Committee. In September, the first moves were made toward ending the Corporation's involvement with running bus services and handing over operations to the Tyneside Passenger Transport Executive (PTE). This was the operating organisation of the Authority created by the Transport Act, 1968, on 1 October 1969 to assume among other matters the functions of Newcastle and South Shields municipal transport undertakings, one of four PTAs in existence at that time. The Local Government Act, 1972, created the metropolitan areas and districts that were to come into existence on 1 April 1974. This Act would also dissolve the Tyneside PTA and vest all its functions and properties in the Tyne and Wear County Council on that date. Sunderland Corporation's public transport functions would pass to the new Tyne and Wear PTE on 1 April 1974 in any case, but the Council was becoming increasingly eager to rid itself of the transport system before that date. It was decided on 30 November 1972 that the PTE should take over on 1 April 1973, although the Council would still have to make up any deficit incurred by the former Corporation buses during the year ending 31 March 1974. Among other matters to be ironed out was the SCT fare structure which differed from that of the PTE.

The number of forward-engined double deckers and 30ft-long saloons was continuing to diminish. Ironically, although there had been early misgivings in some quarters about the quality of the five bodies built locally by Associated Coachbuilders on Daimler chassis in 1954, the last survivor of the DBR-registered Daimler and Guy batches was one of the ACB-bodied examples, 171, withdrawn during 1972. Eighteen years' service was creditable. The final wartime Guy, 238, rebodied by Roe, was also withdrawn, its 29-year-old chassis being the longest-serving one on Departmental record. It is not known when rebodied Guy 237 or Daimler snowplough bus 239 (originally 59/72) were discarded.

Just a fortnight before the end of the Corporation's bus-operating activities, on 17 March 1973, a National Bus Company Joint Mileage Pool was set up in order to eliminate any imbalance of mileage on services operated jointly between the Corporation and NGT or SDO. Two journeys on these services were transferred to NGT. The last day of March was the final day of municipal transport operation in Sunderland after 73 years. A civic ceremony was held to mark the handing-over of the Transport Department to the PTE. Council members, officials, staff and guests assembled at the Civic Centre at 22.30, then travelling by special buses to the Central Bus Station where the Mayor, Cllr Leslie Watson, signalled away the last service departures at 23.00. The party went on to the Wheat Sheaf and Dr Tony Ridley, Director General of the PTE, there "received" the municipal undertaking. A buffet was then put on at the Civic Centre. In contrast to the trams, the buses were not held in popular nostalgic affection and there were no cheering, souvenir-hunting crowds. Next day, the bus services were being run by the South Division of the PTE although nothing appeared to be different immediately. Mr Wright became an Associate Director and the Divisional Manager. 55 double deck and 118 single deck vehicles, identified in Appendix 1, passed into PTE ownership (not including training vehicles).

Appendix 1

The Bus Fleet

Table 1 Fleet list

Notes

Date new. This may be either date first registered or date delivered where known.

Retention of parts. Some pre-war double deck buses were dismantled by SCT for spare parts. Some others had their engines removed for further use or to be kept as spare. Details are given where known.

Depot. F=Fulwell, H=Hylton Rd, denoting allocation of vehicles in service at opening of Hylton Rd as operational bus depot, 1954, and subsequent new ones. Initial allocation only given. Buses withdrawn to end of 1954 all remained at Fulwell.

Body frames. All bodies to 1958 timber-framed except where otherwise stated. All subsequent bodies metal-framed.

Rebuilding. This term refers to the extensive reconditioning of some wartime and early post-war bodies, including re-seating where mentioned. Date given is that of re-entry into service after rebuilding.

Re-seating. Wartime buses re-seated had wooden-slatted seats replaced by leathercloth-upholstered ones. Many post-war buses were re-seated without being rebuilt. DBR/EBR-registered buses that were re-seated were altered by their coachbuilder and fitted with a revised design of staircase (168-172 were not treated).

Green livery. This was introduced 1 Dec 52. Subsequent new and rebodied vehicles were delivered in it and existing vehicles were repainted into it except for centre entrance double deckers, pre-war single deckers, rebodied Guys with their original bodies and several others mentioned below.

Delicensing. Many vehicles were temporarily delicensed at various times for recertification, overhaul or repair. Mention of delicensing is made only where this was for a significant length of time or purpose.

Chassis	Body	Fleet No	Reg No	Unladen Wt t. c. q	Date new	Date withdrawn	Depot from 1954	Remarks (Note: cost given for each vehicle to nearest £1 unless stated otherwise. To 1960 amount given is actual price. From 1961 it is contract price)
Leyland	Leyland B32F	1	BR 7131	4.15.0	May 29	1935		1-12: cost £1,290 complete. May have had folding doors which were removed before or soon after entry into service. 2 now privately preserved
		2	BR 7132	4.14.3	"	1934		
		3	BR 7133	4.15.1	"	Jan 38		
		4	BR 7134	4.15.0	"	1935		
		5	BR 7135	"	"	Jul 38		
		6	BR 7136	4.15.2	"	1935		
		7	BR 7137	4.14.3	"	Nov 43		To 28 perimeter seats + 28 standing, Nov 41
		8	BR 7138	4.15.0	Jun 29	Jan 38		
		9	BR 7139	4.17.3	"	"		
		10	BR 7140	4.18.0	"	Nov 43		To 28 perimeter seats + 28 standing, Nov 41
		11	BR 7141	"	Jul 29	Nov 39		
		12	BR 7142	"	Jun 29	1935		

Fleet No	Make	Body	Reg	Chassis No	New	Withdrawn	Notes
13	Thornycroft LB	Th'croft? B29F	TY 4418	5.4.2	1928	1945	Acquired from W Ankers, Winlaton-on-Tyne, Nov 29. Cost £325. Some fleet lists give original layout as B26F but SCT records say B29F. Rebodied 1935 - see Table 2. May have been renumbered 5 at about same time. Converted to ARP mobile canteen Feb 41. Returned to SCT by Feb 45
14	Leyland Lion LT2	Roe B32F	BR 8001	5.5.2	Jun 30	May 44	Gardner 4LW diesel fitted 17 Nov 33
15			BR 8002	"	"	Oct 43	14-19: cost £1,325 complete. Original folding doors removed soon after entry into service
16			BR 8003	"	"	Apr 44	
17			BR 8004	"	"	Nov 43	To 28 perimeter seats + 28 standing, Nov 41. Withdrawn 24 Mar 43, reinstated 6 May 43
18			BR 8005	"	"	"	
19			BR 8006	"	"	"	
20	Leyland Tiger TS2	Roe B32F	BR 8007	5.5.2	Jun 30	Nov 44	20/21: cost £1,325 complete. Folding doors fitted
21			BR 8008	"	"	Oct 44	
22	Dennis HS	Massey L24/24R	PG 6564	6.10.0	1929	Sep 35	Former Dennis demonstrator. Operated from Apr 30, acquired Jun 30. Cost £1,400. Some sources state chassis HV type. Fitted with engine from 25 (BR 8295) Sep 35, converted to tower wagon 19 Jan 37. Chassis sold 15 Nov 38. 22-25 lowbridge, height c13'6"
23	Dennis HV	Massey L24/24R	BR 8293	6.4.3	Jul 30	1935	23-25: cost £1,660 complete. 24 or 25, or both, believed to have had "herringbone" upper saloon seats.
24			BR 8294	"	Aug 30	1936	24 converted to pole and tram rail carrier 1936. Disposal date not known
25			BR 8295	"	"		25 to Gardner 5LW diesel Apr 34. Original engine to 22 (PG 6564) Sep 35.
-	Guy Wolf CF20	Guy B20T	GR 1156	-	31 Jul 34	1954	GR 1156/57: cost £366 complete. Original bodies toastrack but known as tram-o-cars. Both converted to ARP mobile canteens Apr/Mar 41 respectively. GR 1156 returned to SCT 4 Jul 45. GR 1157 later to National Fire Service, returned to SCT 7 Jun 45. Both rebodied 1947 - see Table 2. Fleet-numbered 1/2 at same time
-			GR 1157	-	"	"	
26	Daimler COG5	Roe H26/22C	GR 1189	6.14.2	14 Dec 34	30 Apr 52	26/27: cost £1,075 chassis, £760 body. All double decks 1934-58 highbridge, height c14'6". 26-37 had Roe "recessed V-front" profile. All Daimlers placed in service 1934-53 had right-hand quadrant gear selector
27			GR 1190	6.14.1	30 Nov 34	"	
-	Guy Wolf CF20	Guy B20T	GR 1774	-	31 May 35	Dec 50	GR 1774/1775: cost £395 complete. Originally as GR 1156/1157. Both rebodied 1938 - see Table 2. Fleet-numbered 3/4 at same time. Both loaned to S Shields CT 1943/44 and possibly for earlier period(s) during war
-			GR 1775	-	"		
28	Daimler COG5	Roe H26/22C	GR 2085	6.13.2	31 Jul 35	1 Sep 53	28/29/31/32: cost £1,015 chassis. £745 body. 28: engine kept after withdrawal
29			GR 2086	6.14.1	"	"	Engine kept after withdrawal
30			GR 2087	6.13.0	Sep 35	24 Jan 50	Reconditioned engine from new. Cost £800 chassis, £745 body + cost of engine. Bus dismantled for spares after withdrawal. Engine believed then fitted to 1947 Crossley 13 (see below)
31			GR 2385	6.15.2	16 Dec 35	30 Jun 53	Engine kept after withdrawal
32			GR 2386	6.16.0	"	28 Aug 50	Bus dismantled for spares after withdrawal
33			GR 2781	6.16.3	29 Jun 36	30 Apr 53	33: after withdrawal, chassis to driving school for display. Disposed of c1960
34			GR 3038	6.16.2	"	30 Nov 53	33-37: cost £979 chassis (exc tyres), £773 body. 34: engine kept after withdrawal
35			GR 3039	6.16.3	"	1 Sep 53	Engine kept after withdrawal

Chassis / Body	No	Reg	Code	Date	Date	Withdrawn		Notes
	36	GR 3525	6.18.2	21 Dec 36		28 Feb 53		Coronation illuminated bus 1953 then snowplough until sold 11 Jan 60
	37	GR 3526	6.18.1	"		31 Dec 53		Used briefly as snowplough after withdrawal. Engine kept before disposal
Crossley Mancunian Eng Elec FH25/23C	24	GR 3739	7.4.1	15 Apr 37		31 Dec 51		24/25: cost £1,084 chassis, £866 body. Full fronts removed between 1940-43, possibly when engines converted from indirect to direct injection and apparently exchanged between chassis Apr 43. 25 dismantled for spares following early withdrawal, due to chassis frame fracture
	25	GR 3740	7.2.3	"		22 Oct 46		
Daimler COG5 Roe H26/22C	38	GR 3881	6.17.0	7 Apr 37		17 Jun 54		38-41: cost £979 chassis (exc tyres), £775 body. 38 had wind-tone horn. Engine kept after withdrawal
	39	GR 3882	"	29 Apr 37		31 May 54		Engine kept after withdrawal
	40	GR 3883	6.17.3	3 May 37		1 Nov 56	H	Disposed of minus seat cushions
	41	GR 3884	6.18.0	29 May 37		30 Jan 54		Loaned to S Shields CT 1951-53. 41-55 (except 47): engines kept after withdrawal
	42	GR 4713	7.2.3	29 Nov 37		30 Jun 54		Cost £979 chassis (exc tyres), £819 body. Exhibited at 1937 Commercial Motor Show. Special fittings and initial use - see text.
	43	GR 5214	7.0.0	6 May 38		31 Dec 54		43-49: cost £1,078 chassis, £810 body. 43 used briefly as snowplough following withdrawal
	44	GR 5215	7.0.0	"		31 Aug 54		
	45	GR 5216	7.0.1	"		31 Jul 54		
	46	GR 5217	7.0.2	"		"		
	47	GR 5218	7.1.1	"		28 Feb 57	H	Longest continuous-serving bus in fleet with original body
	48	GR 5219	7.0.2	"		28 Feb 54		
	49	GR 5220	7.0.0	"		"		
	50	GR 6073	7.0.0	6 Dec 38		30 Apr 54		50-53: cost £1,060 chassis (exc tyres & spare wheel), £810 body
	51	GR 6074	7.0.1	16 Dec 38		"		
	52	GR 6075	7.1.3	"		"		
	53	GR 6076	7.1.2	"		1 Sep 53		
	54	GR 7102	6.18.2	3 Aug 39		31 Jul 54		54/55: cost £1,043 chassis (exc tyres & spare wheel), £790 body. 55 had klaxon horn
	55	GR 7103	6.18.2	"		30 Sep 54		
Crossley Mancunian Blagg B32F	22	GR 7100	5.18.1	3 Oct 39		31 Oct 54		22/23: cost £925 chassis, £540 body. 22: engine converted to direct injection Nov 44. Body altered by SCT for driver-only operation and to B34F, 2 Mar 53. Believed still in existence with preservationist mid-1990s
	23	GR 7101	5.18.1	"		31 Jan 54		Engine converted to direct injection Jun 44
Leyland Titan TD7 Roe H26/22C	56	GR 7499	7.7.0	30 Mar 42		24 Nov 54		56-58 were wartime "unfrozen" buses. All buses delivered 1942-44 (56-81) finished in grey primer, repainted red & cream post-war. 56/57: cost £1,200 chassis, £1,034 body
	57	GR 7500	"	12 Jun 42		31 Dec 54		
Leyland Titan TD7 Leyland H30/26R	58	GR 7501	6.18.2	26 Jun 42		27 May 57	F	Cost £1,200 chassis, £1,025 body which was metal-framed and to Western SMT specification. Used for fuel tests 1954 (see footnote 2) then as driver trainer as well as PSV for some months prior to withdrawal
Guy Arab I 5LW Roe H26/22C	59	GR 7692	7.9.1	30 Jan 43		1 Feb 67	F	Cost £1,297 chassis, £1,020 body which was to W Hartlepool spec - see text. Rebodied 1954 - see Table 2. Renumbered 237 in 1966
Daimler CWG5 Massey H30/26R	60	GR 7707	7.11.0	10 Mar 43		24 Mar 58	H	60-81 were wartime "utility" buses. All those rebuilt were given new-style destination indicators, without rear

No.	Chassis	Body	Reg		In	Out		Notes
61	Guy Arab II 5LW	Massey H30/26R	GR 7708	"	2 Apr 43	31 Dec 56	H	service number, at same time and except 72, were delicensed for short periods prior to and during rebuilding. 60/61: cost £1,635 chassis, £920 body. Rebuilt: 60 - Mar 53, 61 - Feb 53. Neither re-seated. 61 disposed of minus engine, gearbox and differential
62	Guy Arab II 5LW	Massey H30/26R	GR 7722	7.11.0	17 Jul 43	30 Apr 58	F	62/63: cost £1,300 chassis, £910 body. 62 rebuilt & to H32/26R 30 Jul 55
63			GR 7723	7.12.0	20 Jul 43	1966	F	Rebodied 1954/55 - see Table 2
64			GR 7739	7.13.2	4 Oct 43	31 Jan 62	F	64-66/69/70/74-79: cost £1,395 chassis, £910 body. 64 rebuilt & to H32/26R 10 Dec 53. Delicensed 31 Jan 58 then driver trainer until withdrawal
65			GR 7740	7.13.2	"	30 Apr 63	F	Rebuilt & to H32/26R 31 May 55. Used for training as well as PSV from May 58
66			GR 7741	7.13.0	15 Dec 43	14 Feb 58	F	Not delivered until 4 Jan 44. 6LW engine fitted c1950. Rebuilt & to H32/26R 14 Sep 54
67	Guy Arab II 5LW	Pickering H30/26R	GR 7742	7.8.0	30 Oct 43	Oct 72 D	F	67/68: cost £1,395 chassis, £870 body. 67 rebodied 1954/55 - see Table 2. Renumbered 238 in 1966. Latterly delicensed and used as trainer. D - disposal date
68			GR 7743	"	3 Oct 43	30 Jun 64	F	6LW engine fitted c1950. Rebuilt & to H32/26R 1 Mar 55. Temporarily driver trainer May 58. Converted to open-top (H32/26RO) for seaside tours 1 Jul 58, cost c£200. SCT diamond jubilee illuminated bus 1960.
69	Guy Arab II 5LW	Massey H30/26R	GR 7744	7.13.0	24 Dec 43	30 Sep 63	F	Rebuilt & to H32/26R 1 Oct 53. Temporarily delicensed and driver trainer Jun 57. Relicensed Jul 57. Used for training as well as PSV from May 58. Delicensed 31 Aug 61 then trainer. Relicensed 23 Nov 61. Trainer from withdrawal untill disposal Oct 64. Served as long as Daimler 47 overall but not continuously licensed
70			GR 7745	7.14.0	29 Dec 43	30 Apr 58	F	Rebuilt & to H32/26R 1 Aug 53. Temp delicensed and used as driver trainer Jun 57. Relicensed Jul 57
71	Daimler CWA6	Duple H30/26R	GR 7746	7.9.0	30 Oct 43	31 Aug 59	F	71-73: cost £1,655 chassis, £889 body. 71: 5LW engine fitted Apr 54 (becoming type CWG5). Rebuilt & to H32/26R 1 Dec 55. 5LW engines fitted to 71/72 were from pre-war Daimlers
72			GR 7747	"	30 Nov 43	Dec 58	F	Delicensed 1 Feb 55-24 Mar 56. Rebuilt & to H32/26R and 5LW engine fitted 25 Mar 56 (becoming type CWG5). Delicensed 31 Aug 58 following low bridge accident. Converted to open-top (not as PSV) and used as snowplough. Renumbered 239 in 1966 but this number not carried. Disposal details not known.
73			GR 7748	"	18 Dec 43	31 Jan 55	F	Not rebuilt or re-seated. Withdrawn following collision damage. Disposed of Aug 56, still in red livery
74	Guy Arab II 5LW	Massey H30/26R	GR 7770	7.13.0	29 Feb 44	31 Jan 62	F	Rebuilt & to H32/26R 1 May 54. Delicensed 31 Oct 57 then driver trainer until withdrawal
75			GR 7771	"	3 Mar 44	30 Apr 58	F	1 Jul 54
76			GR 7772	7.15.0	6 Apr 44	"	F	1 Nov 54
77			GR 7773	"	11 Apr 44	"	F	1 Jan 55
78			GR 7774	7.14.2	18 Apr 44	Feb 66 D	F	Rebodied 1954/55 - see Table 2. D - disposal date
79			GR 7775	7.15.0	"	Oct 70 D	F	Rebodied 1954/55 - see Table 2. Delicensed by 31 Jul 64 then driver trainer until withdrawal. Renumbered 240 in 1966. D - disposal date.
80	Guy Arab II 6LW	Massey H30/26R	GR 7806	7.10.3	4 Aug 44	30 Apr 58	F	80/81: cost £1,450 chassis, £955 body. 80: rebuilt and to H32/26R 1 Mar 54
81			GR 7807	7.8.2	"	1969	F	Rebodied and fitted with 5LW engine 1954 - see Table 2. Delicensed by 31 Jul 64 then trainer until withdrawal. Renumbered 241 in 1966
15	Daimler CWD6	Massey H30/26R	GR 8097	7.9.3	22 Mar 46	28 Feb 58	F	15-18: cost £1,572 chassis (exc tyres), £1,182 body.
16			GR 8098	7.9.2	"	"	F	
17			GR 8099	7.9.2	8 Mar 46	"	F	

Chassis	Body	No	Registration		In	Withdrawn		Notes
		18	GR 8100	7.9.2	22 Mar 46	"	F	
Crossley DD42/3	Cravens H30/26R	19	GR 8250	7.5.0	27 Sep 46	31 Oct 62	H	19-21: cost £1,499 chassis, £1,278 body, metal-framed. 19 fitted with 5LW engine Dec 53. All 5LW engines fitted to post-war Crossleys, possibly except 11, removed from pre-war Daimlers
		20	GR 8251	7.5.0	"	31 May 61	H	5LW engine fitted Jun 54
		21	GR 8252	7.6.0	6 Sep 46	31 May 63	H	1955
Crossley DD42/3	Crossley H30/26R	9	GR 9003	7.10.0	1 Apr 47	30 Nov 61	H	9-14: cost £1,662 chassis, £1,824 body. Crossley standard Manchester-style bodies, metal-framed. 9 fitted with 5LW engine Mar 54
		10	GR 9004	"	"	31 Dec 61	H	5LW engine fitted Apr 54
		11	GR 9005	"	"	"	H	Mar 53
		12	GR 9006	"	"	31 Mar 62	H	Feb 54
		13	GR 9007	"	"	"	H	Aug 50. To S'land General Purposes Committee 19 Dec 62 for use as mobile polling booth. Disposed of 1972 and still in existence unrestored at North West Museum of Transport, St Helens, mid-1990s
		14	GR 9008	"	"	"	H	5LW engine fitted Apr 54
AEC Regent Mk III O961/2	Roe H31/25R	82	GR 9113	7.7.2	30 May 47	30 Oct 60	F	82-87: cost £1,688 (exc tyres), £1,575 body. All engines derated 1955. All bodies later altered to H33/25R and fitted with new style destination indicators (but not otherwise rebuilt). 82 to H33/25R etc 5 May 56
		83	GR 9114	"	"	29 Feb 60	F	To H33/25R etc 1 Dec 56
		84	GR 9115	"	19 May 47	30 Nov 59	F	22 Jan 57
		85	GR 9116	"	"	"	F	1 Feb 57
		86	GR 9117	"	"	24 Mar 59	F	6 Jun 56
		87	GR 9118	"	30 May 47	30 Nov 59	F	25 Mar 57
Guy Arab I 5LW	Pickering H30/26R	5	ABV 866	7.14.0	5 Apr 43	Apr 55	F	5/6: acquired from Blackburn CT 21 Oct 47 for £1,000 each complete. Were Blackburn 56/57. Entered SCT service 1 Jan 48. Both delicensed 30 Apr 55 then used as driver trainers. Disposed of 5 Jul 57 still in red livery
		6	ABV 867	"	10 Apr 43	"	F	
Daimler CVG6	Massey H30/26R	88	GR 9920	7.5.3	2 Jul 48	31 Mar 64	H	88-99: cost £1,813 chassis (exc tyres), £1,622 body. Those rebuilt were altered to H32/26R and given new-style destination indicators at same time. All were delicensed for short periods prior to and during rebuilding except as mentioned. 88 rebuilt and to H32/26R 18 May 56, others as below
		89	GR 9921	7.6.0	1 Jul 48	31 Aug 61	H	Rebuilt & to H32/26R 1 Sep 56
		90	GR 9922	7.6.1	31 Aug 48	31 Dec 60	H	" 1 Dec 56
		91	GR 9923	7.6.2	2 Jul 48	30 Jun 62	H	" 1 Jun 57
		92	GR 9924	7.6.1	"	31 Jul 64	H	" 1 Jan 56
		93	GR 9925	7.6.0	10 Jul 48	31 Aug 62	H	" 11 Sep 57
		94	GR 9926	7.6.1	31 Aug 48	30 Sep 62	H	" 1 Nov 57
		95	GR 9927	7.6.2	3 Jul 48	31 Oct 62	H	Delicensed Aug 57-Feb 58. Used as driver trainer Aug-Oct 57. Rebuilt & to H32/26R
		96	GR 9928	"	14 Aug 48	1966	H	Delicensed Mar 58-Dec 60. Relicensed 1 Jan 61 with body transferred from 98. Original body never rebuilt
		97	GR 9929	"	31 Aug 48	1962	H	Delicensed Dec 57-Nov 59. Rebuilt & to H32/26R 30 Dec 59 and uniquely fitted with small drainage holes at bottom of upper saloon front panelling due to problems with ingress of water
		98	GR 9930	7.6.1	30 Jul 48	Feb 59	H	Delicensed Aug 57-May 58. Used as driver trainer Aug 57-Jan 58. Rebuilt & to H32/26R 1 Jun 58. Chassis damaged in collision 22 Feb 59 and disposed of 2 Mar 61. Body removed and fitted to chassis of 96, Dec 60
		99	GR 9931	7.6.0	"	31 May 63	H	Rebuilt and to H32/26R 1 Nov 58

No.	Chassis	Body	Reg	UW	Into service	Withdrawn	Type	Notes
100	Crossley DD42/7C	Crossley H30/2R	ABR 433	7.19.0	1 Feb 49	31 Oct 62	H	100-105: cost £3,824 complete (exc tyres). Liverpool-specification bodies. 100 fitted with 5LW engine Oct 53. To S'land General Purposes Committee 19 Dec 62 for use as mobile polling booth. Disposed of 1972 and still in existence unrestored at NW Museum of Transport, St Helens, mid-1990s
101			ABR 434	"	"	30 Apr 63	H	5LW engine fitted Sep 53
102			ABR 435	"	"	"	H	Dec 53
103			ABR 436	"	"	"	H	May 55
104			ABR 437	"	"	"	H	Nov 53
105			ABR 438	"	"	30 Nov 62	H	Jun 54
25	Leyland Titan TD7	Roe H26/22C	EUP 881	7.9.0	29 Jul 42	30 Apr 57	F	Acquired from Stockton CT 20 Dec 49, entered service 1 Jan 50. Cost £500 complete plus further £75 on preparation for service in S'land. Was Stockton 85. Body to WHCT specification - see text. Used for livery experiments Oct 1952 but remained in red. Final centre-entrance bus to be withdrawn.
106	Daimler CVG6	Roe H31/25R	AGR 456	7.14.0	4 Feb 50	31 Jul 64	H	106-109: cost £1,884 chassis (exc tyres), £1,827 body. 106 altered to H33/25R and fitted with new-style destination indicators (but not otherwise rebuilt) 1 Jan 55, others as below
107			AGR 457	"	8 Feb 50	"	H	To H33/25R etc 14 Jan 55
108			AGR 458	"	"	30 Aug 64	H	2 Feb 55
109			AGR 459	"	"	"	H	1 Mar 55
7	Guy Arab III 6LW	Roe B35F	AGR 667	6.10.0	19 Apr 50	31 May 65	F	7/8: cost £1,729 chassis (including £110 extra for preselective gearbox, exc tyres), £1,379 body. Both fitted with 5LW engine Oct 52 then converted by Roe to driver-only operation, 7 in Sep 53, 8 in Oct 53, cost £224 each. UW of 8 then recorded as 6.13.2
8			AGR 668	"	"	"	F	
110	Daimler CVG6	Roe H31/25R	BBR 353	7.16.0	1 Nov 50	30 Sep 64	H	110-115: cost £1,905 chassis (exc tyres), £1,790 body. 110 altered to H33/25R and fitted with new-style destination indicators 1955 but seating capacity on road fund licence not altered until 1 Sep 57. Others altered as below
111			BBR 354	"	8 Nov 50	"	H	To H33/25R etc 30 Jun 55
112			BBR 355	"	1 Nov 50	30 Sep 65	H	10 Oct 55
113			BBR 356	"	8 Nov 50	30 Sep 64	H	c12 Sep 55
114			BBR 357	"	1 Nov 50	30 Sep 65	H	31 Oct 55
115			BBR 358	"	8 Nov 55	30 Sep 64	H	1 Aug 55
116	Daimler CVG6	Roe H31/25R	BGR 416	7.19.1	1 Sep 51	31 Jan 66	F	116-127: cost £1,880 chassis (exc tyres), £1,948 body. First buses 8' wide and 27' long in fleet and first new vehicles to have Gardner 6LW 'K' engine, becoming standard for all future deliveries of LW range. 116 altered to H33/25R 25 Mar 56 but not otherwise changed. Others altered as below
117			BGR 417	"	"	"	F	To H33/25R 17 Apr 56
118			BGR 418	"	"	"	F	4 May 56
119			BGR 419	"	"	"	F	1 Jun 5
120			BGR 420	"	1 Oct 51	"	F	7 Jun 56
121			BGR 421	"	"	"	F	20 Jun 56
122			BGR 422	"	"	"	F	Centrifugal clutch fitted experimentally mid-1950s. To H33/25R 11 Jul 56
123			BGR 423	"	"	12 Sep 66	F	To H33/25R 14 Sep 56
124			BGR 424	"	1 Nov 51	30 Sep 56	F	2 Oct 56

Guy Arab III 6LW — Roe H33/25R (125–127 continued)

Fleet No	Reg No	Code	Date new	Date of disposal		Event date
125	BGR 425	"	12 Oct 51	"	F	8 Oct 56
126	BGR 426	"	"	"	F	8 Oct 56
127	BGR 427	"	1 Nov 51	"	F	by 31 Oct 56

Guy Arab III 6LW — Roe H33/25R

Fleet No	Reg No	Code	Date new	Date of disposal	
128	CBR 528	8.0.0	10 Oct 52	30 Sep 66	F
129	CBR 529	"	1 Dec 52	18 Oct 66	F
130	CBR 530	"	10 Oct 52	"	F
131	CBR 531	"	1 Dec 52	"	F
132	CBR 532	"	10 Oct 52	30 Sep 66	F
133	CBR 533	"	1 Dec 52	"	F
134	CBR 534	"	10 Oct 52	"	F
135	CBR 535	"	1 Dec 52	31 Oct 66	F
136	CBR 536	"	"	"	F
137	CBR 537	"	"	"	F
138	CBR 538	"	"	"	F
139	CBR 539	"	"	Oct 72 D	F

128-138: cost £2,205 chassis (exc tyres), £1,864 body. Preselective gearbox

128-139: first in fleet to exceed £4,000 cost. Chassis price nett of £3 reduction for modified springs

Cost £2,153 chassis (exc tyres), £1,864 body. Constant mesh gearbox. Fitted with Cave-Browne-Cave heating/ventilation system Apr 59 - see footnote 2. Renumbered 242 in 1968. Used latterly as driver trainer as well as PSV. D - disposal date. Privately preserved.

Daimler CVG5 — Roe H32/25R

Fleet No	Reg No	Code	Date new	Date of disposal	
140	DBR 40	6.19.2	30 Jun 53	31 Oct 66	H
141	DBR 41	"	1 Aug 53	"	H
142	DBR 42	"	30 Jun 53	"	H
143	DBR 43	"	1 Aug 53	"	H
144	DBR 44	"	"	31 Jul 67	H
145	DBR 45	"	"	"	H
146	DBR 46	"	1 Jul 53	"	H
147	DBR 47	"	1 Aug 53	"	H

140-147 cost £2,252 chassis (exc tyres), £1,991 body. See footnote 2.

Daimler CVG5 — Roe H33/25R

Fleet No	Reg No	Code	Date new	Date of disposal		To H35/28R
148	DBR 648	7.3.1	1 Mar 54	Feb 68	H	To H35/28R
149	DBR 649	"	1 Jan 54	"	H	21 Apr 55
150	DBR 650	"	1 Feb 54	"	H	18 Apr 55
151	DBR 651	"	1 Jan 54	"	H	19 Apr 55
152	DBR 652	"	4 Feb 54	"	H	7 Mar 55
153	DBR 653	"	1 Jan 54	"	H	6 Apr 55
154	DBR 654	"	1 Feb 54	"	H	7 Apr 55
155	DBR 655	"	5 Feb 54	"	H	28 Mar 55
156	DBR 656	"	1 Feb 54	Jul 68	H	31 Mar 55

148-167: cost £2,325 chassis, £1,492 body, Park Royal metal-framed. Altered by Roe to H35/28R at cost of £208 each, 148 on 27 Apr 55, others as below. 173-201/203-208 altered similarly. All fitted with 202-type staircase but UW not changed. Daimlers from 148 had left-hand gear selector. See footnote 3

	Fleet No	Reg	Code	In service	H/F	Withdrawal	Date
	157	DBR 657	"	25 Mar 54	H	"	25 Mar 55
	158	DBR 658	"	"	H	Aug 68	22 Mar 55
	159	DBR 659	"	12 Feb 54	H	"	21 Mar 55
	160	DBR 660	"	25 Mar 54	H	"	11 Mar 55
	161	DBR 661	"	"	H	"	14 Mar 55
	162	DBR 662	"	"	H	"	9 Mar 55
	163	DBR 663	"	1 Mar 54	H	"	2 Mar 55
	164	DBR 664	"	25 Mar 54	H	"	28 Feb 55
	165	DBR 665	"	"	H	Dec 68	23 Feb 55
	166	DBR 666	"	1 Mar 54	H	Feb 68	24 Jan 55
	167	DBR 667	"	12 Feb 54	H	Dec 68	21 Feb 55
Daimler CVG5 ACB H33/25R	168	DBR 668	7.11.0	1 Jan 54	H	Dec 68	168-172: cost £2,325 chassis, £2,345 body (greater than chassis price), Metal Sections metal fames; 168: entered service 26 Jan 54. See footnote 3
	169	DBR 669	7.5.1	25 Mar 54	H	"	
	170	DBR 670	"	"	F		Delivered 9 Feb 54 but returned to ACB for rectification. Entered service 25 Mar 54
	171	DBR 671	"	"	F	Oct 72	
	172	DBR 672	"	1 May 54	F	Dec 68	

Date of withdrawal

	Fleet No	Reg	Code	In service	H/F	Withdrawal	To H32/26R	To H35/28R
Guy Arab IV 5LW Crossley H32/25R	173	DBR 673	7.4.0	1 Jan 54	F	31 Oct 66	173-184: cost £2,325 chassis, £2,178 body, steel-framed lower saloon, aluminium alloy upper. See footnotes 3/4. Altered by SCT to H32/26R, 173 on 7 Jul 54, others as below. Later altered by Crossley to H35/28R at cost of £225 each, 173 on 18 Jan 56, others as below.	
	174	DBR 674	"	"	F	30 Nov 66	1 Nov 54	25 Jan 56
	175	DBR 675	"	"	F	"	18 Nov 54	6 Feb 56
	176	DBR 676	"	"	F		27 Jul 54	9 Feb 56

Date of disposal

	177	DBR 677	"	"	F	Sep 67	1 Jun 54	7 Feb 56
	178	DBR 678	"	"	F	"	19 Oct 54	17 Feb 56
	179	DBR 679	"	"	F	Aug 67	1 Oct 54	"
	180	DBR 680	"	"	F	Nov 67	9 Sep 54	29 Feb 56
	181	DBR 681	"	"	F	Aug 67	13 Aug 54	
	182	DBR 682	"	"	F	Feb 68	21 Aug 54	1 Mar 56
	183	DBR 683	"	"	F	Aug 67	1 May 54	12 Mar 56
	184	DBR 684	"	"	F	Feb 68	7 Jul 54	13 Mar 56

P=passed to PTE 1 Apr 73

	Fleet No	Reg	Code	In service	H/F	Disposal	To H35/28R	
Guy Arab IV 5LW Crossley H33/25R	185	EBR 185	7.3.1	14 Sep 54	F	Dec 68	185-196: cost £2,198 chassis, £2,130 body, steel-framed lower saloon, aluminium alloy upper. All altered by Crossley to H35/28R at cost of £225 each, 185 on 22 Mar 56, others as below.	
	186	EBR 186	"	"	F	Oct 70	23 Mar 56	
	187	EBR 187	"	1 Oct 54	F	Aug 68	3 Nov 55. Delicensed Sep/Oct 55, believed to be following collision damage	
	188	EBR 188	"	"	F	Jul 68	5 Apr 56	

87

No.	Reg	Chassis				Notes
189	EBR 189	"	14 Sep 54	Dec 68	F	6 Apr 56
190	EBR 190	"	1 Oct 54	Jul 68	F	16 Apr 56
191	EBR 191	"	14 Sep 54	Dec 68	F	17 Apr 56
192	EBR 192	"	"	Oct 70	F	25 Apr 56
193	EBR 193	"	"	Feb 74*	FP	26 Apr 56. *Stored from withdrawal, 1972. Not operated by PTE
194	EBR 194	"	"	Jul 68	F	4 May 56
195	EBR 195	"	1 Oct 54	Aug 68	F	7 May 56
196	EBR 196	"	"	"	F	16 May 56

Daimler CVG5 Roe H33/25R

No.	Reg	Chassis				Notes
197	EBR 197	7.3.1	1 Sep 54	Dec 68	F	197-208 (except 202): cost £2,255 chassis, £2,140 body, all Park Royal metal-framed. All except 202 altered by Roe to H35/28R at cost of £208 each, 197 on 14 Jan 55, others as below
198	EBR 198	"	"	Jul 68	F	To H35/28R 24 Jan 55
199	EBR 199	"	1 Aug 54	Dec 68	F	" 29 Jan 55
200	EBR 200	"	"		F	"

Roe H37/28R

201	EBR 201	"	1 Sep 54	Feb 74*	FP	31 Jan 55. *Stored from withdrawal, 1972. Not operated by PTE
202	EBR 202	7.1.3	1 Oct 54	Oct 70	F	202: cost £2,268 chassis (modified springs), £2,343 body (additional seats and modified staircase). Exhibited at 1954 Commercial Motor Show (demonstration park). See text

Roe H33/25R

203	EBR 203	7.3.1	9 Jul 54	Aug 68*	F	To H35/28R 14 Feb 55. *Severe collision damage to roof
204	EBR 204	"	"	1974	FP	9 Dec 54. First to be altered following rear-end collision damage. Not operated by PTE
205	EBR 205	"	"	Aug 68	F	" 7 Feb 55
206	EBR 206	"	1 Aug 54	"	F	" 9 Feb 55
207	EBR 207	"	"	"	F	" 15 Feb 55
208	EBR 208	"	"	"	F	" 18 Feb 55

Guy Arab LUF 5HLW Burlingham B42D

26	EBR 226	6.6.0	1 Oct 54	Jul 68	F	26-29: cost £2,202 chassis, £2,186 body, metal-framed
27	EBR 227	"	23 Oct 54	"	F	
28	EBR 228	"	1 Oct 54	"	F	
29	EBR 229	"	23 Oct 54	Oct 68	F	Loaned to Dundee CT for 1 week, late 1954

Atkinson L644LW EXL Roe B41F

30	GGR 230	5.4.1	1 Aug 56	Nov 66	F	30: cost £1,819 chassis (exc tyres), £2,359 body.
31	JBR 631	5.5.2	14 Oct 57		F	31: cost £1,900 chassis (exc tyres), £2,369 body. 30/31: bodies Park Royal metal-framed. Dual-width doors.

n=not known

Daimler CVG5 Roe H35/28R

209	HGR 209	6.17.3	1 May 57	Feb 74	FP	209-215: cost £2,505 chassis, £2,150 body, Park Ryoal metal-framed
210	HGR 210	"	"	n	FP	
211	HGR 211	"	"	By Sep 74	FP	
212	HGR 212	"	"	n	FP	
213	HGR 213	"	"	By Sep 74	H	Withdrawn 1972
214	HGR 214	"	"	Feb 74	HP	Withdrawn 1972. Not operated by PTE
215	HGR 215	"	"		HP	Withdrawn 1972. Not operated by PTE
216	HGR 216	7.1.2	31 May 57	Nov 70	H	Cost £2,557 chassis, £2,150 chassis. SCG semi-automatic gearbox, additional cost of which not known

Chassis	Body	No.	Reg.		In	Out		Notes
Daimler CVG5	N Counties H35/28R	217	JGR 217	6.18.2	1 Mar 58	Jan 71	H	217-224: cost £2,525 chassis (exc tyres), £2,357. Steel-framed lower saloon, aluminium alloy upper. 217 fitted with lock-up flywheel-centrifugal clutch by 1959, giving 4% better fuel consumption
		218	JGR 218	"	"	"	H	
		219	JGR 219	"	"	"	H	
		220	JGR 220	"	"	"	H	
		221	JGR 221	"	"	"	H	
		222	JGR 222	"	"	"	H	
		223	JGR 223	"	"	"	H	
		224	JGR 224	"	"	"	H	
Daimler CVG5	Roe H35/28R	225	JGR 625	7.2.3	25 Mar 58	n	HP	225-230: cost £2,425 (exc tyres), £2,300 body. 225-236: teak-framed lower saloon, aluminium alloy upper
		226	JGR 626	"	"	Feb 75	HP	
		227	JGR 627	"	"	"	HP	Fitted with Twiflex centrifugal clutch
		228	JGR 628	"	"	-	HP	
		229	JGR 629	"	1 May 58	"	FP	Fluorescent lighting in lower saloon
		230	JGR 630	"	"	By Sep 74	FP	
Guy Arab IV 5LW	Roe H35/28R	231	JGR 631	7.2.3	1 May 58	Feb 74	FP	231-236: cost £2,348 (exc tyres), £2,300 body. Left-hand preselector quadrant lever
		232	JGR 632	"	"	Jun 72	F	
		233	JGR 233	"	"	Mar 71	F	
		234	JGR 634	"	"	Jun 72	F	
		235	JGR 635	"	"	"	F	
		236	JGR 636	"	"	"	F	One upper saloon ceiling panel experimentally of ICI "Darvic" material, resistant to nicotine stains. Two seat backs in each saloon impregnated with normal interior colour and with standard antique hide marking
AEC Reliance 2MU3RV	Roe B41D	32	PGR 332	5.16.2	10 Jan 61	Dec 73	FP	32-34: cost £2,109 chassis, £2,768 body. Synchromesh gearbox
		33	PGR 333	"	6 Jan 61	n	FP	Withdrawn 1972. Not operated by PTE
		34	PGR 334	"	14 Jan 61	Feb 74	FP	
AEC Reliance 2MU2RA	Willowbrook B41D	35	RGR 35		Jan 62	n	FP	35-41: £2,077 chassis, £2,725 body. Semi-automatic gearbox. 35 withdrawn 1971. Not operated by PTE
		36	RGR 36		Aug 61	Dec 73	FP	Withdrawn 1972. Not operated by PTE
		37	RGR 37		"	Feb 74	FP	Withdrawn 1972. Not operated by PTE
		38	RGR 38		Jan 62	Dec 73	FP	
		39	RGR 39		Aug 61	Feb 74	FP	
		40	RGR 40		Jan 62	Dec 73	FP	Withdrawn 1972. Not operated by PTE
		41	RGR 41		Jul 61	"	FP	Withdrawn 1972. Not operated by PTE
Daimler Fleetline CRG6LX	Roe H39/31F	250	SGR 250	8.15.0	Apr 62	Aug 76	FP	Cost £3,170 chassis, £3,310 body

Chassis	Body	Fleet No	Registration		In	Out		Notes
AEC Reliance 2MU3RV	Willowbrook B41D	42	TBR 442	6.0.0	Jun 62	Dec 73	FP	Withdrawn 1972. Not operated by PTE
		43	TBR 443	"	"	Apr 69	F	Burned out and withdrawn 1968
		44	TBR 444	"	Jul 62	Dec 73	FP	
		45	TBR 445	"	"	"	FP	
Daimler Fleetline CRG6LX	Roe H39/31F	251	TGR 551	8.15.0	Oct 62	*see note	FP	251-264: cost £3,202 chassis, £3,387 body. 251 displayed at 1962 Commercial Motor Show. *Withdrawn 1975, dismantled for spares 1976
		252	TGR 852	"	Nov 62	Aug 76	FP	
		253	TGR 853	"	"	"	FP	
		254	TGR 854	"	"	"	FP	
		255	TGR 855	"	"	"	FP	Fitted with lower saloon luggage rack and upper saloon extractor fans, Feb 64. See text
	Roe H43/34F	256	UGR 856	"	May 63	"	FP	Some published lists give seating layout incorrectly as 44/33
		257	UHR 257	"	"	*see note	FP	*Withdrawn 1975, dismantled for spares 1976
		258	UGR 258	"	"	Aug 76	FP	
		259	UGR 259	"	"	Feb 77	FP	Fitted with new upper saloon following collision damage, Oct 71
		260	UGR 260	"	"	Apr 77	FP	
		261	UGR 261	"	"	Feb 77	HP	
		262	UGR 262	"	"	"	HP	
		263	UGR 263	"	"	"	HP	
		264	UGR 264	"	"	"	HP	
Atkinson BPL746H	Marshall B45D	46	WBR 46	7.1.0	Dec 63	Jul 77	FP	46-48: cost £2,680 chassis, £2,823 body. 46 fitted with semi-automatic gearbox in place of original constant mesh unit Jul 64 at nett cost of £250. Disposed of for preservation
BPL746HF		47	WBR 47	7.4.0	Jan 64	"	FP	47/48 fitted with semi-automatic gearbox new at extra nett cost of £250 each
		48	WBR 48	"	"	"	FP	Disposed of for preservation
Daimler Fleetline CRG6LX	Roe H43/34F	265	XGR 865	8.15.0	Jul 64	*See note	HP	265-276: cost £3,212 chassis, £3,521 body. 265 withdrawn 1976, dismantled for spares Feb 77
		266	XGR 866	"	"	Feb 77	HP	
		267	XGR 867	"	"	Apr 77	HP	
		268	XGR 668	"	"	Jul 77	HP	
		269	XGR 669	"	"	Aug 77	HP	Severely damaged 24 Aug 64 and delicensed. Altered by Roe to H43/30D and fitted with flat one-piece windscreen, total cost £611. Re-entered service 20 Mar 65. Subsequently damaged and repaired again.
		270	XGR 670	"	"	Oct 77	HP	
		271	ABR 271B	"	Aug 64	Oct 77	HP	
		272	ABR 272B	"	"		FP	
		273	ABR 273B	"	"	Apr 78	FP	
		274	ABR 274B	"	"	May 78	FP	
		275	ABR 275B	"	"	"	FP	
		276	ABR 276B	"	"	Apr 78	FP	
Leyland Panther Cub	Marshall B45D	49	BBR 49C		May 65	Feb 77	FP	49-51: cost £2,634 chassis, £2,980 body

Model	Body	No	Reg				Notes	Op
PSURC1/1R		50	BBR 50C		"	"		FP
		51	BBR 51C		"	Jul 77		FP
Daimler Fleetline CRG6LW	Roe H43/34F	277	DGR 89D	8.14.0	Feb 66	Jul 77	277-288: average cost £6,814 complete. Final double deckers for SCT	FP
		278	DGR 90D	"	"	"		FP
		279	DGR 79D	"	"	"		FP
CRG6LX		280	DGR 80D	8.15.0	"	Jul 78		FP
		281	DGR 81D	"	Mar 66	Apr 78		FP
		282	DGR 82D	"	"	Jul 78		FP
		283	DGR 83D	"	"	Apr 78		FP
		284	DGR 84D	"	"	May 80	PTE training bus from May 78.	FP
		285	DGR 85D	"	"	Jul 78		FP
		286	DGR 86D	"	"	May 78		FP
		287	DGR 87D	"	"	Apr 78		FP
		288	DGR 88D	"	"	Jul 78		FP
Leyland Panther PSUR1/1R	Strachans B47+19D	52	FBR 52D	7.15.0	5 Sep 66	Sep 77	HP 52-84: cost £3,025 chassis, £3,394 body	HP
		53	FBR 53D	"	"	*see note	HP *Withdrawn 1977 and disposed of for preservation Aug 78	HP
		54	FBR 54D	"	"	Apr 78	HP	HP
		55	FBR 55D	"	"	n	HP Withdrawn 1977	HP
		56	FBR 56D	"	"	Feb 77	HP	HP
		57	FBR 57D	"	"	Jul 78	HP	HP
		58	FBR 58D	"	24 Oct 66	n	HP Withdrawal date not known	HP
		59	FBR 59D	"	14 Nov 66	May 78	HP	HP
		60	FBR 60D	"	25 Oct 66	Jul 78	HP	HP
		61	FBR 61D	"	19 Sep 66	Apr 78	HP	HP
		62	FBR 62D	"	18 Oct 66	Jul 77	HP	HP
		63	FBR 63D	"	4 Oct 66	"	HP	HP
		64	FBR 64D	"	19 Sep 66	Jul 78		FP
		65	FBR 65D	"	18 Oct 66	Apr 78		FP
		66	FBR 66D	"	7 Nov 66	Oct 77		FP
		67	FBR 67D	"	"	Jul 77		FP
		68	FBR 68D	"	1 Nov 66	Jul 78		FP
		69	FBR 69D	"	"	Nov 77		FP
		70	FBR 70D	"	"	Oct 77		FP
	"	71	FBR 71D	"	25 Nov 66	Feb 79		FP
		72	FBR 72D	"	1 Nov 66	Apr 78		FP
		73	FBR 73D	"	14 Nov 66	Feb 79		FP
		74	FBR 74D	"	28 Nov 66	Oct 77		FP

91

Chassis	Body	No	Registration	Length	New	Withdrawn	Depot	Notes
		75	FBR 75D	"	23 Nov 66	Jul 77	FP	
		76	FBR 76D	"	1 Dec 66	Apr 78	FP	
		77	FBR 77D	"		Jul 77	FP	
		78	FBR 78D	"	6 Dec 66	Apr 78	FP	
		79	FBR 79D	"	14 Nov 66	Apr 79	FP	
		80	FBR 80D	"	6 Dec 66	"	FP	
		81	FBR 81D	"		Jan 80	FP	
		82	FBR 82D	"	13 Dec 66	Jul 77	FP	
		83	FBR 83D	"	"	May 78	FP	Damaged by fire Sep 69. Delicensed then rebuilt. Re-entered service May 72
		84	FBR 84D	"	22 Dec 66	Feb 79	FP	
Daimler Roadliner SRC6	Strachans B47+19D	85	FBR 85D	7.16.2	13 Oct 66	*see note	FP	85-87: cost £3,333 chassis, £3,394 body. *85 delicensed by SCT Aug 70, reinstated Oct 72, delicensed by PTE Jul 73, reinstated Jun 74, dismantled 1974, remains disposed of Feb 75
		86	FBR 86D	"	17 Oct 66	Feb 75	FP	
		87	FBR 87D	"	13 Oct 66	"	FP	Displayed at 1966 Commercial Motor Show
Leyland Panther PSUR1/1R	Strachans B47+19D	88	GGR 88E	7.15.0	Aug 67	May 79	FP	88-97: cost £3,116 chassis, £3,712 body
		89	GGR 89E	"	Jul 67	Apr 79	FP	
		90	GGR 90E	"	"	May 79	FP	
		91	GGR 91E	"	Aug 67	"	FP	
		92	GGR 92E	"	"	"	FP	
		93	GGR 93E	"	"	Apr 79	FP	
		94	GGR 94E	"	Jul 67	May 79	FP	
		95	GGR 95E	"	"	Jul 79	FP	
		96	GGR 96E	"	Aug 67	Jul 78	FP	
		97	GGR 97E	"	Jul 67	Apr 79	FP	
Bristol RELL6G	MCCW B47+19D	98	JBR 98F	7.9.2	Jan 68	Jul 78	FP	98-107: cost £3,324 chassis, £3,681 body
		99	JBR 99F	"	"	Apr 78	FP	
		100	JBR 100F	"	"	Oct 77	FP	
		101	JBR 101F	"	"	"	FP	
		102	JBR 102F	"	"	"	FP	
		103	JBR 103F	"	"	"	FP	
		104	JBR 104F	"	"	Jul 79	FP	
		105	JBR 105F	"	"	Oct 77	FP	
		106	JBR 106F	"	"	Jul 78	FP	
		107	JBR 107F	"	"	Jul 79	FP	
Leyland Panther PSUR1/1R	Strachans B47+19D	108	KGR 508G	7.19.0	Aug 68	Mar 80	HP	108-131: cost £3,403 chassis, £3,470 body
		109	KGR 509G	"	"	Jul 79	HP	
		110	KGR 510G	"	"	"	HP	

No.	Registration		In	Out		Notes
111	KGR 511G	"	"	"	HP	
112	KGR 512G	"	Sep 68	"	HP	
113	KGR 513G	"	Aug 68	"	HP	
114	KGR 514G	"	"	May 79	HP	
115	KGR 515G	"	Sep 68	Jul 79	HP	
116	KGR 516G	"	"	May 79	HP	
117	KGR 517G	"	Aug 68	May 80	HP	
118	KGR 518G	"	"	Jul 79	HP	
119	KGR 519G	"	Sep 68	n	HP	
120	KGR 520G	"	"	Jul 79	HP	
121	KGR 521G	"	"	May 79	HP	
122	KGR 522G	"	"	Jul 79	HP	
123	KGR 523G	"	"		HP	
124	KGR 524G	"	"	Nov 79	HP	
125	KGR 525G	"	"		HP	
126	KGR 526G	"	"	Jul 79	HP	
127	KGR 527G	"	"	Feb 80	HP	
128	KGR 528G	"	Oct 68	Nov 79	HP	
129	KGR 529G	"	"	Jan 80	HP	
130	KGR 530G	"	"	"	HP	
131	KGR 531G	"	"	Feb 80	HP	
AEC Swift MP2R		Strachans B47+19D				
132	KGR 532G	7.8.1	Nov 68	Apr 78	FP	FP 132-141: cost £3,245 chassis, £3,490 body.
133	KGR 533G	"	"	Apr 79	FP	
134	KGR 534G	"	"	Jul 79	FP	
135	KGR 535G	"	"	May 79	FP	
136	KGR 536G	"	"	Apr 79	FP	
137	KGR 537G	"	"	Jun 79	FP	
138	KGR 538G	"	"	Apr 79	FP	
139	KGR 539G	"	"	Apr 78	FP	Collision-damaged 1971, reported withdrawn, repaired and returned to service 1972
140	KGR 540G	"	"	n	FP	Withdrawn 1979
141	KGR 541G	"	"	n	FP	Withdrawn 1979
Leyland Panther PSUR1A/1		Marshall B47+19D				
142	PBR 142J	"	Oct 70	Apr 80	FP	FP 142-150: cost £3,727 chassis, £4,077 body (less 25% bus grant on total)
143	PBR 143J	"	"	"	FP	
144	PBR 144J	"	"	"	FP	
145	PBR 145J	"	"	By Mar 80	FP	
146	PBR 146J	"	"	Feb 80	FP	
147	PBR 147J	"	"	Apr 80	FP	
148	PBR 148J	"	"	Dec 79	FP	
149	PBR 149J	"	"	Jun 80	FP	
150	PBR 150J	"	"	Mar 80	FP	

Footnotes

1 - Heating and ventilation system fitted to Guy 139. In April 1959, 139 was fitted with a Cave-Browne-Cave heating and ventilation system by NCME, cost £230. It was then distinguishable by its front destination display. The system, developed by Wing Commander T R Cave-Browne-Cave, Professor of Engineering at University College, Southampton, used waste heat from the engine and the forward motion of the bus to introduce warmed fresh air into both saloons and did not simply warm the air already inside. The normal radiator (but not its conventional grille and shell) was replaced by a header tank, the coolant passing up from this to the heat exchangers behind the two apertures. Air entering the apertures went through the exchangers before being admitted to the saloons. With this system, the humid air from the presence of passengers, worse in wet weather, was virtually pushed out via the open rear platform and condensation was minimised. In warm weather the heating action could be shut off and cool air admitted to the saloons. Conductors on 139 suffered from headaches which may have been why, after about two years, partial blanking plates were fitted to the intake apertures. Otherwise it was an effective system although no other bus in the fleet was to be fitted with it.

2 - Weight reduction. The period from about 1953 was a time of interest in saving weight as an economy measure. While 140-147 were kept below 7ton, most later examples were not. The Roe and Crossley bodies of 148-167, 173-208 (except 202) were $53^{1}/2$-54cwt, within the specified 55cwt although the other ACB bodies were $55^{1}/2$cwt. Other builders were producing much lighter bodies, MCW's Orion having severely spartan versions weighing 46cwt or less, and Saro a better-finished body weighing 43cwt, for instance. A 1954 report by Mr Morton stated that the newest buses weighed a ton less than previous deliveries (in fact they did not quite) and this would improve fuel consumption by 10 per cent, representing £70 per bus each year. (Fuel consumption tests had been carried out during Feb/Mar 54 using all-Leyland bus 58 which was experimentally fitted with wooden cradles under most of the transverse seats. Into these frames were placed weights aggregating one ton. 58 then ran for a month weighing 7.18.2 unladen instead of 6.18.2.)

3 - Engine modifications. The 5LW 'K' engines of 148-184 were adjusted to give slower idling speed for improved fuel consumption. One report states that the engines of the whole fleet were treated similarly by April 1954, although a later report suggests that only those with preselective gearboxes were treated. SCT bus engines spent an average of 23% of their time each day idling. In order further to improve economy, drivers were instructed to avoid reaching maximum revolutions before each upward gear change, to avoid idling through the fluid transmission with the bus in gear (and yet idling in gear was standard practice on London Transport with more than 7,000 preselective buses), to switch off the engine at termini and when refuelling in the depot, to drive steadily rather than "on the brakes" and finally, to report cases of engines emitting black smoke.

4 - Seating capacity of Crossley-bodied Guys 173-184. The specification was for 58 seats and Crossley records quote this figure. A contemporary trade press report of their delivery states 58 also. Departmental records, however, say they were 57-seaters (32 over 25), the seat over the offside rear wheel arch being for two passengers. SCT documents also state that at various dates during May-Nov 54, the lower saloon seating capacity was increased from 25 to 26. Whether this was a material change or one on paper only is not clear. A former SCT employee, Mr John Hogarth, who worked in the body repair section and would have been involved in any physical alteration, has no recollection of there being any change to the seats.

5 - Centrifugal clutches. In further search of greater economy, SCT experimented with alternative forms of transmission for buses with epicyclic (preselective and semi-automatic) gearboxes. Trials with a centrifugal clutch in place of the normal fluid flywheel had been carried out on Daimler 122 as far back as 1953, although it appears to have reverted to original condition by 1959. The mechanism had been developed by the Self Changing Gears concern in conjunction with Daimler. In providing a positive coupling between the engine and transmission, eliminating fluid flywheel "slip", the centrifugal clutch offered potential savings in fuel consumption. There were, however, some drawbacks in the form of increased maintenance costs which seemingly cancelled out some of the the fuel economy. By the late 1950s, however, technology had progressed and SCT again experimented. NCME-bodied Daimler 217 was fitted with a lock-up flywheel clutch. This comprised a normal fluid flywheel which operated until a predetermined speed was reached, after which a centrifugal clutch would engage. The bus was driven in the normal way. With its modification 217 was reported to give a 4% improvement in fuel consumption. The question arising here is whether 217's original fluid flywheel was in fact exchanged with the original equipment fitted to semi-automatic Roe Daimler 216 which during this period acquired a normal fluid flywheel. Extant records do not say, but it is just feasible that the lock-up flywheel clutch which clearly did not work well in 216 was tried in the preselective 217 and found to be more successful. Another experiment involved Roe-bodied Daimler 227 which was fitted with a Twiflex clutch. This eliminated the fluid flywheel altogether but gave jerky starts and gear changes. Drivers did not like the Twiflex equipment and from the passenger's standpoint also, the fitting of it was a retrograde step. It is possible that these changes of specification to 217/227 were not permanent. Some other municipalities carried out tests of this kind. In 1952, Halifax had tried out a centrifugal clutch in a preselective single deck Daimler Freeline, and Bolton had some 1957 CVG6 chassis delivered new with the Twiflex clutch, drivers there disliking them, too.

Table 2   Rebodied chassis

Note.   In the case of the wartime Guys, date rebodied means date delivered with new body.

Fleet No(s)	Chassis	Original body details	Year new	New body details	Date rebodied	New UW	Remarks (cost given for each new body to nearest £1)
13	Thornycroft LB	Th'croft? B29F	1928	Eng Elec B29F	Jun 35	-	Cost £315. Used as tram-o-car. Altered to B26F in 1938.
1/2	Guy Wolf CF20	Guy B20T	1934	ACB B20F	Jul 47	2.11.3	Cost £544. Fleet numbers not allocated until rebodied. Suitable for driver-only operation
3/4	"	"	1935	Blagg B20F	Oct 38	3.1.0	Cost £258. Fleet numbers not allocated until rebodied. Suitable for driver-only operation
59	Guy Arab I 5LW	Roe H26/22C	1943	Roe H33/28R	30 Dec 54	7.5.3	New bodies on wartime Guys: cost £1,880
63	Guy Arab II 5LW	Massey H30/26R	"	"	7 Jan 55	"	
67	"	Pickering H30/26R	"	"	4 Jan 55	"	
78	"	Massey H30/26R	1944	"	7 Jan 55	"	
79	"	"	"	"	4 Jan 55	"	
81	"	"	"	"	30 Dec 54	"	Original engine 6LW. Altered when rebodied

Table 3 Details of chassis types

Note   In the gearbox column, the figure indicates the number of forward speeds, "slid" = sliding mesh, "con" = constant mesh, "syn" = synchromesh, "pre" = preselective, "s-auto" = direct-acting semi-automatic

Years in service with SCT	Make & model	Engine	P = petrol D = diesel	Gearbox	Wheel-base	Length	Width	SCT fleet No(s)	Remarks
1929-43	Leyland Lion LT1	Leyland 5.1-litre	P	4-slid	16' 81/4"	27'6"	7'6"	1-12	
1929-45	Thornycroft LB	Th'croft MB4	P	4-slid	c17'6"	27'6"	7'6"	13	Normal control
1930-44	Leyland Lion LT2	Leyland 5.1-litre	P	4-slid	16'6"	27'6"	7'6"	14-19	
1930-44	Leyland Tiger TS2	Leyland 6.8-litre	P	4-slid	17'6"	26'0"	7'6"	20/21	
1930-36	Dennis HV	Dennis S6CIP	P	4-slid	16'63/4"	25'0"	7'6"	22-25	
1934-54	Guy Wolf CF20	Meadows 3.3-litre	P	4-con	12'6"	c200"	7'6"	-	Normal control
1934-39	Daimler COG5	Gardner 5LW	D	5-pre	16'35/32"	26' 0"	7'6"	26-55	All Daimlers numbered up to 147 had quadrant gear-change
1937-51	Crossley Mancunian double deck	Crossley VR6	D	4-pre	16'71/2"	26'0"	7'6"	24/25	
1939-54	Crossley Mancunian single deck	Crossley VR6	D	4-con	16' 71/2"	27'6"	7'6"	22/23	
1942-57	Leyland Titan TD7	Leyland E166	D	4-con	16'6"	26'0"	7'6"	56-58, 25	
1943-72	Guy Arab I & II	Gardner 5LW or 6LW	D	4-slid	16'3"	26'0"	7'6"	59/62-70/ 74-81, 5/6	By special dispensation, long-bonneted wartime Guy Arabs were several inches over the maximum permitted length, applying to all except 5/6/59. 6LW engines - 80/81, others 5LW. Gearboxes: see footnote to this table.
1943-58	Daimler CWG5	Gardner 5LW	D	4-pre	16'35/32"	26'0"	7'6"'	60/61	
1943-56	Daimler CWA6	AEC A173	D	4-pre	16'35/32"	26'0"	7'6"	71-73	71/72 later converted to CWG5 specification
1946-58	Daimler CWD6	Daimler CD6	D	4-pre	16'35/32"	26'0"	7'6"	15-18	
1946-63	Crossley DD42/3	Crossley HOE7/1	D	4-con	16'71/2"	26'0" *A*	7'6"	19-21, 9-14	All engines replaced by Gardner 5LW, 1950-55. *A* - 9-14 were 25' 51/8" long.
1947-60	AEC Regent Mk III O961/2	AEC A208	D	4-pre	16'4"	26'0"	7'6"	82-87	
1948-66	Daimler CVG6	Gardner 6LW	D	4-pre	16'35/32"	26'0" *B*	7.6' *B*	88-99, 106-127	*B* - 116-127 were 27'long and 8' wide and had 6LW 'K' engine from new

Years	Chassis/Model	Engine	D	Gearbox	Wheelbase	Length	Width	Fleet numbers	Notes
1949-63	Crossley DD42/7C	Crossley HOE7/4	D	4-syn	16'7½"	25'5⅛"	7'6"	100-105	All engines replaced by Gardner 5LW, 1953-55
1950-65	Guy Arab III single deck	Gardner 6LW	D	4-pre	17'6"	27'6"	7'6"	7/8	Engines replaced by 5LW, 1952
1952-72	Guy Arab III double deck	Gardner 6LW 'K'	D	4-pre *C*	16'3"	27'0"	8'0"	128-139	*C* - 139 had 4-con gearbox
1953-73	Daimler CVG5	Gardner 5LW 'K'	D	4-pre *D*	16'3⁵⁄₃₂" *D*	26'0" *D*	7'6"	140-172, 197-230	*D* - Buses from 148 had "gate" gear-change and were 27' 0" long. 197-230 had 16'4" wheelbase. 216 had a semi-automatic gearbox - see text
1954-68	Guy Arab LUF 5HLW	Gardner 5HLW 'K'	D	4-pre	16'4"	30'0"	8'0"	26-29	
1956-66	Atkinson L644LW EXL	Gardner 4LW 'K'	D	4-syn	18'3¼"	29'11"	7'5¾"	30/31	Body 30'0" x 8'0". David Brown gearbox
1961-73	AEC Reliance 2MU3RV	AEC AH470	D	5-syn	16'4"	30'0"	8'0"	32-34, 42-45	
1961-73	AEC Reliance 2MU2RA	" "	D	4-s-auto	"	"	"	35-41	
1963-73	Atkinson BPL746H	Gardner 6HLW 'K'	D	5-con		33'8"	8'2½"	46	4-s-auto gearbox fitted Jul 64
1964-73	Atkinson BPL746HF	" "	D	4-s-auto		"	"	47/48	
1965-73	Leyland Panther Cub PSURC1/1R	Leyland 0.400(H)	D	4-s-auto	16'6"	33'5"	"	49-51	
1966-73	Leyland Panther PSUR1/1R	Leyland 0.600(H)	D	4-s-auto	17'6"	36'0"	"	52-84, 88-97, 108-131, 142-150	
1966-73	Daimler Roadliner SRC6	Cummins V6-200	D	4-s-auto	18'6"	"	"	85-87	
1967-73	Bristol RELL6G	Gardner 6HLX	D	4-s-auto	"	"	"	98-107	
1968-73	AEC Swift MP2R	AEC AH505	D	4-s-auto	17'6"	"	"	132-141	

Footnote.

Wartime Guy gearboxes. Originally these had 1st/2nd gear positions on the right side of the 'H' (ie, nearer the driver), with 3rd/4th on the left side. In 1946 all SCT examples were modified so that these positions were transposed, ie, 1st/2nd were on the left and vice versa. However, about 1953 Guy 80 reverted to the original arrangement but it has not been possible to confirm whether this was permanent.

Appendix 1, continued

Table 4   Details of engine types

Years in service with SCT	Make	Type	Cyls	Bore x stroke (inches unless stated otherwise)	Swept volume (litres)	Power output (bhp @ rpm)	RAC rating (hp)	Remarks
Petrol engines								
1929-44	Leyland	5.1-litre	4	4¼ x 5½	5.1	62 @ 1,800	28.9	
1929-45	Thornycroft	MB4	4	4¾ x 6	6.97	59	36.1	Exceptionally large 4-cyl engine!
1930-44	Leyland	6.8-litre	6	4 x 5½	6.8	90 @ 2,000	38.8	
1930-36	Dennis	S6CIP	4	110 x 150mm	5.7	70	30	
1933-54	Meadows	3.3-litre	4		3.3	50 @ 2,400	20	
Diesel engines								
1933-66	Gardner	4LW	4	4¼ x 6	5.6	68 @ 1,700	29	4, 5 & 6LW developed from Gardner 4, 5 & 6L2 marine engines in 1931. Exceptional economy and reliability throughout Gardner range. 'K' version of 4LW introduced 1950 - 75bhp
1933-73	Gardner	5LW } 5HLW}	5	4¼ x 6	7.0	85 @ 1,700	36.5	'K' version (introduced 1950) - 94bhp. Most older engines converted on overhaul. 5HLW used from 1954
1937-54	Crossley	VR6	6	4⁷⁄₁₆ x 5½	8.365	100 @ 1,700	47.3	Originally indirect injection, converted by SCT to direct injection 1943
1942-57	Leyland	E166	6	4½ x 5½	8.6	98 @ 1,900	48.6	Exceptionally smooth-running engine
1943-56	AEC	A173	6	105 x 130mm	7.585	86 @ 1,800	41	Marketed as 7.7-litre unit. Output quoted is wartime economy setting, normally 98bhp
1944-73	Gardner	6LW } 6HLW}	6	4¼ x 6	8.4	102 @ 1,700	43.5	'K' version (introduced 1950) - 112bhp. Most older engines converted on overhaul. 6HLW used from 1963
1946-58	Daimler	CD6	6	4½ x 5½	8.6	100 @ 1,800	48.6	A quiet and smooth-running engine
1946-55	Crossley	HOE7/1 HOE7/4	6	4½ x 5½	8.6	100 @ 1,750	48.6	All replaced by Gardner 5LW 1950-55
1947-60	AEC	A208	6	120 x 142mm	9.6	125 @ 1,800	53.5	Derated by SCT 1955
1961-73	AEC	AH470	6	112 x 130mm	7.685	112 @ 2,000	46.7	Marketed as 7.75-litre unit. SCT examples may have been derated to 103bhp @ 1,800rpm by SCT.
1962-73	Gardner	6LX	6	4¾ x 6	10.45	150 @ 1,700	54.2	New design, introduced 1958. Interchangeable with 6LW.
1965-73	Leyland	0.400	6	4.22 x 4.75	6.54	125 @ 2,400	42.7	
1966-73	Leyland	0.600	6	4⅘ x 5½	9.8	125 @ 1,800	55.3	
1966-73	Cummins	V6-200	6	5½ x 4⅛	9.63	150 @ 2,100	72.6	Bus version. Cylinders in V-formation
1968-73	AEC	AH505	6	116 x 130mm	8.2	145 @ 2,200	50.1	This design developed from AH470 (see above)

Table 5   Buses hired-in during World War II

Chassis	Body	Engine P=petrol D=diesel	From	Home Fleet No	Reg No	Unladen Wt t. c. q	Date new	Date to SCT	Date returned	Remarks
Crossley Condor	Met-Cam/Crossley L26/26R	6.8-lit P	Manchester CT	260	VU 635	6.12.2	Nov 30	8 Jul 40	Sep 40	Body fitted new Mar 35
"	"	9.1-lit D	"	265	VU 770	"	"	"	Apr 42	Historic bus: took Paris delegates from Manchester to Dover Oct 1930. Body fitted new Oct 35.
"	"	"	"	259	VU 7412	"	Feb 32	"	"	Originally No349. Body built 1935 and transferred to this chassis from bus 259 (VR 644) keeping original fleet number, Feb 39.
"	"	"	"	195	VU 7413	"	Jan 32	"	Sep 40	Originally No350. Body new 1935 and transferred to this chassis from bus 195 (VR 6014) keeping original fleet number, Oct 37
AEC Regent	Tilling or Dodson H27/25RO	6.1-lit P	London PTB	ST 851	GJ 2027		1930	Dec 41	26 Aug 42	New to Thomas Tilling. To LTPB on its formation, 1933
"	"	"	"	ST 879	GJ 2055		1930	Apr 42	"	As above
"	"	"	"	ST 966	GK 6242		1931	"	"	As above
Leyland Tiger TS11	Roe B30R	8.6-lit D	Leigh CT (Lancs)	A	A		1940	1942	1942	A-either 78, 79 or 80 (ETJ 107, 108 or 109). Precise dates not known

Appendix 1, continued

Table 6   Demonstration buses loaned to SCT

Reg No	Chassis	Body	Engine type	Eng sw vol (lit)	Gearbox	Owner	Year new	When loaned to SCT	Remarks
OTC 738	Leyland Tiger Cub PSUC1/1T	Saro B44F	Ley O/350	5.76	4-con	Leyland	1952	Dec 53	
LJW 336	Guy Arab LUF	Saro B44F	Gardner 5HLW	7.0	5-con	Guy	1953	Dec 53	Subsequent order for 4 Guy Arab LUF 5HLW chassis
PHP 220	Daimler CVG6	N Counties H33/38R	Gardner 6LW	8.4	4-pre	Daimler	1954	1955	Subsequent order for 8 Northern Counties bodies
VDA 32	Guy Warrior LUF	Willowbrook B44F	Meadows 4HDC330	5.4	5-con	Guy	1957	Jan 58	
PNR 891	AEC Reliance MU3RV	Duple (Midland) B44F	AEC AH470	7.75	5-syn	Duple (Mid)1958	1958	Mar 58	Subsequent orders for 14 AEC Reliance chassis
NM 606	Bedford SB8	Duple (Midland) B40F	Leyland 0.350	5.76	4-syn	Vauxhall	1958	Sep 58	
VKV 99	Daimler CVG6LX-30	Willowbrook H41/33R	Gardner 6LX	10.45	see note	Daimler	1956	Oct /Nov 58	4-speed "Daimatic" SCG-designed epicyclic gbx with fully- and semi-automatic modes. Chassis originally used for testing, not bodied until 1957. Semi-low height build (14'0"); no conventional body underframe. See footnote
116 TMD	AEC Bridgemaster B3RA	Park Royal H45/31R	AEC AV590	9.6	4-syn	ACV	1959	May 59	
398 JTB	Leyland Atlantean PDR1/1	Weymann H44/34F	Leyland 0.600	9.8	4-s-auto	Leyland	1959	Sep 59	
7000 HP	Daimler Fleetline RE30	Weymann H72F	Daimler CD6 Mk VIII	8.6	4-s-auto	Daimler	1960	May 61	Engine turbocharged. Seating capacity altered later. Loaned to SCT in May 65 when fitted with Cummins engine. Gardner 6LX fitted later. 39 Fleetline chassis acquired 1962-66
WJU 406	Leyland Leopard LR1	Willowbrook B45F	Leyland 0.600H	9.8	4-syn	Willowbrook	1961	Jul 61	
4599 VC	Daimler Fleetline CRG6LX	N Counties H44/33F	Gardner 6LX	10.45	4-s-auto	Daimler	1962	Jul/Aug 63	
SGD 669	Leyland Atlantean PDR1/1 Mk II	Alexander H44/34F	Leyland 0.600	9.8	4-s-auto	Leyland	1962	Sep 63	
CHN 341C	Bristol RELL6G	ECW B54F	Gardner 6HLX	10.45	4-s-auto	United AS	1965	Aug 65	Loaned on behalf of the chassis manufacturer. Subsequent order for 10 Bristol RELL6G chassis
FGW 498C	AEC Swift MP2R	Willowbrook B53F	AEC AH505	8.2	4-s-auto	ACV Sales	1965	Jan 66	Subsequent order for 10 AEC Swift chassis Nov/Dec 66
LYY 827D	" "	Marshall B48D						1966	
KKV 800G	Daimler Roadliner SRP8	Plaxton DP53F	Perkins V8	8.36	4-s-auto	Daimler	1968	Mar 69	V-formation eight-cylinder engine.
SDU 930G	Daimler Fleetline SRG6-36	Alexander B45D	Gardner 6LX	10.45	4-s-auto	Daimler	1968	Mar 69	Single deck version of Fleetline chassis
VWD 452H	Metro-Scania BR111MH	Metro-Cammell B31D	Scania D11	11.0	*see note	MCW	1969	Oct 70	*Torque-convertor transmission
ABU 451J	Seddon Pennine RU	Pennine B45D	Gardner 6HLX	10.45	4-s-auto	Seddon	1970	Nov 71	

In Feb 60, the first Guy Wulfrunian, OHL 863 (on Guy Motors trade plates 093 UK), visited Sunderland. This revolutionary type of low-height double decker was not operated by SCT and came for inspection only.

Footnote

VKV 99. Special mention is made of this bus as its performance was analysed in detail while with SCT. It ran on 12 days exclusively on service 24 (Durham Road - Seaburn via Fulwell Road). Fully automatic drive was used for only four days. Fuel consumption was found to be 9.54mpg in fully automatic and 9.94 in semi-automatic control. At that time SCT's 6LW-engined buses of comparable weight were returning 9.74mpg alongside 10.78 from the 5LW-powered vehicles of 1954 onwards. The 6LX engine represented Gardner's response to the need for greater power in larger and heavier goods and passenger chassis and was designed to fit into the same space as the 6LW. Although VKV 99 carried 10.1 per cent more passengers and generated 10.8 per cent more revenue during the period, Mr Morton believed that some of these may have been extracted from other buses and he doubted whether the figures would have been the same had all the vehicles on the service been 74-seaters. He did not accept the argument that using larger buses on reduced frequencies was a long-term economy because the result, he believed, would be a more rapid loss of passengers.

Table 7   Ancillary vehicles

Vehicles acquired new except where indicated otherwise. List may not be exhaustive.

Reg No	Make	Year built	Description	Purchase price	Date acquired	Date of disposal	Remarks
BR 1006	Edison 2-ton	1920(?)	tower wagon		1920(?)		Battery-electric chassis.
BR 3649	Albion 30-cwt	1924	lorry	£547	1924	15 Nov 38	Sold for £6.
BR 5662	Morris 12-cwt	1927	van	£170	Apr 27	10 Jul 34	Scrapped
BR 6267	Karrier CY2	1928	2-ton tipping lorry	£425	Jan 28	29 Apr 36	Sold to S'land Cleansing Dept for £10.
CD 6891	Tilling-Stevens TS6	1922	tower wagon	£125	Aug 29	22 Apr 36	New as bus to Southdown. Petrol-electric chassis. To S'land via manufacturer. Tower wagon body possibly from BR 1006. Chassis (CD 6891) sold for £15.
CD 4866	Tilling-Stevens TS3	1919	lorry	£125	Feb 30	20 Jan 37	New as bus to Southdown. Petrol-electric chassis. Lorry body possibly from another chassis.
GR 1080	Morris 14hp	1934	15-cwt van	£179	Jun 34	30 Apr 41	Sold for £5.
GR 2793	Austin 16 Hertford	1936	saloon car	£261	Apr 36	4 Mar 42	Sold to ARP for £100.
GR 2898	Thornycroft CF	1936	3-ton tipping lorry	£421	May 36	7 Mar 52	Sold for £10.
PG 6564	Dennis HS	1929	tower wagon	see Table 1	19 Jan 37	15 Nov 38	Originally Dennis demonstrator bus with Massey body. Some documents state HV type. Acquired by SCT as No22, Jun 30 (see Table 1). Converted to tower wagon 19 Jan 37, possibly with body from CD 6891. Chassis sold for £12.
GR 5929	Thornycroft CF	1938	3-ton tipping lorry	£433	Aug 38	12 Mar 53	Sold for £25.
GR 5930	Thornycroft CF	1938	3-ton tower wagon	£641	Oct 38	24 Feb 56	Sold to Boro' Engineer's Dept for £100.
BR 9868	Austin	1933	van		Sep 39		New to S'land Electricity Dept. UW 11cwt 12lb. Possibly not used by SCT.
GR 430	Morris 10hp	1934	goods saloon car	£5	Sep 39	11 Nov 42	New to S'land Electricity Dept. Dismantled by SCT.
GR 645	Morris 10hp	1934	10-cwt van	£5	Sep 39	30 Apr 41	New to S'land Electricity Dept. Could also carry 4 persons.
GR 1119	Austin	1934	van		Sep 39		New to S'land Electricity Dept. UW 11cwt 96lb. Possibly not used by SCT.
GR 4761	Leyland Cub	1937	tower wagon				Loaned by Electricity Dept for duration of War.

Registration	Make/Model	Year	Type	Price	In	Out	Notes
DPT 376/377	Bedford HC 10hp	1938	12cwt vans	£170 ea	Apr 41	19 Apr 44	Origins not known. Sold for £12 each.
EBB 574	Austin 18 Hertford	1937	saloon car	£145	Feb 42	28 Aug 53	Origin not known. Sold for £105.
GR 7804	Ford 10hp	1944	10-cwt van	£212	23 Jun 44	3 Sep 55	
GR 2579	Wolseley 14	1935	saloon car	£30	18 Jan 45	22 Apr 50	Possibly acquired from Mr H W Snowball. Sold for £42.
GR 80	Morris 10hp	1934	saloon car	£20	29 Jan 45	24 Feb 49	Believed acquired from ARP. Sold by SCT for £28.
GR 9860	Morris 18hp truck	1943(?)	compressor lorry	£230	Apr 48	29 Feb 56	Ministry of Supply specification. New to War Department. Reg'd in S'land 1948. Believed stored unused prior to acquisition.
ABR 724	Thornycroft ER4	1949	tipping lorry		1949	1966	
ABR 881	Austin A40	1949	10-cwt van	£313	1949	1961	Sold for £42.
ENE 747	Rover 12hp	1938	saloon car	£350	1 Mar 50	17 Dec 52	Origin not known. Sold for £155.
CBR 598	Morris Minor	1952	saloon car	£642	1952	1959	Sold for £310.
DBR 72	Morris Oxford	1953	saloon car	£731	1953	1959	Sold for £341.
FBR 715	Austin LDO	1955	1-ton van	£800	1955	1964	Sold for £50.
KGR 191	Morris Oxford	1959	saloon car	£893	1959	1964	Sold for £252.
KGR 981	Morris LDO	1959	30-cwt van	£909	1959		
WBR 400	Austin LDO	1963	van	£780	1963		
JGR 76F	Morris 1000	1968	10-cwt van		1968		
JGR 607F	Austin LDO	1968	30-cwt van		1968		
MBR 694/695G	Bedford Beagle HA	1969	10-cwt vans		1969		
MGR 529H	Bedford	1970	lorry		1970		Converted to breakdown tender by PTE, c1977.

1948 Massey-bodied Daimler CVG6 89, minus mechanical components, undergoes body rebuilding at the newly-opened Wheat Sheaf central works during the summer of 1956 while a 1954 Crossley-bodied Guy, possibly 193, has a collision repair carried out. Attending to 89 are (from nearest camera) George Cook (chargeman bodybuilder), Gordon Gunn (joiner), David Armstrong (coachbuilder, with saw) and Ralph Carr (joiner, on staging). The bus has already had its side and rear panelling and some rotten pillars and rails removed. A new panel incorporating the standard display will replace the original one with twin apertures at the front of the upper saloon with a corresponding one at the rear. Alf Cairns (handyman) sees to the Guy. *(Copyright Busways Travel Services)*

Busy in the foreground are handymen Bill Chambers (left) along with Alf Cairns (right) who has on his bench the tin front from the Crossley-bodied Guy mentioned previously. Behind him are the wings and there are Daimler and Guy radiator shells by the rail. In the engine overhaul bay (left background), bareheaded, are Peter Bell (left, apprentice fitter) and Billy Leckenby (right, fitter). The buses in the docking bay (right), all Roe-bodied, are (left to right) Daimler 119, AEC 87, Guy 131 and Daimler 120. Normally the centre ground would contain buses also. *(Copyright Busways Travel Services)*

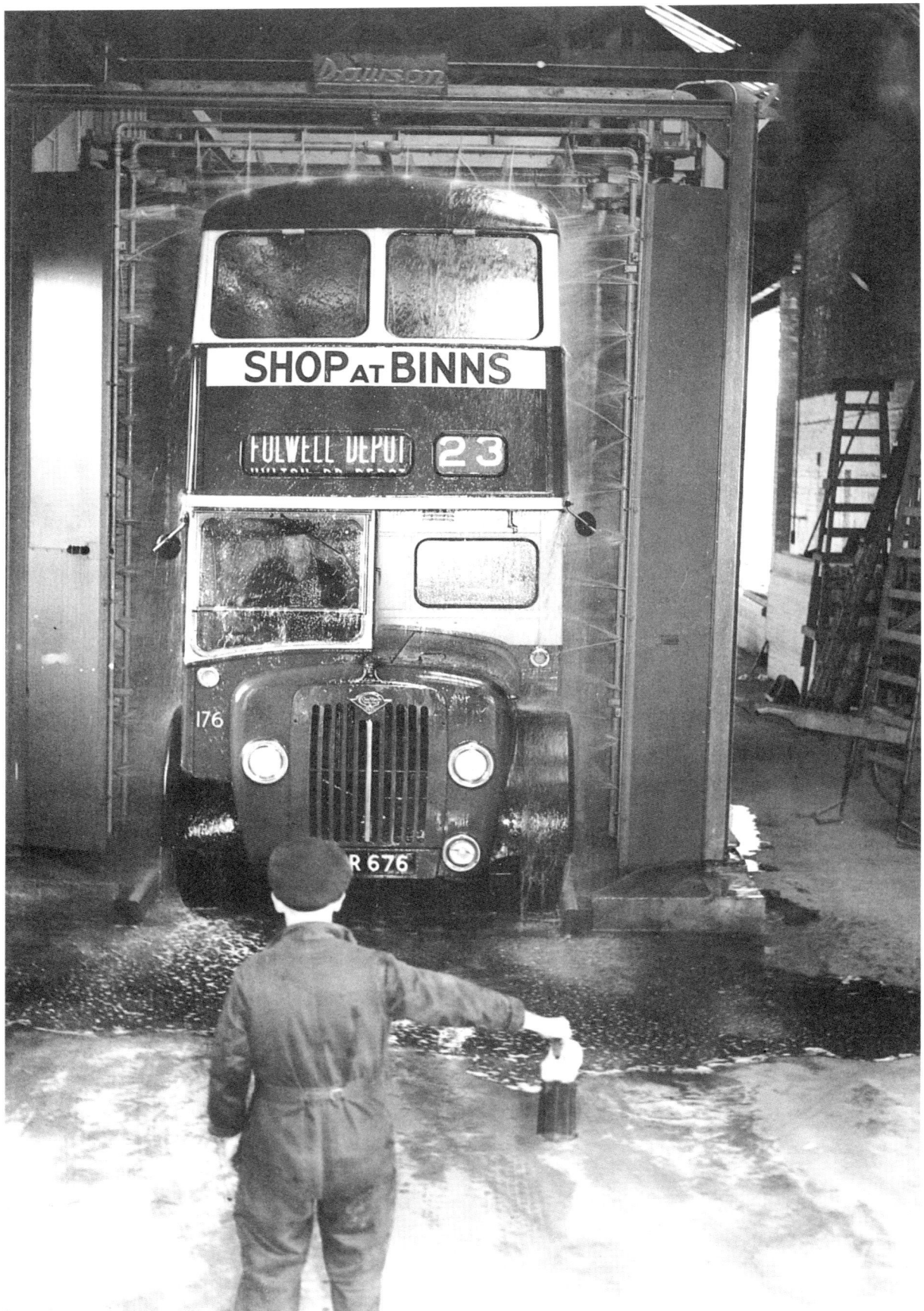

Despite what its destination indicator says, Crossley-bodied Guy 176 is trying out the wash-and-brush-up facility in Hylton Road depot, driven by 'Skip' O'Brien (depot handyman). The guiding is being done by George Laidler (depot foreman) but this is for posing purposes only. Buses were taken through by the driver unaided, the metal tyre guides (on floor, left and right of bus) ensuring that a straight course was followed.

(Copyright Busways Travel Services)

Appendix 2

Transport Department Performance

Table 1: Summary of principal statistics
Table 2: Income from wartime hiring out

Summary of principal statistics

Table 1

Note. Trams included for comparison. Some figures rounded slightly for clarity. Col 3 does not include special bus routes (eg. schools). Col 13 may include some withdrawn vehicles

1 Year ending 31 Mar		2 Population served by Corporation	3 Route mileage	4 Mileage operated	5 Passgrs carried	6 Average pass/mile	7 Total revenue £	8 Av traff rev/mile	9 Working expenses £	10 Av wkg exps/mile	11 W exps as % of traff rev	12 Nett balance £	13 Vehicles in fleet	14 Remarks
1928	buses	180,000	2.0	14,898	225,565	15.1	862	13.9d	799	12.2d	92.7	63	none	Services commenced 6 Feb 28 using buses hired from NGT
	trams		12.24	1.701M	30.921M	18.1	128,899	17.8d	101,361	14.3d	79.9	13,584	83	
1929	buses	190,000	7.7	229,034	2.202M	9.6	9,946	10.4d	11,868	12.2d	119.3	Dr 1,922	none	Services operated by hired NGT buses
	trams		12.24	1.629M	29.337M	18.0	122,422	17.7d	99,256	14.6d	82.5	10,100	83	
1930	buses	190,000	11.05	249,150	2.910M	11.7	13,753	13.2d	11,612	11.2d	84.5	Dr 942	13	SCT bus operations commenced 8 May 29. Hiring of NGT buses ceased after 3 Aug 29
	trams		12.02	1.723M	30.814M	17.9	128,819	17.6d	105,873	14.7d	83.8	9,824	83	
NGT →				46,297	373,310	8.1	1,838	9.5d	2,364	12.3d	128.6	-	-	
1931	buses	184,000	12.95	584,406	7.268M	12.4	33,645	13.2d	24,899	10.2d	74.0	4,898	25	First full year of SCT bus operation
	trams		11.84	1.688M	29.181M	17.3	122,657	17.1d	108,003	15.3d	89.9	5,612	81	
1932	buses	187,600	12.95	657,944	7.542M	11.5	34,547	12.6d	27,470	10.0d	79.5	1,644	25	High unemployment and poor summer weather 1931
	trams		12.07	1.665M	27.504M	16.5	116,192	16.4d	82,742	11.9d	72.8	23,511	75	
1933	buses	188,200	16.01	702,673	6.974M	9.9	32,872	11.2d	29,261	10.0d	89.0	Dr 4,121	25	High unemployment
	trams		12.07	1.729M	27.166M	15.7	115,157	15.6d	81,818	11.4d	72.7	24,343	76	

1 Year ending 31 Mar	2 Population served by Corporation	3 Route mileage	4 Mileage operated	5 Passgrs carried	6 Average pass/mile	7 Total revenue £	8 Av traff rev/mile	9 Working expenses £	10 Av wkg exps/mile	11 W exps as % of traff rev	12 Nett balance £	13 Vehicles in fleet	14 Remarks
1934	187,400	buses 16.01 / trams 12.07	569,291 / 1.914M	4.239M / 29.770M	7.4 / 15.6	21,914 / 126,582	9.2d / 15.6d	22,951 / 82,930	9.7d / 10.4d	104.9 / 66.8	Dr 8,420 / 34,583	25 / 80	High unemployment. Good summer 1933 but bus passengers & revenue per mile lowest so far. Some bus traffic lost to trams
1935	186,650	16.88 / 12.07	568,562 / 1.916M	4.904M / 30.174M	8.6 / 15.8	24,794 / 128,778	10.4d / 15.8d	22,573 / 86,607	9.5d / 10.9d	91.3 / 68.6	Dr 3,117 / 30,715	25 / 80	Reduced unemployment except at Castletown colliery. Poor summer 1934
Tram-o-cars →		11.89	2,310	14,560	6.3	132	13.7d	119	11.8d	90.2	-	2	
1936	185,100	19.15 / 12.07	734,431 / 1.938M	6.612M / 31.298M	9.0 / 16.1	33,534 / 133,455	10.8d / 16.2d	27,940 / 93,323	9.1d / 11.6d	84.7 / 71.3	328 / 28,792	24 / 81	Local trade still improving.
Tram-o-cars →		15.23	6,547	23,582	3.6	364	13.4d	424	15.6d	116.5	Dr 254	5	
1937	184,200	19.4 / 12.07	877,085 / 1.996M	8.727M / 33.683M	10.0 / 16.9	43,830 / 152,453**A**	11.9d / 17.0d	35,219 / 101,877**B**	9.6d / 11.4d	80.7 / 66.8	5,265 / 39,620	27 / 84	Improved employment and local trade. Poor summer 1936. **A**-includes £8,424 illuminations. **B**-includes £7,831 illuminations
Tram-o-cars →		38.33	4,275	8,185	1.9	241	13.5	289	14.6d	119.1	471	5	
1938	182,900	23.4 / 12.88	1.062M / 2.169M	10.309M / 35.644M	9.7 / 16.4	52,569 / 150,269**A**	11.8d / 16.6d	39,878 / 116,345**B**	9.0d / 11.4d	76.2 / 68.4	6,448 / 36,686	33 / 82	Bus mileage now exceeds 1M and is almost 50% of tram mileage. Bus passengers now exceed 10M. **A**-includes £11,132 illuminations. **B**-includes £13,542 illuminations
Tram-o-cars →		38.33	2,169	5,000	2.3	118	13.0d	199	20.1d	168.4	Dr 492	5	
1939	182,400	23.45 / 12.88	1.246M / 2.286M	11.976M / 36.179M	9.6 / 15.8	61,273 / 163,757**B**	11.7d / 16.0d	46,623 / 131,506**C**	9.0d**A** / 12.4d	76.8 / 77.5	5,878 / 21,342	40 / 84	**A**-actual figure 8.978d and lowest ever. **B**-includes £8,888 illuminations. **C**-includes £13,463 illuminations
Tram-o-cars →		38.33	2,612	6,876	2.6	146	13.4	181	16.6d	124.1	Dr 435	5	
1940		29.2 / 12.88	1.374M / 2.109M	14.058M / 34.967M	10.2 / 16.6	71,301 / 149,744	12.4d / 16.8	55,996 / 125,471**A**	9.5d / 14.3d	79.0 / 84.8	2,680 / 13,305	46 / 84	Tram-o-car figures integrated except in fleet total. **A**-includes illuminations expenses (amount not ascertainable) All working exps 1940-47 include allowances to men in HM Forces
1941		c29.2 / 12.88	1.395M / 1.971M	15.926M / 33.304M	11.4 / 16.9	83,996 / 141,683	13.9d / 17.0d	67,825 / 118,135**A**	11.1d / 14.4d	84.0 / 84.5	3,299 / 12,296	46 / 84	Route mileage figure 1941-45 approximate. **A**-includes illuminations expenses £1,791
1942		c29.2 / 12.88	1.456M / 2.076M	19.562M / 38.682M	13.4 / 18.6	103,491 / 164,514	16.9d / 18.9d	80,735 / 134,847**A**	12.8d / 15.9d	78.5 / 82.6	Dr 2,126 / 21,764	46 / 84	**A**-includes illuminations expenses £3,002
1943		c29.2 / 12.88	1.480M / 2.077M	21.231M / 43.241	14.4 / 20.8	112,292 / 183,534	18.1d / 21.0d	87,828 / 138,663	13.9d / 16.0d	78.9 / 76.2	24,464 / 39,015	51 / 84	
1944		c29.2 / 12.88	1.486M / 2.019M	23.077M / 47.389M	15.5 / 23.5	123,038 / 200,223	19.8d / 23.6d	91,254 / 144,318	14.3d / 17.2d	74.6 / 72.6	31,784 / 53,048	60 / 84	
1945		c29.8 / 12.88	1.535M / 2.075	25.094M / 49.688M	16.4 / 23.9	133,702 / 210,784	20.7d / 24.2d	101,064 / 166,716	15.8d / 19.8d	75. / 79.7	32,638 / 42,805	64 / 83	Passengers per mile highest ever for buses and trams

Year ending 31 Mar	Population served by Corporation		Route mileage	Mileage operated	Passgrs carried	Average pass/mile	Total revenue £	Av traff rev/mile	Working expenses £	Av wkg exps/mile	W exps as % of traff rev	Nett balance £	Vehicles in fleet	Remarks
1946	175,590	buses	29.85	1.625M	26.133M	16.1	140,591	20.6d	111,638	16.4d	79.6	28,953	66	
		trams	12.88	2.248M	50.520M	22.5	218,435	23.1d	186,190	19.8d	85.6	30,998	83	
1947	175,820	buses	31.25	2.326M	33.333M	14.3	188,071	19.1d	222,691	16.2d	85.5	30,436	69	Crossley bus 25 withdrawn but still on stock. Large increases in bus mileage and passengers carried
		trams	12.88	2.653M	53.111M	20.0	233,160	20.8d	157,635	20.1d	96.9	9,352	87	
1948	178,530	buses	31.35	2.502M	36.340M	14.5	207,368	19.7d	190,836	18.3d	93.1	16,532	84	*First-ever deficit incurred by trams*
		trams	13.24	2.705M	54.308M	20.1	238,774	21.0d	255,909	22.7d	108.2	Dr 18,398	91	
1949	180,000	buses	34.25	2.712M	38.453M	14.2	235,978	20.7d	224,378	19.9d	96.1	10,292	102	Bus Col 11 highest since 1934
		trams	13.73	2.754M	51.947M	18.9	270,576	23.4d	269,366	23.5d	100.5	Dr 187	91	*Tram route mileage at its maximum*
1950	181,340	buses	35.72	2.998M	41.059M	13.7	273,633	21.6d	243,375	19.5d	90.0	18,033	107	Bus mileage now more than tram mileage
		trams	13.73	2.791M	48.877M	17.5	300,632	25.3d	274,840	23.6d	93.3	23,979	91	
1951	178,100	buses	37.37	3.282M	44.389M	13.5	299,598	21.6d	285,352	20.9d	96.5	Dr 1,065	113	Bus mileage more than double 1946 figure
		trams	12.55	2.633M	44.103M	16.7	268,613	24.2d	248,649	22.7d	93.7	18,118	90	*Trams now in decline*
1952	180,000	buses	40.31	3.720M	49.343M	13.3	361,357	23.0d	350,973	22.6d	98.3	Dr 8,863	122	Highest ever vehicle total (210). Bus mileage and total passengers now leaping ahead of trams but tram passenger volume still higher
		trams	11.64	2.297M	38.266M	16.7	247,341	25.6d	247,285	25.8d	101.0	Dr 1,685	88	
1953	180,400	buses	47.99	4.184M	53.769M	12.9	443,296	25.2d	414,029	23.6d	94.4	3,338	131	Bus mileage now more than double tram mileage
		trams	10.14	2.054M	31.414M	15.3	234,892	27.2d	223,964	26.2d	96.3	9,223	61	
1954	181,550	buses	63.84	4.911M	62.923M	12.8	531,260	25.7d	485,652	23.7d	92.3	11,559	164	192,000 more bus & tram passgrs carried; first rise since 1948 but television now having effect. Trams down to one section after 28 Mar
		trams	2.71	1.501M	22.453M	15.0	171,243	27.2d	158,283	25.3d	93.2	2,073	29	
1955	181,800	buses	77.25	6.303M	82.003M	13.0	683,209	25.8d	626,713	23.9d	92.6	Dr 3,883	175	Bus Col 5 increase c30% but Col 6 only c1.5%. Combined passgr total down 460,240.
		trams	-	0.215M	2.912M	13.5	22,057	24.4d	31,875	35.6d	144.5	-	-	*Tram operations ceased 1 Oct 54*

107

1 Year ending 31 Mar	2 Population served by Corporation	3 Route mileage	4 Mileage operated	5 Passgrs carried	6 Average pass/mile	7 Total revenue £	8 Av traff rev/mile	9 Working expenses £	10 Av wkg exps/mile	11 W exps as % of traff rev	12 Nett balance £	13 Vehicles in fleet	14 Remarks
1956	182,000	80.63	6.645M	87.884M	13.2	781,621	28.0d	685,662	24.8d	88.5	16,245	169/6	First full year buses only. Col 8 increase more than double Col 10 increase. Fleet total includes three utilities out of service (5/6, 73)
1957	182,800	81.79	6.539M	87.993M	13.5	832,228	30.2d	735,852	27.0d	89.3	15,442	166/7	Col 5 figure highest ever. Other figures affected by Suez crisis 1956/57
1958	183,800	86.07	6.819M	87.284M	12.8	854,110	29.8d	797,879	28.1d	94.3	Dr 18,694	177/8	Some figures affected by 'flu epidemic, winter 1957/58. Col 6 down by nearly 5%
1959	185,100	86.98	6.923M	87.496M	12.6	914,309	31.4d	813,027	28.2d	89.7	15,530	177/8	Col 5: second and final peak (see also 1957)
1960	186,600	89.11	6.876M	85.284M	12.4	892,838	30.9d	790,898	27.6d	89.4	18,576	171/8	Col 4 down for first time since 1934. Col 10 down slightly on 1959
1961	188,000	94.13	6.567M	81.712M	12.4	904,601	32.8d	807,711	29.5d	90.1	4,047	167/11	Col 5 down 7% since 1957
1962	189,600	91.59	6.572M	80.209M	12.2	916,542	33.1d	854,743	31.2d	94.2	Dr 8,194	161/18	Route mileage down for first time ever
1963	190,580	92.14	6.372M	74.581M	11.7	891,956	33.2d	843,100	31.8d	95.7	Dr 25,966	157/22	7% fall in Col 5 - highest proportion since 1934 (15% since 1957)
1964	190,510	92.04	6.444M	74.149M	11.5	951,557	35.0d	893,875	33.3d	95.0	Dr 22,991	158/25	Passenger loss minimal
1965	189,630	97.39	6.484M	74.056M	11.4	962,199	35.2d	944,936	35.0d	99.3	Dr 50,019	157/25	Col 11 uncomfortably high
1966	192,056	98.83	6.337M	70.883M	11.2	1.008M	37.8d	1.012M	38.3d	101.5	Dr 80,054	157/26	Col 6 lowest since 1941. Cols 7/9 exceed £1M for first time. Col 11 exceeds 100% for first time since 1934
1967	191,550	103.7	6.243M	67.413M	10.8	983,106	37.4d	1.085M	41.7d	111.5	Dr 195,932	132/60	Route mileage exceeds 100
1968	191,550	102.28	6.138M	62.916M	10.3	1.066M	41.0d	1.106M	43.2d	105.4	Dr 159,655	111/8	Population does not include 27,720 in added areas
1969		101.01	5.879M	57.533M	9.8	1.234M*	50.4d	1.132M	46.2d	91.7	Dr 79,514	76/109	*Traffic revenue. S/d exceed d/d buses for first time since 1938
1970											Dr 20,800	74/109	Omitted information from 1970 not available
1971			5.836M	50.536M	8.7	1.371M	56.4d				Dr 127,186	65/118	Col 8 = 23.5p
1972			5.457M*	44.843M*	8.2**						Dr 167,315	60/118	*SCT estimate. **Based on Cols 4/5
1973			5.209M*	43.000M*	8.3**							55/118	4 d/d & 6 s/d buses to PTE as withdrawn vehicles

Appendix 2, continued

Table 2

Income from wartime hiring-out

Note   Details for 1945 not available. All figures to year ending 31 March.

Income from	1941	1942	1943	1944	1946
Hire of commandeered buses	£2,745	-	-	-	-
Buses loaned out	-	£114	£210	£106	£636*
Tram-o-cars loaned out	£192	£252	£247	£190	-

*Presumably in respect of loan of Crossley bus 23 to South Shields, June 1945 - January 1946

Appendix 3

Some of the People

Charlie Parnaby

"I started working for Sunderland Corporation as a tram conductor number 272 on 22 January 1937 and finished as bus bus driver with the Tyne and Wear PTE on 21 January 1977," said Charlie. "My real name's Oliver but they've always called me Charlie. I'd just served my time as a motor mechanic and I was hoping for a start as a bus fitter. Why man, I lived right opposite the depot in Fulwell Road! Anyway, they said the only vacancies they had were for conducting on the trams and so that's what I had to do. The tram depot was at the Wheat Sheaf. My starting wage was £3 3s 9d a week. I put in for a transfer to the buses and got it about a year later and I was then number 337 because bus and tram crews were numbered in separate series. I had badge AA 1468. You've seen that famous photo taken outside the museum just before the war, the one that has a Leyland Lion in it and has been published in a few books? Well, if you look at those two bus conductors across the road, I'm the tall one on the right. I was on the Docks Circle that day, round the East End. A lot of the East Enders were moving to new houses at Ford and such places at that time. They were too poor to hire removal vans. They'd take larger articles on a hired barrow but buy an all-day ticket and go up and down the whole day long with items that were not too big to be lifted on to a bus. There was one duty on the Docks service where you did 34 trips. It was Sunday tablet number 3 and you signed on at 11.42, left the Depot at 11.52, left the Museum at 12.02 and then did four trips an hour without a break until 8.32, which was the last. Nobody liked that tablet!

"I remember once, I conducted two buses together! Yes, we were up at Humbledon on the Sea Lane service with two buses and two drivers but only one conductor. It was a warm summer's day and the crowds were starting to flock to the beach. I set off on the first bus, a centre-entrance Daimler double decker. The other one, which was a Leyland single decker, followed behind. When we got to Barnes Park Road I hopped off and got on the single decker. By the time it got to Kayll Road I'd collected all the fares so I got back onto the double decker and did this, going from one to the other, all the way to Sea Lane and I never missed a fare.

"I spent the war years in the Army and became a Normandy veteran. When I came back, I went on to bus driving. Driving Instructor Frank Hodson put me through my PSV training on a wartime Guy. After I'd passed my test he took me out on a Daimler to familiarise me with the preselector routine. I was then driver 1207, badge number AA 13616 but later 19184 because I lost my original driver's badge. After I was married I lived in Francis Street, right next to the depot, so I never had far to go to work or to go home until we moved in 1970.

"My favourite type to drive? Oh, the Daimlers. They had a nice, easy gearchange. Those four with Daimler engines, numbers 15 to 18, were the best and d'you know why? Because they had an access flap on the engine cover in the cab by the driver's left leg. It was right alongside the exhaust manifold and on a cold day you could open it and keep yourself lovely and warm. Mind you, with a Daimler you had to be careful about pressing the gear-change pedal right down the full length of its travel. If you didn't, it would spring back further than normal and give you a nasty knock on your left foot or shin! It only ever happened to me once and luckily I was unhurt but another time, going to Grangetown, I pulled up at Mackie's Corner traffic lights behind another bus going to the Docks. When the lights changed that bus didn't move. I got out to see what was the matter and the driver, a little fellow, said the gear change pedal had come out and he couldn't get it back. I swopped places with him and using all the strength of my left leg and pulling myself down with the steering wheel, pushed the thing back in again. That was the technique.

"Otherwise, though, they were good buses and I only wish they'd put six-cylinder engines in those later Daimlers and Guys instead of five-cylinder ones. They were slow going up banks. I wasn't keen on those double deck Leylands. Oh yes, they had a nice, smooth engine but the gear-changing took too long. They weren't a suitable bus for town service. My brother Ralph who's dead now, used to drive the night service single decker when it first started. He was well-known on the Corporation. I remember when Norman Morton wanted to make the Alexandra Road service one-man in 1953. There was a lot of fuss about it. 'It's nothing new,' I told them. 'It's already been done. They had two little Guys one-man operated on that service before the war and there was no fuss about it then!'

"What are my main impressions, looking back? Well, I remember getting up at 3.45 every morning to drive the staff bus. That was my regular job for many years in addition to my normal duty, early or late, because I lived so close by. Another impression that comes back is the smell those lovely fish and chips we used to get down at the Docks, and another is taste of the nice tea that used to be made for all the crews by the wife of a Doxford's worker at the Humbledon terminus when we were on the morning Doxford's special. We went back to Humbledon and we had about half an hour's layover before our next trip. When we arrived, there were always two mugs of steaming tea on the gateposts! Then one silly idiot had to go and end it for everybody by knocking on the door to ask for more sugar. Oh, and there was one occasion when I had a utility Guy 77 on my way to Grangetown from Ford. I was just going round Watson Street corner at Pallion and luckily very slow because the steering wheel came right off the column! Well, it was like the Keystone Cops. I turned round with it in my hands to show the conductor who was in the lower saloon. You should have seen the looks on the passengers' faces! I put it back on and held it down, going steady all the way. I stopped to 'phone for a change-over to meet me in John Street. It was there when I arrived and the fitter said to me, 'What's the matter with it?' So I thrust the steering wheel into his hand and said, 'There you are, that's what's the matter with it!'

"Another time, I was on the last bus to the Docks one night, 11pm from High Street. Some of the passengers were a bit rowdy, shouting and singing. I turned round and told them that if they wanted to get home they'd have to be quiet so we could hear the Town Hall clock striking eleven. There was silence and then I checked my watch and left for the Docks. 'I never heard the clock strike,' someone shouted. 'No,' I replied, 'They took it down two months ago!' I also recall in later years having to take most of the Bristols down to Birmingham for Metro-Cammell, the bodybuilder, to repair the splits in the roofs when they were fairly new. Those were long journeys! But overall, I enjoyed my work on the buses. Not everybody could stick the job. There were many of them, they came and went quickly because they didn't like the early starts and late finishes and weekend work. But I managed to stay for forty years."

Charlie and his wife Muriel were living in contented retirement at the time of the author's communications with them during the 1990s and it has been a pleasure to keep up contact with both.

Spencer Bradwell

Spen at work. A smile and a cheerful word could always be expected of Driver Spencer Bradwell on the driver-only operated services during the 1950s and early 1960s. He then became an inspector. "Not bad for a young lad!" he would reply in retirement and aged 80 when asked how he was.

(Copyright S Bradwell)

"Before the war I was working down south, driving lorries," Spencer began. "I drove Army wagons during the war and had one or two narrow escapes in North Africa! Never mind, I got back unscathed, returned to Sunderland and applied to work on the buses. I started as a conductor in January 1946 and was working on wartime Guy 75 when it ran over a little lad and killed him going down Stoney Lane. I was just changing the back indicator when the bus did an emergency stop and I felt it going over him. Fred Smith was the driver. I'd seen a lot during the war of course but the sight of that bairn was a real shock." *(Author's note: that was on 20 February 1946 and the child was George Henry Davis, aged eight years. See Chapter 4.)*

"I was driving within three months. Frank Hodson, the Driving Instructor, trained me for PSVs and I passed my test on wartime Guy 65. He then gave me a run out in a Daimler to learn about preselecting. My badge number was AA 13526. One early driving experience that sticks out in my mind was with one of those two pre-war centre-entrance Crossleys that had a centre accelerator pedal. You remember the ungated level crossing that used to be at the top of Silksworth Row bank, where that electric loco used to pull the coal wagons across for the power station? Well, one day I was just approaching the crossing in Crossley 25 when I suddenly saw on my left a stray wagon running away slowly from the sidings! If I'd tried to stop, it would have rammed the bus so I accelerated and it just caught the nearside back corner and did some slight damage. In fact there were two other wagons coupled to it and the shunter was running after them, trying to get a brake on. They nearly sacked me because at first they thought I'd gone past the red flag!

"My mother-in-law, Mrs Taylor, lived down at the Docks and that was very handy for a can of tea when I was on the Docks service. Bus crews always enjoyed a drink of tea. I had no particular preference as to type of bus. If it had four wheels I just got in and drove it. I became spare one-man driver in 1955, regular one-manner in 1958 and inspector in 1962. There was a lot of bad feeling against one-man bus drivers during the early years. Some of the others thought it was taking conductors' jobs away but of course there was always a shortage of them anyway. Eventually it was accepted and the Union agreed to total one-manning in the end. I retired in January 1976, just thirty years after starting."

Author's personal recollection. When driver-only operated service 6 was extended from Barnes Park Road to Southwick in 1955, I began to travel on it regularly and mentioned to a school pal that one of the drivers was particularly bright and cheerful. "Oh, that's Spencer!" he replied. I don't know how he knew his name, but I began to look forward to seeing Spencer at the wheel of buses on service 6. He would always wait for intending passengers and nothing seemed too much trouble for him. People appreciated his polite and happy manner. In those days many households had coin-operated gas meters. One afternoon, aboard Roe-bodied Guy 7 or 8, Spencer gave a female passenger some change and remarked, "There's some pennies for the gas. *Now dinna gan an' gas yersel'!*" Spencer's brother, Alf, had started bus driving in the early 1930s and was one of the pre-war one-man drivers. He became an inspector during the early 1950s. I knew him by sight and subsequently I was to have contact with him through church connections. Contact was lost following my leaving the town soon afterward. Alf died in 1990 but to my great delight I met up with Spencer in 1992. He was still the same as he ever had been, helpful, cheery and genuinely interested in my plan to write the history of the town's municipal bus operations. I have enjoyed becoming acquainted with his wife, Jean, also.

John Hogarth

"I started working in the bodybuilding section at the bus depot in Fulwell Road on 20 March 1950, beginning my apprenticeship as a joiner-coachbuilder on 30 December that year and finishing it on 29 December 1955," John recalled. "I did my National Service in the RAF between 1956 and 1958 and then went back to repairing buses. Oh, it was a fantastic job! I've had some interesting experiences. One of my first tasks was with Billy Storey, a joiner, taking out those troublesome half-drop windows on some of the pre-war and utility bodies and replacing them with sliding vents. Then when they wanted an illuminated bus for the Coronation in 1953, pre-war Daimler 36 was the one and I worked on it with Leslie Garrick who was also a joiner and Norman Harrison, a coachpainter. I made some decorations and light supports. Those Roe bodies were very good and their teak framing gave little trouble. I couldn't say the same about the utilities, though. Most of them were Masseys and they needed a lot of rebuilding in the early 'fifties. You couldn't get seasoned timber during the war. The builders just had to use what was available and because it was "green", it soon tended to warp or rot. The post-war Massey bodies, as well, had to be stripped down and thoroughly rebuilt." *(Author's note: in peacetime this may have been due to the inability of all but the largest coachbuilders to tie up considerable amounts of capital in seasoning timber. Massey Bros were not alone here.)* "But the metal-framed bodies we had, Cravens, Crossleys, the 1954 Roe ones, Northern Counties and even the ACBs, were all pretty trouble-free.

"We had some real characters working in the depot in those days. There was Tommy Craig, the depot foreman, who never said much but was all right with you if you got on with your work; Billy Watson, the foreman bodybuilder, a very clever and inventive man who made that model of number 86 tram in the Museum and many other useful things for the Department; there was Harry Robinson, the chargeman, he's still alive and over 90, and the rolling stock engineer, Albert Wass. They were very strict and you had to do each job properly. Billy Watson was keen on keeping things original as far as possible when doing repairs and rebuilding. He used to say, 'What comes out must go back!' However, different people would put different interpretations on some things, and that's how you might have seen minor variations in the appearance of individual buses after rebuilding. In fact, when they rebuilt some of the utilities at Hylton Road Car Works, Geordie Cook, the chargeman on the trams side, used up some tram body parts on the buses.

"One day I was working on the upper saloon emergency window of a centre-entrance bus and I think it was Leyland 56. It was parked over the pit in the depot yard and I held the window open while Walter Nichol, another of the joiners, shaved a bit off the bottom of the frame because it wouldn't shut properly. He was outside, perched on plank between two stagings. Well, Skip O'Brien, the handyman, got into the cab and drove the bus away, leaving poor Walter frozen in a precarious position and not daring to move! I dashed forward and rang the bell. They couldn't climb up to rescue Walter in case they made him fall. The bus had to be reversed carefully up to the plank to give him a hand-hold. That was a big scare. Another time, Norman Thwaites was on the roof of a bus in the repair shop, mending a vent, and somebody drove that one away to park it in the top shed. Norman had to lie flat and cling on to the vent because there wasn't much clearance under the shed entrance!

"When the central works were set up at the Wheat Sheaf I moved there, and later I went on to repairing other departments' vehicles when the Transport Department became responsible for them. When the PTE took over in 1973 I went to work in the Ambulance Service but returned as a coachbuilder in 1978. I finally took redundancy at deregulation in 1986, but my experience had stood me in good stead for my hobby which is preserving old and rallying old vehicles." John's wife Bernice, son Ian and daughter Anita are also involved in that activity and all have been most kind and helpful in the preparation of this material.

Mrs Mary Shield

Generally known by her maiden name, Molly Parker, this bus conductress was awarded the British Empire Medal for her wartime service to transport. She was possibly the best-known of Sunderland's clippies and a popular figure with thousands of regular passengers, including the author, on account of her consistently cheerful and courteous manner. Molly was recorded as having worked up to 96 hours a week during the difficult war years. She had a particularly effective way of calming down boisterous and aggressive drunken passengers without giving offence. In February 1960, when her bus stopped at the scene of an accident in which a cyclist had been hurt, Molly crossed the road to give assistance but was herself hit by a passing car and fatally injured.

Speedy Robson

A small, swarthy man, this conductor was of course always known by the diminutive of his first name which was Speedman. Few people of such humble rank as that of bus conductor could have had their decease headlined with a photograph in the local press, but it happened to Speedy. He was at Hylton Road Depot for sixteen years and during that time he became renowned as an entertainer of passengers. Joker of the pack? Speedy was more a packer of the jokes and had a quip for every occasion. He it was who would invite passengers to sit upstairs *"in the gas chamber!"* Speedy had his own descriptions of bus stops, such as *"Duncan's, for cheap ham shanks!"* On cold days he would greet the queuing assembly with, *"Ha'way! Gan downstairs aside the fire!"* Then there was that time when the house at a Ford bus stop, said to be haunted, was featured on television with Cliff Michelmore on the "Tonight" programme. Speedy had his own theory. *"It was the sun shinin' on a cuppa tea, reflectin' up the wall. They thowt it was a ghost!"*

One winter's evening aboard Roe Daimler 113 going along Pallion New Road, Speedy stood at the front and put on a show that had the passengers almost falling into the gangway with laughter. Two women had been waiting for his bus after a weary day in a factory, he said, and they were slow in climbing aboard. He encouraged them by saying that if they didn't hurry up, their husbands would be home before them. One of them replied that she wished he would. *He'd been dead eighteen years.* Yes, and Speedy had the knack of *timing* in the recounting of a tale to best effect in producing a laugh. In his younger days, he had been famous in the town as an amateur boxer. Speedy joined the Merchant Navy in 1925 and served on ocean liners, including the Mauritania and the Olympic, aboard which he took part in boxing displays and won trophies. He died after an illness on 25 October 1970 at the age of 64.

James E Watson

Jim was a bus driver with Sunderland Corporation for 19 years, nicknamed 'Colonel' Watson by his colleagues because of his smart, militaristic bearing. Having learned to drive in 1913, he had been an Army driving instructor during World War II, teaching hundreds of men and women to drive. One young woman in the ACTS underwent the usual twelve-week course, including maintenance, and learned particularly quickly. Jim had a feeling he knew her somehow but it was several days before it dawned on him who she was. Her name was Elizabeth and she was the daughter of the King! Not many people were able to boast they'd taught an heir to the throne to drive but bus driver Jim Watson could. He retired in 1963.

Mrs Cornelia Watson

Not related to the Queen's driving instructor and affectionately known by all as 'Granny' Watson, this well-known diminutive lady was one of the Corporation's World War I tram conductresses. When women were needed urgently during the next war she was among the first to come forward. Then after a three-year break post-war, 'Granny' Watson returned again for a twelve-year stint on the trams and later the buses. She retired in 1960 at the age of 63 to care for her invalid husband and is believed to have been the last of the Great War conductress finally to retire.

Long service

Three non-operating employees who retired during 1954/55 had given no less than 115 years' accumulated service. They were H Crow (cash collector), J H Wendell (shed foreman) and G Smith (track foreman). This figure was beaten three years later, however, when W Watson (foreman bodybuilder), C Lewis (foreman linesman) and Miss R Turnbull (ticket office supervisor) retired with an aggregate of 117 years behind them. Among members of the Council, in November 1953 Alderman D Cairns achieved 50 years' continuous service on the Tramways/Transport Committee.

Committee Chairmen, Vice-Chairmen and Mayors
during bus-operating years

Tramways Committee 1928-32
Transport Committee 1932-72
Environment Committee 1972-73

Year ending 31 Mar	Chairman	Vice-Chairman	Mayor
1929	Ald G New	Ald R Dixon Jeffrey	Cllr I G Modlin
1930	Ald R Dixon Jeffrey	Cllr J Wilson	"
1931	"	"	Ald E H Brown JP
1932	"	"	"
1933	Ald R Dixon Jeffrey	Cllr J Wilson	Ald E H Brown JP
1934	"	Cllr J R M Dinsdale	Cllr E W Ditchburn JP
1935	"	Cllr J G Potts	"
1936	Ald G Lumsden JP	Cllr J N Lisle	Ald T Summerbell JP
1937	"	Cllr J A Smith	"
1938	Cllr J A Smith	Cllr A Morgan	Ald G Ford JP
1939	Ald R Dixon Jeffrey	Cllr R G Smart	Cllr M Wayman OBE
1940	"	"	"
1941	"	"	"
1942	"	"	Cllr M Wayman OBE, FSS, JP
1943	" (a)	"	"
1944	Cllr R G Smart (b)	Cllr T M Carr	Cllr W L Milburn
1945	Cllr T M Carr	Cllr N Waters	Cllr J young JP
1946	Cllr J A Smith	Cllr T Heil	Cllr J Ritson JP
1947	"	Ald G Lumsden JP	Ald M Walton
1948	Ald G Lumsden JP	Cllr G English	Ald E Johnston JP
1949	"	"	"
1950	"	Cllr T W Atkinson	Ald J Cohen JP
1951	"	"	Ald G H Morgan JP
1952	"	"	Ald W Harvey JP
1953	"	"	Ald A H Suddick JP
1954	Cllr T W Atkinson	Cllr R Wilkinson	Ald M E English JP
1955	"	"	Ald Mrs J Huggins JP
1956	"	"	Ald Miss E E Blacklock JP
1957	"	"	Ald T H Cavanagh JP
1958	"	"	Ald J Hoy MBE, BEM, JP
1959	"	"	Ald E E Wales JP
1960	"	Ald R Wilkinson	Ald N L Allison
1961	"	"	Ald J Tweddle
1962	Cllr T W Atkinson*	"	Ald Mrs K Cohen
1963	Cllr J W Jamieson JP	"	Ald R T Weston MBE
1964	"	"	Ald Mrs J E Hedley
1965	"	"	Ald R Wilkinson
1966	"	"	Cllr A Watson
1967	"	"	Ald F Young
1968	Ald R B Spain	Cllr J G D Bell	Ald N Waters
1969	"	Cllr P R Wood	Ald J W P Wilkinson*
1970	"	"	Cllr Mrs M E Miller
1971	"	Cllr J Miller	Cllr W O Stephenson MBE, JP
1972	"	"	Ald W S Martin
1973	Cllr A Burgham	Cllr A Lumley JP	Cllr L Watson JP
	(a) *Retired Dec 43*	(b) *Took over Jan 44*	*Died in office during year*

114

General Managers
Tramways Dept 1928-29
Tramways & Motors Dept 1929-38
Transport Dept 1938-73

1928	Archibald R Dayson MIEE (appointed 1904)
1929-48	Charles A Hopkins M Inst T
1948-52	Henry W Snowball AMI Mech E
1952-67	Norman Morton B Com, M Inst T, MIRTE
1968-69	Richard E Bottrill M Inst T
1969-73	Alan H Wright B Sc (Tech), C Eng, MI Mech E, MCIT

The Transport Committee undertakes its annual inspection, seen here at Fulwell depot, in 1952 shortly before Mr Morton's arrival as General Manager. Identifiable are Mr S Finkle (Acting General Manager, extreme left), Cllr T W Atkinson (Vice Chairman, second left), Cllr Mrs M Burlinson (right of centre), Cllr R Wilkinson (4th from right) and Mr J Rostron (Traffic Superintendent, extreme right). The buses present no problem. They are utility Guys 80 and 81.

(Copyright Busways Travel Services)

The males in the foreground here about to board the ceremonial last tram, 86, on 1 October 1954 are (left to right) Mr G S McIntyre (Town Clerk), Cllr T W Atkinson (Transport Committee Chairman), Mr N Morton (General Manager) and Cllr R Wilkinson (Vice Chairman). On the platform are Conductor Glendenning and Chief Inspector Roberts. The notice in the window gives details of the replacing bus service on the Town -Fulwell - Seaburn (Dykelands Rd) section.

(Copyright Sunderland Echo)

115

Appendix 4
Miscellaneous Reports
of General Manager to Transport Committee

3 June 1955 - Financial position of Department

Summary

1 - There had not been a general fares rise since 1951.

2 - Increased costs outside the Department's control included wages and salaries (up 38 per cent from 1951) along with National Health Insurance contributions and fuel tax.

3 - Heavy capital expenditure on rolling stock, buildings and the reinstatement of roads after the lifting of tram tracks had been unavoidable in the circumstances and was spread over a number of years according to the various loan periods.

4 - Staff shortage had meant increased costs because of overtime pay.

5 - Due mostly to Company bus operation within the town boundary the total number of passengers carried (including trams up to 1 October1954) had fallen from its 1948 peak of 90.648M to 84.915M in 1955 [but was then to rise above 85M until 1960]; however, some measures had helped to offset the adverse effects of those circumstances.

6 - As to working expenses, the following were down: staff employed during previous 4 years, by 140 (c14%) - fuel consumption 9% - maintenance and cleaning costs nearly 20% - insurance costs £1,000 p/a - ticket costs by nearly £3,000 p/a (due to use of Setright machines).

7 - On capital costs, there were these savings: - new vehicle costs £195,500 (due to a fleet reduction from 210 buses and trams in 1952 to 175 buses by 1955, some 16 per cent) - the building programme £180,000 - road reinstatement nearly £70,000 (by revising the means of apportionment).

Other items: - a planned increase in bus fleet total seating capacity of 14% by 1956 - an actual increase in annual bus mileage from 28,665 in 1952 to 37,247 in 1955 [subsequently the figure was to peak at 38,414 in 1960; the general trend then being downward, falling below 33,000 by 1967].

Suggested measures. Driver-only-operation of selected services - staggering of schools and some works times -   reduced services increased fares, specifically the Universal from 6d to 8d; reducing the distance of the ordinary 1^1/2d from 1^1/2 miles to 1 mile, then ^{1}/2 mile for each ^{1}/2d; the abolition of ordinary transfers.

Additional points

Plainly, fuel economy was a high priority. The average bus figure had improved from 9.24mpg in 1951 to 10.06 in 1954, a nine per cent reduction representing about £10,000. The main factors leading to this were:

    1 - Use of thinner lubricating oil.

    2 - Adjusting engines to run at slower idling speed (mentioned previously).

    3 - Converting all 15 post-war Crossleys from Crossley 6-cylinder to Gardner 5LW engines, saving nearly 20% fuel

    4 - Governing the six AEC Regent 9.6-litre engines down to 1,600rpm and converting to a 3-in exhaust system, saving 5%

    5 - Use of fuel oil with a specific gravity of at least 0.840 giving increased British Thermal Units per gallon, saving more fuel

    6 - Specifying new buses from 1953 to have Gardner 5-cylinder engines and to be much lighter, enabling their average fuel consumption over 12 months to be 10.52mpg (ie, 0.46mpg above overall fleet average).

Maintenance costs were also down by 18 per cent in four years. One factor here was the high proportion of new vehicles but another significant one was the doubling of engine life by the adoption of chromium-plated piston rings along with detergent engine oil. Savings on repairs would have been greater but for the cost of rebuilding the utility bodies during the period in question. Tyre costs had fallen overall during the same time span, although price rises had begun to cause an upward trend again.

(Comment. Increasing the seating capacity may have seemed sound economically but it did not enhance comfort. Apart from reduced leg room, the upper saloon of 8ft-wide Daimlers 116-127, for instance, originally sat 31 passengers within a volume of about 1,200cu ft, averaging about 38.6cu ft per person. In a 7ft 6in-wide bus seating 35 upstairs, the average came down to about 32cu ft each.)

27 August 1959 - Town centre traffic congestion.

Summary

1 - Cause of serious disruption to bus services - during previous 7 years, number of motor vehicles licensed in Sunderland had doubled.

2 - Fawcett Street was main bottleneck - traffic lights at both ends (Mackie's Corner and Gas Office Corner) - situations once regarded as exceptional (eg, football Saturdays) now becoming commonplace on weekdays.

3 - Several recommendations for reference to Highways Committee and Watch Committee, including:

    (a) John Street to be one-way southbound, (b) Fawcett Street to be one-way northbound.

    (Nearly a year and a half were to pass before this proposition was put into effect.)

Appendix 5
1969 Zonal Fare Scheme
Introduced 6 January

Services through or to/from town centre

Service		Zone 3/2 boundary	Zone 2/1 boundary	Zone 1/2 boundary	zone 2/3 boundary
1	Grangetown - Town - Dene Estate	-	Gray Rd	Wheat Sheaf	-
2	Farringdon - Town	Prospect Hotel	Edenhouse Rd	-	-
3	Farringdon - Plains Farm - Town	Prospect Hotel or Premier/Pearl Rds	Health Dept	-	-
4	Downhill - Town - Hendon - Blue House Villette Rd - Tatham St - Town - Downhill	Rmsgte/Redcar Rds	Wheat Sheaf	Hendon School or St Barnabas	-
5	R House N - Town - Tatham St - Villette Rd Blue House - Hendon - Town - Red House N	Rmsgte/Redcar Rds	Wheat Sheaf	St Barnabas or Hendon School	-
7	Docks - Town - Dene Estate	-	-	Wheat Sheaf	-
	Grangetown - Town - Docks	-	Gray Rd	-	-
8	High Barnes - Mount Rd - Town*	-	Edenhouse Rd	-	-
9	Helmsdale Rd - Kayll Rd - Town	-	St Mark's Rd	-	-
10	Pennywell - Town - Hendon - Grangetown } Grangetown - Hendon - Town - Ford }	Front Rd	Wesley Hall	{Hendon School	-
11	Ford - Town - Tatham St - Corporation Rd } Blue House - Hendon - Town - Pennywell }	-		{or St Barnabas	-
15	High Barnes - Cleveland Rd - Town	-	St Mark's Rd	-	-
16	Hastings Hill - Town	Chester/Holborn Rds	St Mark's Rd	-	
17	Hylton Castle - Town }				
28/29	Town End Farm - Town }	Aged Miners' Homes	Wheat Sheaf	-	-
19	Seaburn - Town - Circle	-	Wheat Sheaf	St Mark's Rd	-
		-	Millfield Station**	-	-
20	Prestbury Rd - Town	Round Robin	Millfield Station	-	-
21	Prestbury Rd - Town - Grangetown	Round Robin	Millfield Station	College of Art	-
22	Seaburn - Town - Tunstall Rd	-	Wheat Sheaf	College of Art	-
23	Dene Est - Town - Durham Rd - Thorney Cl	-	Wheat Sheaf	Edenhouse Rd	Prospect Hotel
24	Seaburn C - Town - Durham Rd - Telford Rd	-	Wheat Sheaf	Edenhouse Rd	Prospect Hotel
25	Witherwack - Town - Docks	-	Wheat Sheaf	-	-
26	Helmsdale Rd - Town	-	Millfield Station	-	-
30	Gilley Law - Town	Prospect Hotel	Edenhouse Rd	-	-
	Works journeys to Bartram's	As normal service	As normal service	Barrack St	-

Service 8: school journeys only

**Service 19 was unusual in passing from zone 1 to zone 2 and then back into zone 1 during the same journey and vice versa*

Other services (not via town centre)

Service		Zone 5/6 boundary	Zone 6/7 boundary	Zone 7/8 boundary	Zone 8/9 boundary
6	Witherwack- Grangetown	-	David Brown's	Chester Rd	Bede School
12	Fulwell - Humbledon	Charlton Rd	David Brown's	Chester Rd	-
13	Red House or Hylton Castle - Humbledon	Rmsgte/Redcar Rds or Aged Miners'	David Brown's	Chester Rd	-
14	Fulwell - Humbledon	Charlton Rd	David Brown's	Grindon Mill	-
18	Seaburn Camp - Springwell	Charlton Rd	Pallion Exchange	Bede School	-

Special services, eg, to Football Ground whether via Town or otherwise, observed normal service zonal boundaries

Sunderland Corporation Transport

Route map, 31 Dec 1939

Diagram only. Not to scale.
Some detail omitted or simplified for clarity

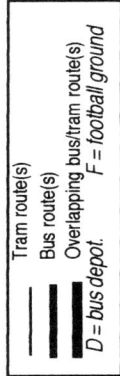

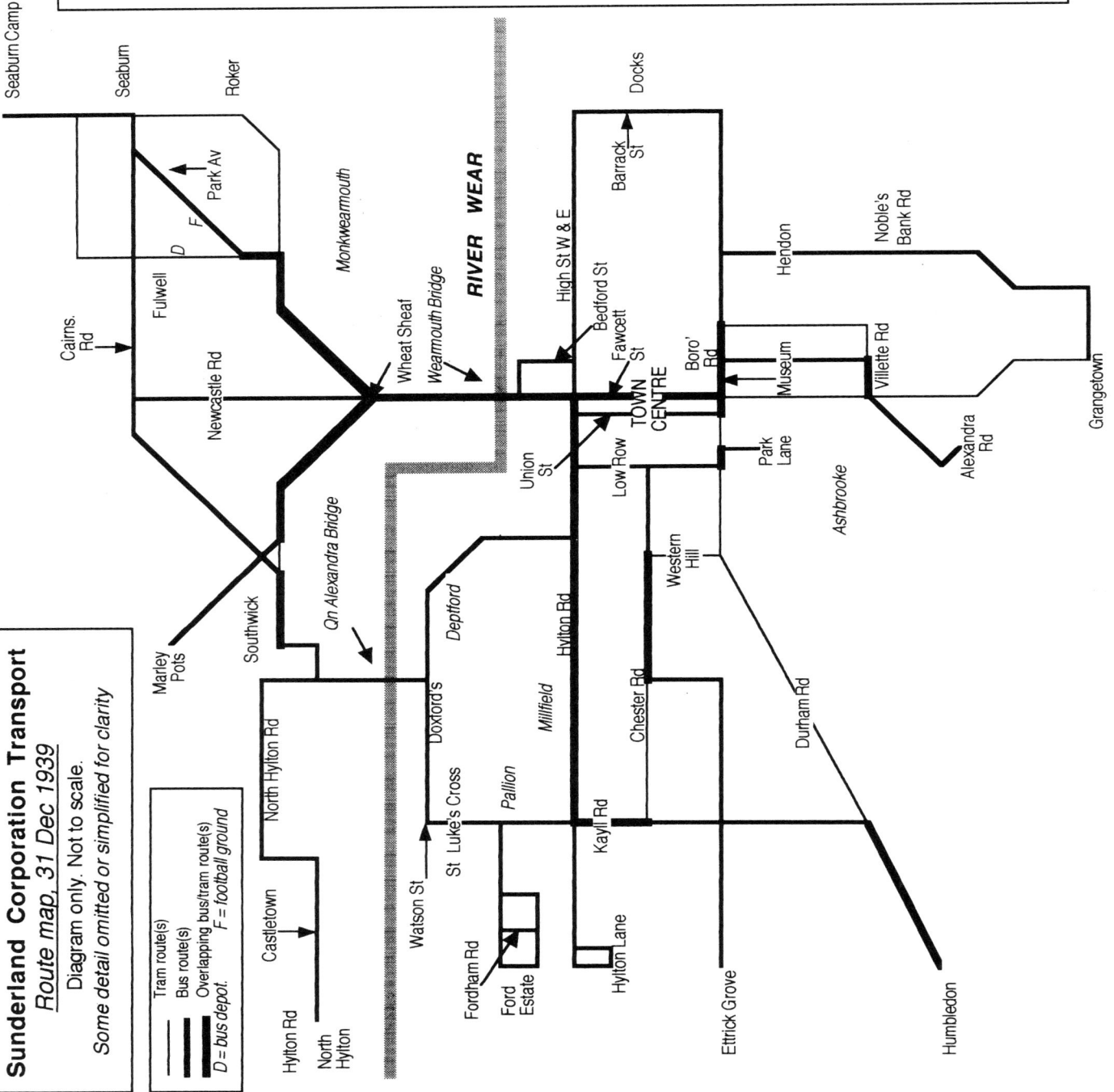

Legend:
- Tram route(s)
- Bus route(s)
- Overlapping bus/tram route(s)
- D = bus depot. F = football ground

Bus & tram services, 31 Dec 1939

Bus

Alexandra Rd - Town (Boro' Rd/Museum) *(suspended)*
Cairns Rd - Newcastle Rd - Town (Boro' Rd/Museum)
Docks Circle
Ettrick Grove - Chester Rd - Town (Union St)
Ford Estate - Pallion - Deptford - Town - Hendon - Grangetown
Humbledon - Pallion - Southwick - Fulwell - Seaburn Camp
Hylton Lane - Millfield - Town (Union St)
Marley Pots - Wheat Sheat - Town (High St W)
N Hylton - Castletown - Southwick - Deptford - Park Lane
Seaburn - Park Ave - Town (Bedford St)

Tram

*Circle - Roker - Seaburn *(suspended Roker - Seaburn)*
Durham Rd - Town - Fulwell - Seaburn
Durham Rd - Town - Southwick
Villette Rd - Tatham St - Town - Southwick
Grangetown - Ryhope Rd - Town - Fulwell

*Circle section: High St W (nth end of station) - Hylton Rd - Kayll
Rd - Chester Rd - Western Hill - New Durham Rd - Fawcett St

Altitudes

bt=bus terminus   tt=tram terminus

21ft	Seaburn bt
22ft	Seaburn Camp bt
53ft	High St E/Barrack St
57ft	Roker tt
77ft	N Hylton bt
95ft	Castletown (Schools)
96ft	Wheat Sheaf
96ft	Qn Alexandra Bridge (centre)
100ft	Boro Rd/Museum
102ft	Fulwell tt
104ft	Villette Rd tt
110ft	Fawcett St/High St W
115ft	Pallion New Rd/Watson St
129ft	St Luke's Cross
132ft	N Hylton Rd/Castletown Rd
132ft	Alexandra Rd/Ashbrooke Range
134ft	Hylton Rd/Trimdon St
136ft	Southwick tt
165ft	Hylton Rd/Kayll Rd
173ft	Chester Rd/Kayll Rd
180ft	Ford Estate bt
240ft	Hylton Rd/Front Rd
252ft	Ettrick Grove bt
260ft	Durham Rd/Ettrick Grove
268ft	Hylton Lane bt

Map labels:
Seaburn Camp, Seaburn, Roker, Park Av, Cairns. Rd, Fulwell, Monkwearmouth, Newcastle Rd, Wheat Sheaf, Wearmouth Bridge, RIVER WEAR, Marley Pots, Southwick, Qn Alexandra Bridge, North Hylton Rd, Hylton Rd, North Hylton, Castletown, Doxford's, Deptford, Millfield, Pallion, St Luke's Cross, Watson St, Fordham Rd, Ford Estate, Hylton Lane, Kayll Rd, Chester Rd, Western Hill, Durham Rd, Etrick Grove, Humbledon, Union St, Low Row, High St W & E, Bedford St, Fawcett St, TOWN CENTRE, Boro' Rd, Museum, Park Lane, Ashbrooke, Villette Rd, Alexandra Rd, Hendon, Noble's Bank Rd, Grangetown, Docks, Barrack St, D, F

Sunderland Corporation Transport
Route map 1 Jan 1960
Diagram only. Not to scale.
Some detail omitted or simplified.

FD = Fulwell Depot. **FG** = Football Ground. **HD** = Hylton Rd Depot.
Plain figures = routes. Bold ringed figures = termini.
ITALIC CAPITALS indicate areas of future service development

Altitudes
bt=bus terminus

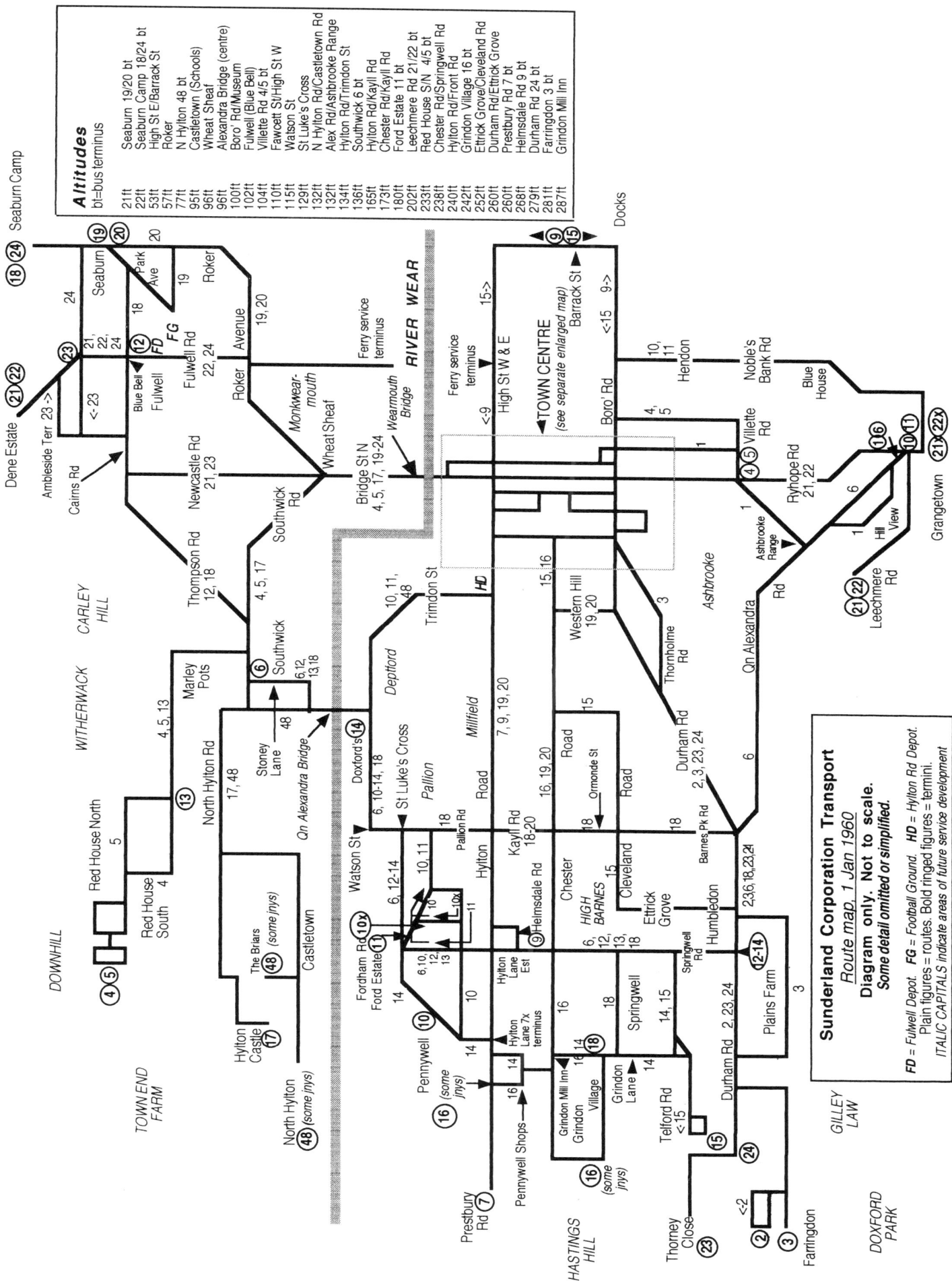

Altitude	Location
21ft	Seaburn 19/20 bt
22ft	Seaburn Camp 18/24 bt
53ft	High St E/Barrack St
57ft	Roker
77ft	N Hylton 48 bt
95ft	Castletown (Schools)
96ft	Wheat Sheaf
96ft	Alexandra Bridge (centre)
100ft	Boro' Rd/Museum
102ft	Fulwell (Blue Bell)
104ft	Villette Rd 4/5 bt
110ft	Fawcett St/High St W
115ft	Watson St
129ft	St Luke's Cross
132ft	N Hylton Rd/Castletown Rd
132ft	Alex Rd/Ashbrooke Range
134ft	Hylton Rd/Trimdon St
136ft	Southwick 6 bt
165ft	Hylton Rd/Kayll Rd
173ft	Chester Rd/Kayll Rd
180ft	Ford Estate 11 bt
202ft	Leechmere Rd 21/22 bt
233ft	Red House S/N 4/5 bt
238ft	Chester Rd/Springwell Rd
240ft	Hylton Rd/Front St
242ft	Grindon Village 16 bt
252ft	Ettrick Grove/Cleveland Rd
260ft	Durham Rd/Ettrick Grove
260ft	Prestbury Rd 7 bt
268ft	Helmsdale Rd 9 bt
279ft	Durham Rd 24 bt
281ft	Farringdon 3 bt
287ft	Grindon Mill Inn

RIVER WEAR

TOWN CENTRE *(see separate enlarged map)*

Map labels and route references:

Seaburn Camp · Dene Estate · Seaburn · Roker Park Ave · Roker Avenue · Ferry service terminus · Monkwearmouth · Wheat Sheaf · Wearmouth Bridge · Bridge St N 4, 5, 17, 19-24 · High St W & E · Barrack St · Docks

Ambleside Terr 23 -> · Blue Bell · Fulwell · Fulwell Rd 22, 24 · *FG* · *FD* · Cairns Rd · Newcastle Rd 21, 23 · Southwick Rd · Bridge St N

DOWNHILL · TOWN END FARM · WITHERWACK · CARLEY HILL · Red House North · Red House South · The Briars · Castletown · Hylton Castle · North Hylton

Thompson Rd 12, 18 · Marley Pots · Southwick 6,12 13,18 · Stoney Lane 48 · Qn Alexandra Bridge · North Hylton Rd 17, 48 · 4, 5, 13 · 4, 5, 17

Pennywell · Pennywell Shops · Grindon Village · Grindon Lane · Telford Rd · Durham Rd 2, 23, 24 · Plains Farm · Farringdon · Thorney Close · HASTINGS HILL · GILLEY LAW · DOXFORD PARK

Fordham Rd · Ford Estate · Hylton Lane Est · Hylton Lane 7x terminus · Watson St · Doxford's · St Luke's Cross · *Deptford* · *Pallion* · Pallion Rd · *Millifield* · Hylton Road · Kayll Rd 18-20 · Helmsdale Rd · Chester Road · *HIGH BARNES* · Springwell Rd · Humbledon · Ormonde St · Cleveland Road · Ettrick Grove · Barnes Pk Rd

Trimdon St · *HD* · 10, 11, 48 · 7, 9, 19, 20 · 16, 19, 20 · Western Hill 19, 20 · Thornholme Rd · Durham Rd 2, 3, 23, 24 · Qn Alexandra Rd · *Ashbrooke* · Ashbrooke Range

Ferry service terminus · Boro' Rd · Villette Rd · Ryhope Rd 21, 22 · Ashbrooke Range · Hendon 10, 11 · Noble's Bank Rd · Blue House · Hill View · Leechmere Rd · Grangetown

The author, who has been fascinated by buses and trams from an early age during World War 2, is a committed enthusiast for public transport and believes that a stable and integrated network can be created and sustained only by radical and co-ordinated policies. Concerned for the preservation of the past as well as for the securing of the future of public transport, he is actively involved in several preservation societies; drives preserved trams at the Heaton Park Tramway, Manchester, in a voluntary capacity; is a member of the Greater Manchester Transportation Consultative Committee and its Buses Sub-Committee, and of the Greater Manchester Passenger Transport Authority Oldham Local Transport Group; and founder and convener of Oldham Transport Users' Forum. For many years he has driven buses and coaches on a casual basis for a former National Bus Company operator, and his other interests lie in poetry, music and writing transport magazine articles. He also manages to do a full-time job in local government.

Other books by the same author
Weekend Bus Driver (Sheaf Publishing)
Manchester Area Buses (Sheaf Publishing)
Oldham Corporation Buses (DTS Publishing)

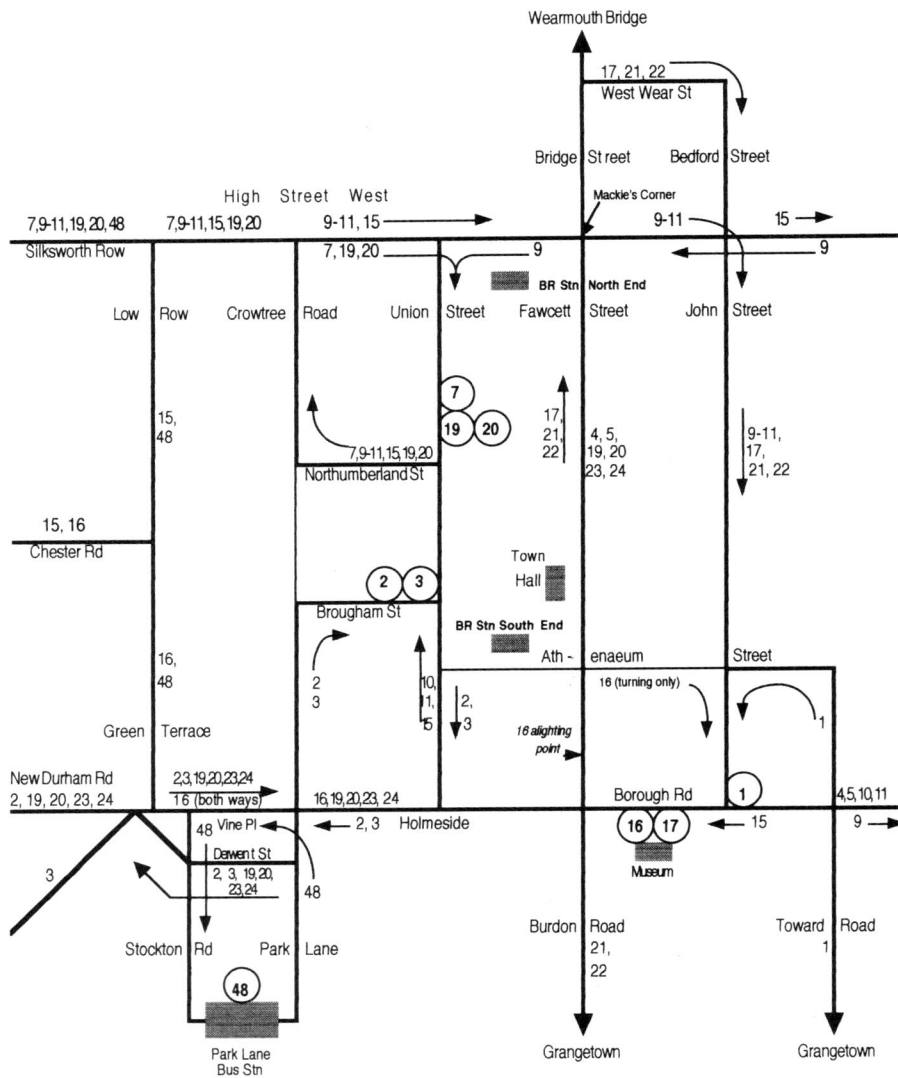

Town Centre

Enlarged route map, 1 Jan 1960

Diagram only. Not to scale

bus routes
other thoroughfares
direction of travel where one-way
Plain figures = routes.   Bold ringed figures = termini